Music, Memory and Memoir

Music, Memory and Memoir

Edited by Robert Edgar,
Fraser Mann and Helen Pleasance

BLOOMSBURY ACADEMIC
NEW YORK • LONDON • OXFORD • NEW DELHI • SYDNEY

BLOOMSBURY ACADEMIC
Bloomsbury Publishing Inc
1385 Broadway, New York, NY 10018, USA
50 Bedford Square, London, WC1B 3DP, UK
29 Earlsfort Terrace, Dublin 2, Ireland

BLOOMSBURY, BLOOMSBURY ACADEMIC and the Diana logo
are trademarks of Bloomsbury Publishing Plc

First published in the United States of America 2019
Paperback edition first published 2021

Copyright © Robert Edgar, Fraser Mann and Helen Pleasance, and Contributors, 2019

Cover design: Louise Dugdale
Cover image: The Crescent Community Venue, York, UK. Photograph by Julia Edgar.

All rights reserved. No part of this publication may be reproduced or
transmitted in any form or by any means, electronic or mechanical,
including photocopying, recording, or any information storage or retrieval
system, without prior permission in writing from the publishers.

Bloomsbury Publishing Inc does not have any control over, or responsibility for,
any third-party websites referred to or in this book. All internet addresses given
in this book were correct at the time of going to press. The author and publisher
regret any inconvenience caused if addresses have changed or sites have
ceased to exist, but can accept no responsibility for any such changes.

Library of Congress Cataloging-in-Publication Data
Names: Edgar-Hunt, Robert. | Mann, Fraser. | Pleasance, Helen.
Title: Music, memory and memoir / edited by Robert Edgar, Fraser Mann and Helen Pleasance.
Description: New York, NY: Bloomsbury Academic, 2019. |
Includes bibliographical references and index.
Identifiers: LCCN 2019009576 (print) | LCCN 2019009948 (ebook) |
ISBN 9781501340659 (ePub) | ISBN 9781501340666 (ePDF) |
ISBN 9781501340642 (hardback: alk.paper)
Subjects: LCSH: Musicians. | Autobiography.
Classification: LCC ML385 (ebook) | LCC ML385 .M815 2019 (print) |
DDC 781.1–dc23
LC record available at https://lccn.loc.gov/2019009576

ISBN: HB: 978-1-5013-4064-2
PB: 978-1-5013-7625-2
ePDF: 978-1-5013-4066-6
eBook: 978-1-5013-4065-9

Typeset by Integra Software Services Pvt. Ltd.

To find out more about our authors and books visit
www.bloomsbury.com and sign up for our newsletters.

*Dedicated to the memory of Dr Nathan Wiseman-Trowse.
A good friend and a fine scholar.*

Contents

List of illustrations ix
Notes on contributors xi

Introduction *Robert Edgar, Fraser Mann and Helen Pleasance* 1

Part 1   Readings

1 Hiatus: Music, memory and liminal authenticity *Robert Edgar* 13
2 Paying more close anxious attention to Joy Division
   Helen Pleasance 25
3 Portrait of the artist as an indie star: Kristin Hersh and the memoir
   of process *Fraser Mann* 39
4 Poet is priest: Julian H. Cope's subversive biography
   Nathan Wiseman-Trowse 53
5 Grace Jones: Cyborg memoirist *Janine Bradbury* 65
6 'Walking the Dead': Memory and self-reflexive intertextuality
   in late-style David Bowie *Kevin Holm-Hudson* 81
7 Memory, graffiti and The Libertines: A walk down
   'Up the Bracket Alley' *Benjamin Halligan* 99
8 Reading lyrics, hearing prose: Morrissey's *Autobiography*
   Laura Watson 119
9 'Glory Days': Memory-related processes and the performance
   of memory in the work of Bruce Springsteen *Nicola Spelman* 133

Part 2   Recollections

10 Time machines *Barbara Frost* 151
11 Meeting your idols 1: Growing up addicted in York *Karen Woodall* 165
12 Meeting your idols 2: Teenage dreams *Steve Leedale* 169
13 Meeting your idols 3: The soldier in the box *Kate Ramsay* 175
14 Meeting your idols 4: Culture Clash *Peter Cook* 179
15 Meeting your idols 5: Goodbye Tupac *Jerry Ibbotson* 183

16	'What Do I Do Now?': Encountering ourselves in music memoir *Jon Stewart, Louise Wener and Benjamin Halligan*	187
17	Exploding the myth *Tom Hingley*	201
18	Remembrance Sunday *Bill Drummond*	211
19	Confessions of metal and folk: Remembering and contextualizing the creative process *Kimi Kärki*	223

Index   240

Illustrations

7.1	Up the Bracket Alley in 2012	99
7.2	Grove Passage becomes Up the Bracket Alley	100
7.3	From 'Up the Bracket' (opening sequence, Grove Passage/Hare Row, 2002)	101
7.4	The location in April 2012	101
7.5	From 'Up the Bracket' (opening sequence)	102
7.6	Concert/party in the living room, from 'Up the Bracket'	104
7.7	2 Cold Fingers: Libertines lyrics as graffiti on Up the Bracket Alley	106
7.8	Miriam's tattoo adapts lyrics from 'Time for Heroes' by The Libertines (2003)	106
7.9	'I get along just singing my song people tell me I'm wrong … FUCK 'UM' (lyric)	107
7.10	'The Arcadian dream will never fall through. X. 13/2/12'; 'I lived my dreams today'; 'What became of the likely lads?' (lyrics)	108
7.11	'The Arcadian dream has fallen though, BUT the Albion sails on course … THANX SO MUCH! Betina & Bienie. 7/8/2011'	109
7.12	Sophie Thunder's design for the 2003 'Freedom Gig'	110
7.13	'Pete Doherty is Innocent'	111
7.14	'Thought you might like to know you broke my heart' (lyric)	112
7.15	'If you've lost your faith in love and music, the end won't be long' (lyric)	113
7.16	'Stylist kids in the riot' (lyric)	113
7.17	'I'm so clever but clever ain't wise' (lyric)	114
7.18	'Time for Heroes [song title] – Pete you changed my life I love you more than you could imagine thank you'	115
7.19	From 'Up the Bracket' (closing sequence)	116
16.1	Sleeper receive British Phonographic Industry gold discs awards for certified sales of 100,000 copies of their debut album, *Smart* in 1995 (Jon Stewart far left, next to Louise Wener). Credit: Andy Willsher: http://www.andywillsher.com/	188

16.2 Louise Wener (centre) and Jon Stewart (right) on stage at the London Shepherd's Bush Empire sound check, 2 December 2017. Credit: Thomas Brooker: http://www.tlbrooker.com   189
16.3 Sleeper reunion gig, London Shepherd's Bush Empire, 2 December 2017. Credit: Thomas Brooker: http://www.tlbrooker.com   189

Contributors

Dr Janine Bradbury teaches literature at York St John University. She specializes in African-American women's writing and American Studies and she is especially interested in constructions and representations of race, gender and sexuality in contemporary literary and cultural texts. She is currently working on her monograph *Contemporary African American Women Writers and Passing* (forthcoming) and her work on drag and American professional wrestling has been published recently.

Peter Cook moved from Hull to London to study at the National Film and Television School. From there he moved to Leeds to work at Yorkshire Television where he forged a career as a documentary maker. Following this he moved into education where he trained a new generation of film-makers.

Bill Drummond is a Scottish musician, music industry figure, writer and artist. He is best known as co-founder of 1980s avant-garde pop group The KLF and its 1990s media-manipulating successor, the K Foundation, with which he burned a million pounds in 1994.

Dr Robert Edgar is an Associate Professor in the School of Humanities, Religion and Philosophy at York St John University. He has published a range of topics, including popular music. His books include *The Music Documentary* (2013) and *The Arena Concert* (2015). He has published a series of texts with Fairchild/Bloomsbury on film-making, including studies on Screenwriting, Directing and Film Language. His co-authored book on *Film Adaptation for Screenwriters* is forthcoming.

Barbara Frost was born in South London. She met her future husband Frank Tovey (aka Fad Gadget) at St Martin's School of Art and spent twenty years as his partner in crime: photographer, vocalist, lyricist, accountant and tour manager. Later: teaching. Most recently: writing.

Dr Benjamin Halligan is Director of the Doctoral College for the University of Wolverhampton. His books include *Michael Reeves* (2003) and *Desires for Reality* (2016), and five co-edited collections on music since 2010.

Tom Hingley is a musician and author. In 2012 Tom published the book *Carpet Burns*, a memoir about his time as singer with the internationally acclaimed band The Inspiral Carpets. He taught popular music at the University of Salford and Manchester Metropolitan University. He continues to perform as a solo artist and with the Tom Hingley Band and as the singer of the Inspiral Carpets tribute band, The Karpets.

Dr Kevin Holm-Hudson is Associate Professor of Music Theory at the University of Kentucky. He is the author of *Music Theory Remixed: A Blended Approach for the Practicing Musician* and *Genesis and 'The Lamb Lies Down on Broadway'*, as well as editor of *Progressive Rock Reconsidered*.

Jerry Ibbotson is still trying to work out what he wants to do when he grows up. He's been a radio journalist at the BBC, worked in the games industry and has written two novels and numerous short stories. He is currently working on a new novel.

Dr Kimi Kärki holds a PhD in Cultural History from the University of Turku and works as a Coordinator on the International Institute for Popular Culture. Kimi has most recently published on the history of popular music, especially live music, and is co-editor of *Peter Gabriel: From Genesis to Growing Up* (2012). He contributed to *The Arena Concert* (2015) and has recently undertaken a Fulbright Scholarship in the USA.

Steve Leedale lives and works in Doncaster. He has spent many years as a DJ specializing in independent music. He is currently working on a book of John Peel memories.

Dr Fraser Mann is a Senior Lecturer in literature at York St John University. He is a specialist in war literature with particular interests in testimony, gender and trauma. He has published research on a range of literary figures such as James Jones, Norman Mailer and Ernest Hemingway. His teaching interests include American Studies, autobiography and twentieth- and twenty-first-century war writing.

Dr Helen Pleasance teaches Creative Writing and English Literature at York St. John University. Her research interests include Contemporary Fiction and Creative Non-Fiction in all its forms, especially memoir, biography and true crime. She has published on memoir as a form, biographical representations of Myra Hindley and narrative accounts of the Moors murders. She is currently writing a novel with a country and western soundtrack and researching a project that combines textile and textual histories.

Kate Ramsay lives in her hometown of York. Before her current career as a promoter and DJ, she worked in the music industry. This included time working for Sony Records while living in London and New York.

Dr Nicola Spelman is a Senior Lecturer in Music at the University of Salford where she teaches composition and popular musicology. Her authored book *Popular Music & the Myths of Madness* (2012) identifies links between the anti-psychiatry movement and representations of madness in popular music of the 1960s and 1970s, analysing the various ways in which ideas critical of institutional psychiatry are embodied both verbally and musically in specific songs by David Bowie, Lou Reed, Pink Floyd, Alice Cooper, the Beatles and Elton John. Her recent critical work explores the areas of noise music, music and memory, and audience participation.

Jon Stewart was the founder, guitarist and co-songwriter for Sleeper. He is now the Course Leader BA (Hons) in Music Business and Senior Academic Lecturer at BIMM Institute, Brighton, and a PhD researcher at the University of Southampton. Publications include 'If I Had Possession Over Judgment Day: Augmenting Robert Johnson' in *M/C: A Journal of Media & Culture*, 16/6; 'Oh Blessed Holy Caffeine Tree: Coffee in Popular Music' in *M/C: A Journal of Media & Culture*, 15/2.

Dr Laura Watson is Lecturer in Music and MA Musicology Director at Maynooth University, Ireland. She has published on twentieth-century French music, Irish musical culture, music criticism and current popular-music culture. Research outputs include the forthcoming sole-authored monograph *Paul Dukas: Composer and Critic* (2019) and co-edited collection *Paul Dukas: Legacies of A French Musician* (2019); articles appear in *Twentieth-Century Music, Journal of the Society for Musicology in Ireland, The Musical Times* and

Journal of Music. As a founding member of the Sounding the Feminists Working Group, she campaigns for gender equality in music in Ireland.

Louise Wener is the London-born songwriter, singer and guitarist of platinum-selling Britpop band Sleeper, who have released four albums: *Smart* (1995), *The It Girl* (1996), *Pleased to Meet You* (1997) and *The Modern Age* (2019). Wener has also written four novels: *Goodnight Steve McQueen* (2002), *The Big Blind* (2003), *The Half-Life of Stars* (2006) and *Worldwide Adventures in Love* (2008); a critically acclaimed memoir, *Just For One Day: Adventures in Britpop* (2011); and co-wrote the BBC Radio 4 drama series *Queens of Noise* (2014).

Dr Nathan Wiseman-Trowse was an Associate Professor in Popular Music at the University of Northampton where he led the BA Popular Music programme. Nathan published two monographs, *Nick Drake: Dreaming England* (2013) and *Performing Class in British Popular Music* (2008). He also published work on the music of Nick Cave, the artistic practices of Bill Drummond and the writing of Alan Moore.

Karen Woodall is a psychotherapist and writer who moved from York to live by the river in London. She writes about her therapeutic work with children in her blog (karenwoodall.blog) which is read around the world. When she is not writing, she is usually in Cornwall.

Introduction

Robert Edgar, Fraser Mann and Helen Pleasance

Conception

This collection came together through a series of happy accidents. Shared office space, chats in the pub and similar summer reading lists slowly moved towards something of an academic epiphany. Ostensibly, the three of us in the editorial team work on fairly disparate research interests. We cover everything from American war fiction through film adaptation to the ways that the fabric industry of England's North West has been narrativized. We work across multiple disciplines and engage with a broad range of theoretical paradigms. It seems inconceivable that such divergent pursuits can come together in a project as original and fascinating as the one housed in these pages. However, it turns out that such diversity is highly stimulating and that in interdisciplinary practice lays opportunity for critical and creative elasticity.

Having said all that, we are linked in one crucial way. We are unadulterated, dyed-in-the-wool, never-likely-to-change music fans. Most of our days are governed by playlists that run on our iPods, trickle out of our flimsy office speakers and irritate our next-door neighbours when we are home for the evening. We spend far too much of our time recovering from late nights in sweaty little venues. We spend way too much of our salaries buying tickets, t-shirts and limited editions. Our teenage years and the records we bought have irreversibly shaped who we are and how we like others to see us. Remaining heartbroken about the deaths of Kurt Cobain and Ian Curtis, the closure of treasured record shops and venues, or even Ned's Atomic Dustbin's third album are all signifiers of identity and badges of hard won indie honour. It is this shared heritage and melancholy reminiscence that drew us together as colleagues and collaborators. Our discussions grew, as they tend to do in university departments, into something more analytical and critical. We wanted to examine what all this irrational fandom meant. As people whose days are spent working with words, we also wanted to know how these processes become narrative.

Our memories have shape and they appear concrete and tangible. Yet, they are also an artifice; they are the self-conscious stories we tell. This paradox is central to the chapters contained in his collection. We want to examine why the stories we tell about music are so persistent but also why they are so fascinatingly malleable.

This brings us to the texts, analyses and creative processes that we have gathered here. The last decade or so has witnessed something of a publishing boom. This period has seen a proliferation of music memoirs appear on bookshelves and in literary discussions. More than ever before, musicians are commenting on contemporary culture and writers are using music to shape uneven collective cultural memories. The act of remembering has created conditions for innovative storytelling. Memoirs by a hugely diverse range of musicians, from Morrissey to Grace Jones and Patti Smith to Mark E. Smith, battle for space in high street bookshops. Detailed, loving and lengthy label histories tell stories of mythical Svengalis such as 4AD's Ivo Watts Russell, Creation's Alan McGee or Subpop's Jonathan Poneman and Bruce Pavitt. Scenes in cities such as Detroit, New York City, Manchester and Bristol are evoked in texts that intertwine personal experience with extensive research. In the cinema, fans of Amy Winehouse, Kurt Cobain, Whitney Houston and Bob Marley have been able to witness extended eulogies to their heroes. Meanwhile, BBC4 and Sky Arts have become must-visit television for those interested in everything from the history of British indie music to the country mecca that is Nashville.

Finding commonalities across this tangled mess of storytelling is a daunting prospect but one that this collection aims to achieve. We approach the processes of memorial, commemoration and nostalgia with a range of writers, artists and academics that share an interest in the relationship between music, memory and written memoir. We interrogate the mechanics of storytelling and the manner in which creative non-fiction blurs the lines between music history and music memory and how all of this intersects with cultural memory. The way that music and memory combine to create spaces for alternative voices and alternative ways of remembering are fundamental to this text. We combine scholarly rigour with personal fandom in an innovative and creative model of research that considers the personal and the universal. We establish models that underpin the ways that music and memory are narrated. More than anything, we examine the role that storytelling has in revisiting musical experience and how this functions in structuring personal and broader cultural memory.

Memoir consciously engages with the construction processes involved in turning the past into text. This can simply take the form of the memoirist acknowledging that there are holes and gaps in memory that they refuse to fill with the fiction of coherent narrative, or it can involve more radical textual experimentation. This experimentation can take many forms, such as: critiquing the strategies of realism through pastiche (Morley 2000), undermining the importance of facts by overtly lying to get at metaphorical 'narrative truth' (Slater 2000: 219) or using the techniques of bricolage and hybridity to make connections between the memoirist's life, the lives of others and theories and strategies of remembering (Dillon 2006; Laing 2016; McDonald 2014). Modern popular music often features multidisciplinary artists who work across different forms of text and for whom engaging in multidisciplinary practice is second nature. Cultural authors are therefore constructing their own identity through constructing their own past for a readership that, in turn, constructs their own past in the music and identity of the musician. This, therefore, is a literate artist writing for a literate audience. This process of creating the artist as bricoleur is a key element of the contemporary music memoir; music provides a partial and fractured way into the past and eschews the fiction of narrative coherence.

Perhaps this narrative complexity is best explained with the aid of a metaphor. Made famous by polymath punk rocker Richard Hell, the safety pin serves both aesthetic and practical purposes. Johnny Rotten, in typically understated style, has always maintained that it was an item whose only use was to 'stop the arse of your pants falling out' but this underplays its potential as an act of aesthetic and narrative subversion. Taking a functional object and elevating it to greater political purpose is at the heart of the punk and indie aesthetic revealed and explored in many of the textual analyses and creative contributions in this collection. Following punk's lead, the indie kid's aesthetic of the 1980s and 1990s featured tattered DM boots, sticking plasters on pairs of spectacles or army surplus gear that was well past its best. All of this helped in rejecting mainstream fashion and embracing the strange beauty of busted and broken stuff. The safety pin, as Johnny Rotten confirms, is a way to hold things together; a visible signifier of DIY as practical and pragmatic endeavour. Punks also made use of safety pins as body piercing and in 'stick and poke' tattooing. The incompleteness of the aesthetic is underlined by its status as a work-in-progress.

An object that celebrates process replaces the sleek lines of corporate modernity. In this way, the safety pin operates as analogue for the textual processes at work in the contemporary music memoir. The foregrounding of artifice and the intrusive presence of an uncertain author show that the memoir is also a work in progress. These memoirs never make claims for authority and the curatorship of life's materials is held together by textual safety pins. The safety pin in punk is DIY, it is self-destructive yet inventive; it is endlessly self-deprecating and auto-parodic. The contemporary music memoir is all of these things too.

Memoir: form and methodology

This enables us to suggest how the recent examples of the music memoir with which we are concerned might be understood as formally distinctive and how that formal distinctiveness produces new kinds of knowledge.

We are aiming to move beyond a discursive critical relationship with these texts by adopting a new and fluid methodological approach. We are also aiming to blur the lines between criticality and creativity. As academics, we are interested in exploring the liminal spaces between scholarly investigation of form and cultural narrative. But as music fans, we are also interested in the ways that we construct our own cultural selves through engagement with the textual practices in question. Or, to put it another way, we are interested in memoir both as a form through which the past takes on particular narrative shapes and as a methodology through which the past can be investigated to provide new insights.

We define memoir here as a personal narrative which embraces the partial, mutable, fragmentary and subjective nature of the past events being narrated and the 'self' who is narrating them. As such it subverts, challenges and critiques the fantasy of many other historical forms; that the past is unproblematically available to be re-created seamlessly, whole and intact as text. As a genre it has garnered much academic interest because of this instability (Couser 2011; De Man 1984; Pleasance 2015; Scott 1998; Singer and Walker 2013; Stacey and Wolff 2013; Stanley 1992). It is an instability that challenges two dichotomies; that between fact and fiction and that between the creative and the critical. The ways in which it does this make clear why it is of both generic and methodological interest here.

The instability of memoir provides a textual form through which its writers and readers can play with identity construction. Memoir texts are produced out of the narration of what is remembered and the gaps around that. The selves of memoir emerge out of these two forces – what is remembered and what has been lost to memory and so remains ineffable in any direct way. The narrating author produces a self, or shifting selves, through the ability 'to cobble together a subjectively workable narrative from ideas and memories available to the person' (King, Neilson and White 2013: 446). Such a process is neither fictional nor factual, but it does use the creativity of narrative construction to engage with the world in new and productive ways.

Memoirs that use music in all its cultural and material manifestations as the material through which new identities are constructed highlight just how rich the relationship between music and identity is. Returning to our safety pin metaphor, the producers of these music memoirs might already be understood as bricoleurs through their use of music to 'cobble together' identities. Their memoirs contribute as further acts of bricolage. As texts their interest is triple-fold; they are producing accounts of a significant history of innovative self-creation, they are developing the form of that self-creation further in their own textual strategies and they allow their readers to insert and develop their own identity narratives in relation to them.

Curating the collection

As editors, we are also participants in this process. We are shaping components and constituent parts into something of an academic narrative. This is a self-aware process and one in which we are keen, like classroom mathematicians, to show our working out. We want the edges and sutures in our thinking to be clear, but also want our readers to make links between the critical material loosely gathered together in the 'readings' section and the selection of original memoir collected under the title 'recollections'. Indeed, the two sections also speak to one another as we seek to break down dichotomies and binaries between critical and creative practices.

The critical work included here addresses a range of cultural output and ephemera from a diverse cast of musicians and industry figures. Some of the chapters, such as Robert Edgar's examination of the notion of 'hiatus' or Helen Pleasance's challenge to the myths created around Joy Division and Ian Curtis, offer complex responses to much of the reductive and simplistic discourse that surrounds the nostalgia market and the heritage industry. Other chapters in this section examine particular artists and their idiosyncratic take on memoir writing. Janine Bradbury reads Grace Jones as a knowing manifestation of Donna Haraway's paradigmatic 'cyborg', while Fraser Mann explores indie luminary Kristin Hersh's tale of artistic growth and creative process and Laura Watson proposes a multisensory reading of Morrissey's *Autobiography*. The chapters here are fluid in what they interpret as memoir. Benjamin Halligan, for example, reads the graffiti left on a hidden East London alley as a memorial to the fleeting social significance of The Libertines and Kevin Holm-Hudson sees David Bowie's late-career music as an intertextual homage to his earlier incarnations. The self-conscious use of memory can create portals to real and imagined pasts through carefully selected language and narrative style, and this is something that Nicola Spelman investigates in her reading of Bruce Springsteen as performer and memoirist and that Nathan Wiseman-Trowse visits in his journey through the bizarre and quasi-arcane writing career of Julian Cope.

In all chapters there is a balance between the academic as analyst and fan. Indeed, this approach is one that seeks to collapse the broader dialectic between scholarship and fandom, or between the cultural commentator and the individual who exists within culture. *Writing Otherwise: Experiments in Cultural Criticism* (Stacey and Wolff 2013) recognizes the importance of narrative incoherence as a methodological imperative in identifying the problematic nature of narrative coherence in respect of some cultural forms. The use of 'I' within analysis becomes a central methodological feature of their work and one the contributors to this book embrace.

This approach is one which then seeks to recognize and utilize the relationship between cultural memory as a phenomenon ironically fixed by cultural commentary and individual cultural memory as something which is contingent. This is not then a collection that draws on simplistic notions of nostalgia. Rather it embraces the fractured narratives that typify the contemporary music memoir. Memory is an equally important dimension of this research, not only as a facet of the memoir but as both individual and collective memory, fluid, fractured and as linked by music.

What emerged through research for all contributors was the extramusical dimension of memory. As we explain elsewhere, 'the memoirist cannot write sound and the fan cannot shape conscious memory of sound. This creates the need for an extramusical turn. This term is defined here as the ephemera and material culture that surrounds musical production, performance and engagement' (Edgar, Mann and Pleasance 2019: 181–99). Critical work presented here combines the contributor's personal memories with analysis. Just like the memoir 'genre' itself, this is writing that seeks to explore connections between memory and narrative process.

The 'recollections' section of this collection includes original memoir writing in which those involved in various facets of the music industry participate in self-consciously 'looking back'. This can be seen in Barbara Frost's account of five LPs that are important to her. Her connection to Mute Records and to Fad Gadget forms part of a narrative in which being a fan is equally important. These recollections can be found in varying degrees throughout all contributions; simultaneously providing detail of lives in music and ruminations on the significance of discussing and communicating those very memories. This is present in artists who are themselves published writers; for example, in Tom Hingley's reflection on writing his own memoir and Jon Stewart and Ben Halligan's discussion with Louise Wener about her writing practice.

The contributors to this text are then asking questions about our own construction of self and this in turn raises questions about the critical conclusions they arrive at. This is the nature of the form and an inevitable result of engaging with it. This is most evident in the autoethnography of Kimi Kärki and the interrogation of his own songwriting practice. The nature of fractured narrative is one that is fully embraced in the shorter chapters of original memory written by Peter Cook, Karen Woodall, Jerry Ibbotson, Steve Leedale and Kate Ramsay. These contributors share a connection with northern England and each discusses an experience where music forms part of a broader narrative. The message in each is a similar one; music informing aspiration and transcendence. In each case the experience of music is one that is central and the connection to an event or individual that has taken on socio-cultural significance beyond the time in which it took place. It is quite right that these moments are unrealized or fleeting in these accounts. This is evident in Cook happening to be at the recording of *White Riot* or Ibbotson having to report on the death of Tupac Shakur without knowing who he was.

What this collection does not do is follow the historiographic approach that is so common in music journalism and music commentary. This can be seen in the plethora of aforementioned music documentaries, popular music texts, label histories, 'best of the decade' compilation albums, reunion gigs and rock family trees. This is not to suggest that these forms are invalid or that a historiographic approach to popular music should not be considered. They are, of course, important forms in socio-historic and musicological analysis. For example, the well-established field of subculture research has to draw on a historical approach to discuss the development of local and specific subcultures. However, this is where the memoirist and theorist are fundamentally different from the cultural historian. The living through or being part of an event or movement is the socio-critical core of this methodological approach. What the approach in this collection recognizes is that this 'living through and being part of' a scene or movement is contingent. The experience of engaging with bands such as Joy Division or Nirvana is still possible through the reproduction of their work through musical, extramusical and textual forms. Again the fluidity of memory remains a factor.

This collection, then, represents a variety of forms of writing that suggests a spectrum approach. What links them is a recognition of memory as something which embraces the physical and sensory experience and its problematic relationship through written text; the function of the writer as 'I' located with text and experience; and the uncertainty of memory is inevitable and reflected through narrative form.

References

Couser, G. T. (2011), *Memoir: An Introduction*, Oxford: Oxford University Press.
De Man, P. (1984), 'Autobiography as Defacement', in P. De Man (ed.), *The Rhetoric of Romanticism*, 67–81, New York: Columbia University Press.
Dillon, B. (2006), *In the Dark Room: A Journey in Memory*, London: Penguin.
Edgar, R., F. Mann and H. Pleasance (2019), 'Music, Memory and Memoir: Critical and Creative Engagement with an Emerging Genre', *Journal of Writing in Creative Practice*, 12 (1&2): 181–99.
King, R., P. Neilsen and E. White (2013), 'Creative Writing in Recovery from Severe Mental Illness', *International Journal of Mental Health Nursing*, 22 (5): 444–52.
Laing, O. (2016), *The Lonely City: Adventures in the Art of Being Alone*, Edinburgh: Canongate.
Macdonald, H. (2014), *H is for Hawk*, London: Vintage.
Morley, P. (2000), *Nothing*, London: Faber and Faber.
Pleasance, H. (2015), 'Ghosts of the Real: The Spectral Memoir', in L. Tansley and M. Maftei (eds), *Writing Creative Non-Fiction: Determining the Form*, 71–88, Canterbury: Gylphi.

Scott, J. W. (1998), 'Experience', in S. Smith and J. Watson (eds), *Women, Autobiography, Theory*, 57–71, Madison, WI: University of Wisconsin Press.

Singer, M. and N. Walker (eds) (2013), *Bending Genre: Essays on Creative Nonfiction*, London: Bloomsbury Academic.

Slater, L. (2000), *Spasm: A Memoir with Lies*, London: Methuen.

Stacey, J. and J. Wolff (2013), *Writing Otherwise: Experiments in Cultural Criticism*, Manchester: Manchester University Press.

Stanley, L. (1992), *The Auto/Biographical I: the Theory and Practice of Feminist Auto/Biography*, Manchester: Manchester University Press.

Part One

Readings

1

Hiatus: Music, memory and liminal authenticity

Robert Edgar

Let's open our Melody Maker and scan the list of the Top Twenty: of the recordings which have had the highest sales to our fellow-countrymen and women. What will it tell us of their tastes and dreams? In the week I write this, plenty ... modern troubadours are teenagers, and the reason's not too far to seek: the buyers are teenagers, too. (MacInnes 1961: 49)

Colin MacInnes, writing for *Twentieth Century* in 1958, documented the birth of the teenager in the UK and with this the emergence of recorded popular music as a mass commodity. Much has been written about the emergence of 'the teenager' as a concept and teenagers as an identifiable grouping and their relationship to popular music and the subsequent variety of related subcultures. This is significant in a number of fundamental ways that have an impact on the relationship between individual (what might be crudely identified as personal) and shared/cultural memory. This is furthered by the birth of pop music still being, just, within living memory. MacInnes identifies that, from the advent of rock and roll, there has been an alignment of producer and consumer. This raises questions about the formation of our identity in adolescence and whether there is an initial alignment. The presupposition is that we follow the bands and performers we grew up liking due to a nostalgic drive, or perhaps because we never really become adult. However, recent research has identified that there is the potential for neurological as well as cultural resonances of the music (and associated artefacts) we consume in our youth. When I was growing up it was still common to see middle-aged men traversing the streets dressed as Teddy Boys. They seemed so old, so lost in time and we seemed cutting edge in our post-punk/indie attire, not recognizing it, at the time, for the uniform it was. But it provided localized identity forged in youth. The suggestion that this is not simply a function of nostalgia is important. The drive to continually buy Adidas trainers, plaid shirts and Harringtons, while listening to The Pastels and BMX Bandits on a loop, is more than a clinging to an ever more quickly disappearing youth. The 1960s revival gang shows that tour the seaside towns of Britain have been joined by indie-focused 1990s Shiiine On and Indie Daze one-day events, mini-cruises and festivals at Butlins holiday camp in Minehead. These events reunite and in doing so provide a continuum.

The term hiatus has crept in to common parlance as a way of describing a band reforming or a performer coming out of retirement. What was, perhaps, seen as a final act – the break up – is now arguably seen as a pause, a gap in time but one where a continuum is implied and potential to continue exists. In these terms there is currency in the adherence to something that is present and this problematizes what might otherwise be seen as an act of nostalgia. The reformation is inevitable. That there will be a ready audience for bands/performers is a given, and it is easy to suggest that this is due to financial gain and/or a ready nostalgia market. Whilst this might be true for some performers or might be a by-product of their desire to continue performing, there are many other artists/groups who perform without lucrative financial rewards. In his early discussion of the origins of rock and roll, MacInnes uses the term troubadour. The etymology of this phrase suggests that this is where the writer and performer is often the same person. This classical allusion also implies satire in terms of social commentary and, therefore, substance in confirming a sense of identity. From its origins this form of popular music is one that documents society and comments on itself through form and content. This is perhaps why Simon Reynolds (somewhat playfully) identifies 1963 as the starting point: 'Rock 'n' roll in the fifties sense was both rawer and more showbizzy; 1963, the year of The Beatles, Dylan, The Stones, is when the idea of Rock as Art, Rock as Revolution, Rock as Bohemia, Rock as a Self-Consciously Innovative Form really began' (2011: 403). This suggests an early distinction between that which is thoughtful, reflective, aware or transformative and that which is simply commercial, disposable and transitory. This last definition of transformative focuses on reception as much as it does on production. It is the well-considered argument that meaning, and with it socio-cultural function, is generated between the text (artefact) and the person consuming that artefact. In these terms it is as possible for a stadium behemoth such as Fleetwood Mac, with their origins in the 1960s British blues boom, to have been as transformative as the Dead Kennedys or Take That to have been as formative in creating a sense of youthful connection as, for instance, the Senseless

Things. The substance lies in their reception and other associations made by an audience. The implication is that this is linear; association with a band or artist forms as memory at the intersection between a band's emergence in popular culture and where you encounter them at the same historical moment. This is certainly the case for some individuals, but this simply connected timeline does not capture the broad function of the relationship with popular music and memory. Some of this comes from the reach of the form beyond music simply as a sonic experience. The playful part of Reynolds's discussion of 1963 as the year of his birth; linear time then seems to always function not as a measure but rather as a structuring device.

Perhaps inevitably there has been a tendency to treat popular music as a purely commodified form, with respectful analysis focused on the subcultures that in some ways tend to rally against what might be seen as the dominant: music as simply an industrial form. The trend has led to sociological analysis of the origin of the teenager in the 1950s and the development of the subculture reaching its zenith with punk in the 1970s. The predominance of the texts available from Dick Hebdidge (1979) onwards and the development of a variety of subsequent research networks confirm this. These approaches tend towards an analysis of the collective and, therefore, the individual's inclusion within that collective. More recent analysis has shifted this focus; texts such as *Punk Rock, an Oral History* (Robb 2006) start to capture the testimony of those that were 'there at the time'. Those who were involved, complicit, part of the scene and those who started to define it. This marks a shift or perhaps, in reference to MacInnes, a return. The processes of sociological and journalistic comment conflate in providing a reference point for a range of bands/performers including those that were at the height of commercial success. The emergence of the popular music memoir starts to close the gap. It starts to see the artist as 'real'. The authors are humans discussing aspects of their life away from their music. Often they discuss their life as a fan placing them on a level with those reading the book, making them part of the scene that they also in many ways define. This is the case with books such as Tracey Thorn's *Bedsit Disco Queen* (2014), Viv Albertine's *Clothes, Clothes, Clothes. Music, Music, Music. Boys, Boys, Boys* (2015) or Tim Burgess's homage to vinyl and iconic performers, *Tim Book Two: Vinyl Adventures from Istanbul to San Francisco* (2016). Potential for shared memories is something that is furthered through texts which are formed from diary extracts, such as Miles Hunt's *The Wonder Stuff Diaries 86-89* (2016) or *The Wedding Present: Sometimes These Words Just Don't Have to Be Said* (Houghton and Gedge 2017).

Hunt's work references youth scenes we may have experienced and gigs we may have been at: a portrait of the artist as a Grebo. The Wedding Present text draws on memories from fans and fellow performers, drawing on our memories and re-presenting them back to us and to a wider audience. The advertising notes on The Wedding Present's website identifies that: 'The book gives a real insight in to what it's like to attract – or become one of – a coterie of passionate fans who have followed the group since the beginning. Many have fallen in love with – and to – the band's music. As one fan describes it, "They have been the soundtrack to my life"' (Scopitones.co.uk, n.d.).

This triage of approaches – sociological, historical and personal – creates an intersection where experience is at once personal and collective and where popular music treads the liminal space between the two.

The nature of our memories, as defined by popular music, might easily be seen as trivial; the alignment with a popular cultural or commodified form could easily drive this perception. Discussion of transitory moments in rundown venues seeing obscure bands or queuing outside record shops waiting for the new release might be seen as youthful folly or a moment of experience without fundamental value. How value is ascribed to moments such as this requires consideration regarding what value systems are being applied and, the question remains, value in relation to what? Denis Dutton differentiates between expressive and nominal authenticity as systems of classification, recognition and, from this, of ascribing forms of value (2003). This meta-classification considers perceptions of originality and fake (in Dutton's terms) as the basis for this process of classification. The sense of the original having a time frame is, in these terms, fundamental in legitimizing not an experience but the memory of that experience and with it the holder of the memory. The artefacts of popular music serve as cultural signifiers and with them the nature of time can be specific – a record release or a performance happened at a given time and place and this confers a level of providence. Music provides a structure to experience in that it emerges in a particular time and has particular connotations. This confers authority on the text due to it being genuinely of a moment in time. With this comes (in Dutton's terms) a sense of expressive authenticity; the music was there at that moment and so the individual intersects with a cultural phenomenon. However, the cultural 'event' is a status that is invoked in hindsight. The small crowd that attended the Sex Pistols at the Manchester Free Trade Hall was going to see a small gig, probably because local heroes Buzzcocks organized it. The status of the gig is built in the subsequent canonization of the Sex Pistols as a group and their function in representing punk as a movement. For the individual this moves from nominal authenticity in the moment of engaging with the musical artefact to expressive authenticity in recounting the act. This becomes expressive authenticity when it intersects with the discourse of popular music as expressed through popular memory (newspaper reports, popular journalism, documentary, etc.). For example, seeing The Hoverchairs in 1990 in the Doncaster Toby Jug remains nominally expressive in being representative of a scene and a venue, particularly in respect of the rituals that are associated with it. Dutton cites ritual as a validating part of the process of identifying authenticity. In viewing an obscure band in a dilapidated (and sadly long gone) music venue in a northern British town this might include wearing Doctor Martens, a Smiths t-shirt, an army Parka, Levi 501s, drinking snakebites and dancing in dim light in a strange shuffling motion. (These indie music rituals are considered in *Empire of Dirt* (Fonarow 2006).) This is where there is an additional level of complexity. The eclectic mixing of the artefacts of individual memory compounds the authentic function of the event. However, these levels of authentic expression are problematized when shared and the artefacts of memory which, in popular musical terms, are generally shared. In these terms there has always been a play between the commodified and the personal.

The *True Faith* exhibition in Manchester in 2017 presented artefacts relating to Joy Division and New Order. The range of objects and images used testify to the complex relationship we have with the various aspects of popular music. This sharing takes on different forms, including the sharing of items within a particular sub-group of friends (which we might define as personal), the sharing of items within a subculture (which extends the reach of the artefact) and the sharing of the artefact at a national or international level, for instance with a record or a video. The presentation of Peter Saville's album cover art alongside Rob Gretton's notebooks, alongside a Parka with a New Order album cover hand-painted on the back exemplifies these complex relationships. There is a related and inevitable authentic battle for the individual where these artefacts exist in the same space and yet are of a different order. Their functions as signifiers of cultural memory are varied. Arguably, the albums are universal and their reproduction over time spreads their impact. Ian Curtis's handwritten lyrics for 'Love Will Tear Us Apart' appear to have a different status and the exhibition played with the concept of art in reifying the art object and the artist in the deification of Curtis. The lyrics were the last exhibit presented and were displayed behind glass. The tiny piece of paper took on the aura of the Mona Lisa; or perhaps had much more significance than that. Prior to this, the exhibition engaged us as audience, we had seen objects that we likely own and more than likely have shared with others before being allowed to see (but not photograph) the holy relic. The experience was of seeing the originating point, an object which is expressively authentic, an object which has providence conferred not by its location in the gallery or even as an aesthetic object in its own right but by its cultural significance as a piece of recorded and replicated music. Despite this, the other objects within the space give way in the presence of this 'original' to liminality where they function within and without private space. Deborah Curtis's *Touching From a Distance: Ian Curtis and Joy Division* (2005), Bernard Sumner's *Chapter and Verse: New Order, Joy Division and Me* (2015) and Peter Hook's *Unknown Pleasures* (2016) all provide context and expose a perceived reality of Joy Division and Ian Curtis which collapse in respect of that which is expressively authentic. The power of this form of authenticity is palpable, in seeing New Order perform at Liverpool Olympia on 22 November 2015 the encore was preceded by an iconic image of Curtis above the stage. The black and white image of him smoking a cigarette drew a reverent hush from an otherwise excited and boisterous crowd who were reeling from a Hi-NRG performance of a range of tracks. The quiet remained as the crowd watched, still, as Anton Corbijn's video was projected while the band played 'Ceremony'. This is where, outside the safety of the gallery, the experience exists as liminal authenticity – it exists in reference to that which has providence, but only (to borrow a title) touching at a distance.

Conway and Loveday discuss this phenomenon in relation to neurological functioning and identify a similar conflation of the personal and the collective. In these terms the process of inhabiting what might be determined a collective and individual past is biological in function:

> Autobiographical memory contains autobiographical knowledge, e.g. personal factual knowledge and cultural knowledge, such as the history of our times. It also contains episodic memories, e.g. fragmentary knowledge derived from experience ... As such it forms a major part of the self ... episodic memories are part of general events which in turn are part of lifetime periods which may themselves be part of broader themes such as work or relationship themes and the life story. (2015: 574–5)

Meaning is then generated for the individual who holds that memory – the memory serves a function for the individual who both generates and receives that memory. Conway and Loveday extend their argument to discuss the idea of the memory cue where indirect associations in effect trigger memories. In music terms this can, for instance, connect hearing a track (which may have a known and very specific cultural context) to an experience when we heard the track that may itself have no corollary.

Conway and Loveday's use of the established psychological term 'autobiographical memory' has an important parallel with the development of written memoirs, although there is a distinction between that which is unconscious but neurological (and thus inevitable) and a form such as memoir which is conscious and overtly reflective. There are, of course, narrative rules to follow in both cases, and the expression of a memory to ourselves or to others provides narrative resonance and further levels of meaning. In recounting memory we are forced to use narrative structure (selection/sequence/orientation) and we are all subject to narrative expression. This process of sequencing seems to be crucial to the process of remembering: 'it is only when an episodic memory or set of episodic memories are activated that a constructed memory enters consciousness, i.e. the rememberer becomes consciously aware of the memory' (Conway and Loveday 2015: 575). In these terms our personal memories are expressed in terms of how others will understand them, even if this is only for us to understand them. The 'narrative instinct', if you will, follows the processing and subsequent structuring of collective memory. This inevitably means some form of linearity of expression and thus construction of progression and development, even if this is only at a perceptual level. The idea of progress is philosophically problematic but is implicit in narrative development – stories work towards an end, even if this is not a conclusion. Narratives, once expressed, are also fixed; this is particularly true of the written memoir, forever fixed on paper. What these become is a fixed point in a process where our memories are essentially evolving. There is an instinct to narrativize and this requires a perceptual facet, or an ideological positioning as an inevitable part of the processes of selection. However, this doesn't equate to an ideological positioning of the experience in relation of the music artefact; thus is the nature of the evolution of memory as something that is not fixed and thus where the perceptual aspect changes.

There is a function in addition to memory; the objects we associate with popular music as signifiers have a specific socio-cultural and temporal 'signified' beyond personal connection. The connection is back to the collective, but via an artefact that has a material form. Where these memories intersect with a dominant discourse and broader cultural memories (as inevitably constructed) and legitimized by the physical artefact, the memories take on a liminal quality in that they sit between the private and the public, the contingent and the general, the real and the remembered/imagined. The authentic function is not compromised for the individual as memory but is inevitably changed in expression. The function of 'I was there' is not subjugated by the collective memory of, for instance, 'being there', 'meeting person x', etc. At a neurological level these are already of the same order. The authentic function of the experience is then only ever perceptual and ideological. For example, there are certain gigs that enter the collective memory and via the processes of being collectively remembered they take on the appearance of having a higher cultural value. In theory, this changes the context in which the memory is recalled. For example, seeing Oasis in the back room of a small venue in 1994 is a fixed point as an event for the individual. The memory of this contingent event takes on more significance following their two-day performances at Knebworth in 1996 and the subsequent media interest. The production of the documentary *Supersonic* (Whitecross 2016) confers status on the small venue memory and provides a context in which the memory has broad cultural context. In recalling this there is a 'cue' where the connection is already in existence as the narrative pre-exists. A memory of seeing, for example, The Family Cat and CUD in 1992 in the Tower in Hull will have a different and much more contingent narrative. The collective memory does not exist in the same way that it does for Oasis, but there is still a collective memory. This is despite the fact that The Family Cat and CUD (in this writer's mind) were far superior bands.

Conway and Loveday develop their argument to evaluate the accuracy of memory, although in socio-cultural terms this perhaps marks a point of divergence – where accuracy is forever deferred. As with authenticity, the question is, and to paraphrase Dutton, accurate in relation to what? This leads us to a difficult and contingent definition of 'accurate' which itself is aligned to authentic. The legitimacy of a memory is then via the published recording (in prose and/or image, still or moving and/or audio) of an event where there is a collision between the public (general constructed discourse) and the individual (autobiographical memory). This is further compounded where that memory is already an amalgam of evolving context in that it may develop as cultural memory extends. The danger for the individual is, in discourse or in discussion of the memory, the public carries the authority and the nominal authenticity it carries wins out via providence. If this is the case then the method of conferring value on memory is where it intersects with popular cultural discourse. This function of memory is perhaps suggestive as to why so many people saw the Sex Pistols at the Free Trade Hall. The memory is so well culturally established that they might as well have done. This is not a lie (although it might be) and, while it might be deemed a false memory, the experience of that gig is felt and understood by many, and this in itself is legitimate. The response to the gig is authentic regardless of presence. Music documentaries and music memoirs confer status, the written word perhaps more so than moving images in that they invoke visualization or conceptualization. They then become an authoritative account, where the diary account has the appearance of authority; the linear autobiography is next in the authenticity stakes and where the reflective memoirs of a writer such as Patti Smith (2011) have suitably less authority as memorial texts. Regardless of any potential hierarchy, these documents serve to locate and fix time and experience. Again, providence wins out but this time it is providence provided by author status and form. In these terms the sense of liminal authenticity wins out over the nominal and expressively authentic. The concept of liminal authenticity as previously used in respect of geographical borders suits as an analogy for the hinterland of memory and, in these terms, marks the border between collective and autobiographical memory.

In terms of popular music and memory, we are left in an uneasy position. There are moments that become fixed, but only in the way that we experience the recounting of the memory and then recount our own. Mark Fisher discusses this in reference to Derrida's *Spectres of Marx* and the subsequent field of hauntology. The consideration of memory identified is essentially in relation to an idea of presence via connection. In Derrida's deconstruction (of voice above text) we might also see attendance/experience over association with or alignment to an event. The authentic and value-driven once again appears, '[b]ut hauntology explicitly brings into play the question of time ... one of the repeated phrases in *Spectres of Marx* is from *Hamlet*, "the time is out of joint" ' (Fisher 2014: 18). In the terms identified above, the connection to bands of our youth is not an act of nostalgia. This is something Fisher himself critiques: 'the question has to be, nostalgia, compared to what?' (Fisher 2014: 25). Fisher makes the crucial point that a comparison of the present to the past is not necessarily an act of nostalgia. This supersedes Jameson's definition of the postmodern condition where nostalgia is an inevitable process of the commodification of the past and provides an opportunity for both a nostalgia function to operate in relation to a memory function. There is a question about the simulacra under these circumstances where the memory function dictates that we engage with the past from an authentic origin, whatever the status of that authenticity. Postmodern criticism suggests that the collapse of history is an inevitable consequence of commodification and that contemporary processes of online distribution will further this. Indeed, autobiographical memory function suggests that some form of linearity is inevitable. It is well documented that Spotify sweeps up distinctions between different forms of music, but this is an argument that Ann Kaplan was making in respect of MTV some twenty-five years ago (1990). This doesn't negate theories of the eclecticism of contemporary culture and the raid of the past for commercial purposes. It is perfectly possible for someone to wear an MC5, Ramones or Sonic Youth t-shirt with no idea there is an associated band. This doesn't preclude them from engaging with their own originating music as well as potentially engaging with the music their fashion choices suggest. For those of us who encountered Sonic Youth as youths (us and the band) the status of our autobiographical memory is arguably confirmed and extended by the presence of these cultural referents on the high street. If they are important enough to be copied then our memories have been legitimized, not by the processes of capitalism that might inevitably diminish but by the collective presentation of that which was previously liminally authentic crossing the border and being recognized.

This implies that memory is equally deferred and de-centred. However, in practice there is a continuum. Hiatus implies a gap, not an absence, and raises the question about what provides a continuum and what happens to linearity? There is then a clear distinction to be made between those bands where they can never perform again. This is clearly the case with a band such as Joy Division and perhaps accounts for the reverence for Curtis and the band generally. It is still possible to get close via the artefacts that not only remain but are also reproduced. The fact remains, though, that the band has gone. This suggests that the aura that surrounds the band is furthered by mechanical reproduction. This complex relationship with the band as signifier of the authentic is a complex one. A few short years ago in York, there were two music venues next door to each other, Fibbers and the Duchess. One featured Dr Feelgood, a band who have a direct lineage back to their founding members and a narrative where Lee Brilleaux, evidently knowing he was ill, told them to continue performing – to continue the tradition. In the venue next door, Wilko Johnson was playing. This caused much consternation about who to go and see. This raises a further problematic question about the nature of providence and authenticity in respect of the current act and their connection to the past.

Colin MacInnes discusses the origin of British popular music and, writing in 1958, had no insight into how long Steele and associated acts would continue to perform. The longevity of musical acts provides potential for engagement across time. There is then a tension where there exists potential to bear witness to a band. This perhaps suggests why the term hiatus has become common parlance for bands that previously would have split up never to be seen again. The reformation or comeback tour might be for the love of the fans or music, it might be for financial gain or it could be for both. The reason is somewhat irrelevant. The effect is that there exists potential to elicit autobiographical memory and to confer an authentic status on this memory via its connection to that which is current. This potential exists in this liminal space where collective and thus autobiographical memory can evolve in relation to the legitimacy conferred by the authentic event – the artefacts of popular music. In these terms, buying a band t-shirt for the group you loved as a youth has the same function. What this does suggest is that music and related artefacts shape our sense of self and the focus on music, performers, clothes and scenes that we engaged with in our youth is not simply an act of nostalgia, although that might be part of it. The return to the past, which is our past expressed and experienced through others, is an essential part of the construction of self. There is a question to be asked about what happens when musical acts are no longer with us and where the potential to reconnect disappears. The touring captured by Julien Temple in *The Ecstasy of Wilko Johnson* (2015) highlights the grief caused by the passing of a musical icon (thankfully deferred in this case). This is of a different order to those who have died tragically young through rock and roll excess, misadventure or personal tragedy. These icons are no longer present. Time, rather than history, has outlived them. Written memoirs, documentaries and other methods of engaging with musical acts allow us to perpetuate and develop memory and further legitimize experience. Collective and cultural memories allow for moments where the liminal shifts into expressive authenticity and this in turn authenticates our experience. It provides providence for our lives.

References

Albertine, V. (2015), *Clothes, Clothes, Clothes. Music, Music, Music. Boys, Boys, Boys*, London: Faber and Faber.

Burgess, T. (2016), *Tim Book Two: Vinyl Adventures from Istanbul to San Francisco*, London: Faber and Faber.

Conway, M. and C. Loveday (2015), 'Remembering, Imagining, False Memories & Personal', *Consciousness and Cognition*, 33: 574–81.

Curtis, D. (2005), *Touching From a Distance: Ian Curtis and Joy Division*, London: Faber and Faber.

Dutton, D. (2003), 'Authenticity in Art', in J. Levinson (ed.), *The Oxford Handbook of Aesthetics*, New York: Oxford University Press.

Dutton, D. (2009), *The Art Instinct*, New York: Oxford University Press.

Fisher, M. (2014), *Ghosts of My Life*, London: Zero Books.

Fonarow, W. (2006), *Empire of Dirt: The Aesthetics and Rituals of British Indie Music*, Middletown, CT: Wesleyan University Press.

Hebdidge, D. (1979), *Subculture: The Meaning of Style*, London: Routledge.

Hook, P. (2016), *Unknown Pleasures: Inside Joy Division*, London: Simon and Schuster.

Houghton, R. and D. Gedge (2017), *The Wedding Present: Sometimes These Words Don't Have to Be Said*, London: Red Planet Books.

Hunt, M. (2016), *The Wonder Stuff Diaries 86–89*, London: Independent Records.

Kaplan, E. A. (1990), *Rockin' Around the Clock: Music, Television, Postmodernism and Consumer Culture*, New York: Routledge.

MacInnes, C. (1961), *England, Half English*, London: Penguin.

Reynolds, S. (2011), *Retromania: Pop Culture's Addiction to its Own Past*, London: Faber and Faber.

Robb, J. (2006), *Punk Rock, an Oral History*, London: Ebury Press.

Scopitones.co.uk. (n.d.) Available online: https://merchandise.scopitones.co.uk/product/the-wedding-present-sometimes-these-words-dont-have-to-be-said/ (accessed 29 August 2018).

Smith, P. (2011), *Just Kids*, New York: Bloomsbury.

Sumner, B. (2015), *Chapter and Verse: New Order, Joy Division and Me*, London: Corgi.

Supersonic (2016), [film] Dir: Mat Whitecross, UK: Nemperor.

The Ecstasy of Wilko Johnson (2015), [film] Dir: Julien Temple, UK: The Cadiz Recording Co.

Thorn, T. (2014), *Bedsit Disco Queen*, London: Virago.

True Faith (2017), Manchester Art Gallery, Manchester, 30 June–13 September.

2

Paying more close anxious attention to Joy Division

Helen Pleasance

It is a Friday in early spring 1984; the last day of my second term at Sussex University. I'm living on campus in a hall of residence. There is a carnival atmosphere among the first years today. Most of the halls will be vacated for the holidays and, in our heightened, youthful experience of time, it feels like tomorrow will be a parting of old friends. This, despite the fact that we have only known each other since the preceding October (the Brighton October of Neil Kinnock's fall on the beach, immortalized by *Spitting Image*) and we will all be back in a matter of weeks for the final term.

I'm not sure how or where I hear the news, but by mid-evening the atmosphere has changed. Another first year, a girl I know by name, a friend of friends, has been knocked down by a motorbike on the dual carriageway outside the campus. She and a friend had been heading into Brighton (to see a band, I want to say, but I'm really not sure now), and had taken the short cut across the road to the train station, heading for the gap in the hedge in the central reservation; the route we were all warned against. It is a dangerous road – that is why there is an underpass. But that takes so much longer. Going straight across the road, especially with that tempting gap in the hedge, is almost irresistible, especially if you're in a rush, especially if you know a train is due any minute, especially if it is the last day of term and you're in a carnival mood. But I don't think any of us will ever do it again, certainly not for the rest of our first year. This girl, Mandy, has been knocked down by a motorbike and killed. She's dead. One of us is dead. Someone who has had the same immediate past and, up until that moment, had shared the same immediate future as us, is dead.

Most of the evening has gone now; it can't be pieced back together in any kind of narrative form. Two things remain. My friend John falling to his knees, sobbing inconsolably. John knows Mandy well. John knows everybody well.

He has spent virtually every evening of his time on campus trawling from hall to hall drinking, smoking dope and charming his way into assignations and adventures. I am looking at him, on his knees, head in hands, sobbing, and I realize I don't, can't, feel what he is feeling. I'm not sure I have ever even spoken to Mandy. So I am in shock but am nowhere near the raw, unreachable place that John is in. Then it is later. My boyfriend Malcolm and I are in his room. It is the room of an alti music fan – huge Echo and the Bunnymen poster on the wall, Goth boots and DMs on the floor, a stack of vinyl, copies of the *NME*. Even the Mancunian girlfriend (me) can be interpreted as an alternative music accessory (she's been to the Haçienda, she can translate the dialect words in Fall lyrics). We are lying on the bed. Malcolm didn't know Mandy well either. I'm not sure if he has ever spoken to her. But he also seems to be feeling something I'm not. I have taken on the role of comforter. His emotion is different to John's. He has become silent and distant. His response to Mandy's death seems to have gone beyond it to some kind of greater existential angst. He gets up from the bed, finds the record he wants and puts it on the turntable. The crackle and thud of the outer grooves give way to melody and a voice. It is Joy Division. 'Atmosphere'? 'Love Will Tear Us Apart'? The specific song, like most of the evening, has gone now. But it doesn't matter. The important thing is that it is Joy Division. The soundtrack that Malcolm has chosen for this moment is Joy Division. It is Ian Curtis giving voice to his – I'm not sure what the exact emotion is – grief? angst? pain? It is the sparse Martin Hannett production providing a soundscape for what feels like a staged moment of trauma.

I look at him, knowing that I should take on some kind of attendant role in this moment of heightened emotion. And all I can feel is complete and utter irritation.

****

This opening fragment of memoir enacts for me the kind of 'close anxious attention' that has been, and continues to be, paid to Joy Division and through which a potent experience of trauma is brought forth. There are several things at stake in this narrative moment that I will explore in this chapter. First, there are two nineteen-year-olds, Malcolm and me, who can be characterized as fashioning their identities and relationship out of the music, sensibilities, philosophies and material artefacts of British post-punk culture. Several of these have already been recounted above; their narration ascribing them historical significance. I could also add my move away from British indie bands, via Two-Tone and Dexy's Midnight Runners, to soul, funk and reggae. All of these references serve to make Malcolm and me recognizable as characters shaped by and giving shape to a particular historical and cultural moment. So the recourse of one to Joy Division and the other's irritation by it could be understood as simply a difference in our tastes from the cultural choices available to us (really? Joy Division? Could you not have chosen something a bit more original than that?). And I'm sure there is some truth in this.

But that alone would not make it worthy of the narrative significance I am ascribing it here. In a discussion such as this, memory is best conceptualized as something constructed in the present to give meaning to past events, rather than a mimetic recall of how I actually felt in that bedroom all those years ago (see, for example, Stanley 1992: 62). So, in my memory, my irritation was about how the playing of Joy Division turned a tragedy that was not ours, to which we were peripheral at most, into a narrative that produced it as Malcolm's trauma. Again, this is clearly subjective and contestable; if he remembers it at all, Malcolm might ascribe a very different meaning to his choice of Joy Division or might refute it entirely. But for me, its producer, this memory is emblematic of the power of Joy Division within a peculiarly masculine mythologization of this cultural moment; producing a dominant narrative account of its significance. Nancy K. Miller argues that the significance of memoir lies in the 'interactive remembering' (2002: 10) that it produces. She develops this through a discussion of her own reading of memoirs of women who, like her, came of age in New York in the 1950s, defining a particularly close kind of relationship between reader, text and author: reading 'memoirs of women whose lives were marked by the cultural template of the 1950s, I feel that the book has been written for me' (2002: 11). So, I am offering a moment of memoir as a way of showing lives shaped by a particular cultural template of the late 1970s and early 1980s. I am suggesting that Joy Division had become a particular kind of 'cultural template' through which to modulate emotional experience. In our engagements with Joy Division, Malcolm and I are locating ourselves differently within this cultural template; one of us identifying and the other disidentifying with a particular popular and collective form of remembering that was emerging. Miller notes that both processes are equally as important in the interactive remembering of memoir (2002: 3). And readers of my memoir fragment, with a similar cultural provenance, might reproduce this form of interactive remembering with their own identifications and disidentifications.

I have privileged gender in my interpretation of the irritation I felt at the playing of Joy Division and the narrative of male trauma that I perceived it to express. Some of this irritation is echoed by Tracey Thorn, the singer who came to fame on the post-punk scene of the early 1980s, first with girl band The Marine Girls and then as one half of duo, Everything But The Girl. Her disidentification with Joy Division's canonization is noted by Lucy O'Brien:

> Tracey Thorn was one of the first female rock memoirists to celebrate the 'small story', the one that hadn't yet made the male rock canon. She grew up reading male music journalists and absorbed the idea that they somehow defined the story. 'I read their version of events, like the post punk band that are important are Joy Division. Yeah, I liked Joy Division, but I liked Young Marble Giants better,' she told me recently. 'I had a different version and other people said, "Yeah, yeah, me too!" So I realized it wasn't just me.' (2018)

Indeed, I identify with Thorn's feeling of having her story excluded from a broader historical narrative because the writers of that narrative were defining it in other terms: a kind of feminine identification with our mutual disidentification from 'the male rock canon' and its privileging of Joy Division. But I also want to problematize my disidentification by returning to the writing of the Joy Division myth up to that moment of irritation in a university hall of residence. The figure who problematizes this for me is the music journalist Paul Morley.

All those copies of the *New Musical Express* (*NME*) littering Malcolm's hall of residence room constitute an archive of writing about music in the post-punk era in which new identities were being fashioned. A generation of journalists were writing themselves and their contemporaries into history through small stories. These were the stories with which both Malcolm and I had identified over the previous eight years or so to produce our own post-punk identities, and Paul Morley, a staff writer at the *NME* from 1977 to 1983, was consistently one of the writers through whom we fashioned those identities. Those copies of the *NME* are also a feature of my memoir that should spark identifications for many of our contemporaries. Simon Reynolds describes how he was 'in awe of specific writers' (2018) of this generation of the music press. He cites the *NME* and Paul Morley in particular. He also stresses the innovation and power of this writing as being as important as the music it discussed in constituting the meanings of post-punk, describing it as a 'discursive engine' (2018). He has acknowledged this writing as distinctive from previous music journalism in that it 'seemed to be made of the same *stuff* as the music they championed' (2005: xxvii). Paul Crosthwaite goes even further in characterizing this era of 'pop criticism' (2014:

2) as developing a new kind of discourse, an 'imaginative historicism' (2014), that resists academic modes 'of argumentation, corroboration and citation imposed on scholars of pop, offering instead, readings that are wilfully imaginative, inventive and speculative' (2014: 4). He cites Paul Morley's writing about Joy Division as paradigmatic of pop criticism's imaginative historicism. I would like to add wilfully personal to his list of descriptions. This is why returning to look at the different kinds of anxious attention that have been paid to Joy Division, and, in doing so, paying more close anxious attention to Joy Division, so many years after my irritation with it, illuminates how a series of personal discursive engagements with a particular band produced a complex mythology that traversed collective and individual trauma and wrote a whole generation of young men into history.

Paul Morley's close anxious attention to Joy Division

My chapter title is paraphrased from Paul Morley's memoir, *Nothing*, in which he explains the textual attention he has lavished on Joy Division in relation to his inability to engage with a personal trauma: 'I was thinking deeply about pop music, the newer the better, to avoid thinking deeply about my father. I was paying more close anxious attention to the suicide of the lead singer of Joy Division than I was to the suicide of my father' (2000: 272). *Nothing* engages directly with something that Morley had previously only been able to articulate or approach obliquely: the trauma of his father's suicide in 1977 at just the point when his own career as a music journalist was taking off. 1977 was also the year he became a staff writer at the *NME* after several years as a contributor to and producer of several Manchester fanzines.

1977 became a year in which Morley became a historical agent – contributing to the imaginative historicism of post-punk – and suffered a personal loss so traumatic that he could not express or even, as his memoir suggests, remember it. Writing about Joy Division articulated both. As Morley has subsequently stated: 'During 1977, lost to myself as I was following the creation of this endlessly exciting new scene, my father killed himself. The year split into two. One 1977 where everything collapsed and closed down. One 1977 where the world was opening up' (2006). Morley situates himself very clearly within a mythologization of this moment in Manchester's musical history. He refers to two Sex Pistols gigs at the Lesser Free Trade Hall in the city that are consistently written as foundational moments for the generation of many Manchester punk and post-punk bands and which, in imaginative historicist terms, he identifies as starting the process of post-industrial regeneration of the city: 'Those two shows started the process that led to the actions that inspired the creative energy and community pride that pieced the city back together again and which led to it being filled – splendidly and somehow sadly – with light and lofts and steel and glass and sophistication' (2006).

Joy Division's formation has also been written into this foundational moment. Attendance at these two gigs has been cited as inspiring many of the audience members to form the bands which went on to give voice to the city. These attendees included (if the myth is believed; in the way of mythical events, more people than physically possible now claim to have been there. Perhaps this is another example of imaginative historicism) Mark E. Smith, who went on to form The Fall, Morrissey, who later formed The Smiths, Tony Wilson, who founded Factory Records and Bernard Sumner and Peter Hook, who formed Warsaw, who became Joy Division, whose sound and biography came to epitomize Manchester's post-punk sensibility of 'gloom and decay' (Reynolds 2005: 174).

This kind of writing the city's history through this musical moment, and privileging Joy Division's place in it, has taken on a broader currency in popular discourse. For example, *Not a Guide to Manchester*, which actually is a guide to Manchester, albeit of the alternative kind, gives the band only one sentence: 'It started off in 1976 with Joy Division' (McGarr 2012: 100). The 'it' that is being referred to is the 'Madchester' music scene that developed over the 1980s and 1990s. But the placing of Joy Division at the origin of this narrative is telling with regards to the kind of summative history in which the book is engaging. Joy Division's significance can be gestured toward without having to be either elaborated or justified: it has become a self-evident truth. The story to which McGarr is gesturing has been iterated over multiple engagements with the Manchester music scene that developed out of punk. It is a story about the emergence of Manchester as 'a taste-making rock & roll town' (Haslam 1999: 110). It is the kind of historical narrative Edmund de Waal has characterized by claiming, 'It isn't just getting smoother, it is getting thinner' (2011: 17) through repeated retellings. It is also the kind of engagement with myth that irritated me in the recourse to Joy Division to evoke gloom.

The close anxious attention being paid by Morley as a key author of Joy Division, out of which the band's mythologization emerged, complicates my understanding of this process though. Morley's autobiographical details offer a double coda to the functions that his myth-making served in relation to his personal life. Initially, his engagement with the Manchester music scene from 1977 onwards provided an 'opening up' in contrast to the 'collapse' caused by his father's suicide. But after Ian Curtis's suicide, the narrative of Joy Division weirdly mirrored that personal collapse. His process of mythologizing the band is, partially at least, a way of writing a self that acknowledges and transcends the trauma that threatened to consume and destroy him. Myth serves a really important function of giving the traumatized subject an identity narrative that gives them a future. Morley's obituary of Curtis in the *NME* articulates this. Significantly, it is titled 'The Myth Gets Stronger', emphasizing from the outset how myth stands in for loss and provides a new and abiding status. On his death Curtis will not disappear if he is written into myth. Instead, he is given a clear narrative presence in a story that endows him with wider cultural significance. Morley makes 'collapse' the very subject of his imaginative historicism, through which he gives it discursive expression:

> Joy Division throw us out of balance. Their music is undoubtedly filled with the horror of the times – no cheap shocks, no rocky horror, no tricks with mirrors and clumsy guilt, but catastrophic images of compulsion, contradiction, wonder, fear. The threatening nature of society hangs heavy; bleak death is never far away; each song is a mystery, a pursuit. The music is brutally sensual and melancholically tender. The songs never avoid loneliness, cruelty, suffering; they defy these things. (1980)

Morley's writing about Joy Division, understood through the coda of his memoir, can be interpreted as displaced autobiography; as a way of exploring the emotions around his father's suicide and his own experiences of being a traumatized young man. With even a cursory knowledge of Morley's personal circumstances at the time it is not difficult to see how his writing about Joy Division and Ian Curtis is autobiographical. Just a couple of quotations from his collected writing on the group exemplify this: 'Ian Curtis had mutated into an explosive performer who was dragging his life, his woes, his responsibilities, his fears and anxieties into his songs and then right onto stage' (2016: 18); 'In hindsight *Closer* was a series of blatant suicide notes to a number of people in Ian's immediate vicinity, who at the time simply looked upon the songs as immensely powerful representations of emotional collapse that had appalling, yet liberating clarity – not actually an emotional collapse' (2016: 20). For Morley, writing about Joy Division allowed him to reflect on almost inexpressible, liminal emotional states, especially those of young men, which he saw Joy Division as expressing. It is compelling to see how the writing allowed him to overcome the trauma and write himself a different future to the 'emotional collapse' offered by Curtis. Morley's subsequent career seems to confirm this, both as a writer and as a creative/marketing manager at ZTT Records, where Simon Reynolds described his contribution as 'playful and pretentious (in the best sense)' (2005: 494). This is particularly evident in *Earthbound*, Morley's recollection of using the Bakerloo line from late 1978 onwards when he moved to London from Manchester to work full time for the *NME*. Morley constructs a self that is diffused through the experience of moving to and through London on the underground network, 'working out London and its loaded, scattered ways' (2013: 6). Rather than going back to trace a line of a coherent, remembered self, he goes out, with a nod to psychogeography, on a more playful personal journey. This journey is about self-invention, through the movement to London and the movement through the contemporary music scene on which it is predicated. Morley expresses it in terms of map-making: 'If you were anything like me, you found and made up personal, fluid maps of fast-moving, fast-changing rock music that enabled you to discover ideas and sounds that fitted into and symbolized your life and mind – the life of your mind' (2013: 36).

For him, writing is an act of self-creation that allows him to engage with and transcend trauma: 'I replaced my father with myself, with my own life, with my writing, with my belief in pop music, with my own needs' (2000: 277). That a whole generation of young men seemed to be writing themselves into history through their public and performative engagement with Joy Division bears some attention in order to consider what this was allowing them to do.

Masculinity, Joy Division myths and history

Morley's writing on Joy Division was crucial to the mythologization of the band, and is of particular relevance here because of the account he gives of it in his memoir. The memoir allows for a reading of the mythologization as serving as a powerful exploration of personal trauma. If we read it in conjunction with other key authors of this myth and the terms in which they wrote it, this exploration can be lifted to the level of collective history and trauma. A group of male 'authors' (I put the word in inverted commas because not all these authors were writers) put Joy Division in a discursive frame that has been cited as narrating a moment of crisis for Northern post-industrial society and culture. Leonard Nevarez, for example, has argued that the band came to 'sound like Manchester':

> For many listeners, Joy Division sounds like Manchester. That is to say, their music doesn't just come from the late 1970s Manchester of deindustrialization, a carceral welfare state epitomized by concrete housing estates built in brutalist architecture style, Margaret Thatcher's subsequent class warfare upon Britain's industrial proletariat, and the discovery of expressive and artistic possibilities in the wake of punk – their music recreates and conveys this historic milieu through its sonics and aesthetics. (2011)

Nevarez's interest in Joy Division has some similarities with Crosthwaite's. They both understand the discursive treatment of the band as a form of writing into history a particular group and their experiences. Foucault's concept of 'history below the level of power' (1975: 205) is useful here. Foucault characterized such history as emerging through popular forms and as raising the experiences of ordinary people to a level of historical importance that they could not achieve in history at the level of power in terms of the machinations of national and international politics. History below the level of power gives form to the experiences of ordinary people and allows those experiences to become interpretive devices. Through such history ordinary people can become historical agents.

Nevarez characterizes Morley and Jon Savage at *Melody Maker* as 'journalistic entrepreneurs of Joy Division's Mancunian myth' (2011). He cites the imagery in Kevin Cummins's and Anton Corbijn's photography and the record artwork of Peter Saville, which 'effectively convey a sense of space, albeit an eerily desolate or (in the album cover's case) unreal version of a human landscape' (2011). Together, these connect the external landscapes of a desolate urbanism with personal interior landscapes. Most significantly, there is the sonic 'space' created by Martin Hannett's production on their recordings, which Nevarez considers to be as important as the band's own contribution to their sound. He argues that this is especially important within the predominant 'spatially contained listening experience' (2011) of the bedroom, which would be how most of Joy Division's original audience would have experienced them, given the limitations of vinyl technology. This 'might reinforce the solitary, solipsistic experience of Joy Division's music' (2011).

The juxtaposition of the deeply personal, internalized experience of listening to Joy Division with the collective meaning he identifies in the wider discursive frame of the music suggests why it might be so potent when operating as history below the level of power. It allows individual listeners to engage with the collective at the level of personal affect: each listener *feels* that they are inscribed in and actively inscribing a historical moment. This seems to be corroborated by Jon Savage's reminiscences, which enact this process of inscribing personal experience into historical selfhood: 'Joy Division helped me orient myself in the city' (2014: 9); 'Their first album, *Unknown Pleasures* ... defined not only a city but a moment of social change' (2014: 110).

This alone suggests how powerfully the Joy Division myth has narrated young men's experience into history at a particular moment. The centrality of Ian Curtis's suicide to this myth complicates what is being inscribed into history and offers a radical possibility for what kind of history the music memoir can write and the kind of agency it might offer. Savage's historicization of Ian Curtis's suicide gives a startling insight into how this has lifted personal trauma to the level of collective history. He suggests that the suicide created 'a shock so profound that it has become an unresolved trauma, *a rupture in Manchester's history*' (2014, my emphasis). For the suicide of an individual to be narrated as so historically significant confirms how powerfully the Joy Division myth operates as history below the level of power. What is most significant is that they are raising liminal experiences, usually ineffable, to the level of history. Here, Savage is mirroring Morley's close anxious attention to Curtis's suicide: it is a trauma that can be used to narrate other traumas. But while, for Morley, it allows him to articulate another personal trauma (his father's suicide), for Savage, this has been lifted to the level of history itself. It is a huge claim to suggest that discursive engagement with the suicide of the lead singer of a pop group can put a rupture into history, and what that actually means bears some consideration.

Ian Mathers (n.d.) has linked this to the concept of hauntology. He argues that all recorded music is hauntological in the sense that the sound has been separated from its source and so becomes a sonic experience of absence. But he suggests that Joy Division's second and final album, *Closer*, becomes a project that is concerned with 'the way to make music that reflects and even comments most fruitfully on this metaphysical divide, on the fact of its own absence'. *Closer* was released in July 1980, two and a half months after Ian Curtis's suicide, so that 'Ian Curtis's performance is not merely haunting in the way that all recordings become, sooner or later; almost certainly engineered to be post-mortem from the very beginning, his voice makes absence the central sonic and thematic focus of *Closer*' (Mathers, n.d.). Mathers mirrors Morley in his response to this representation of liminal, almost ineffable states in that it offers a way of engaging with such states; of doing something productive with them: 'It's not simply the bleak fact of despair, but a representation of despair; hence proof that something can be done with sadness' (Mathers, n.d.). If, as Savage does, this is lifted to the level of the historical, it achieves something quite staggeringly radical. It puts something hitherto inexpressible into historical discourse, and allows *something to be done with it*. So, in the same way that Morley created a new self out of the writing with which he responded to his father's suicide, this suggests that bringing a collective or historical rupture into discourse might enable that rupture to be addressed and potentially overcome through the creation of new identities that are born out of that rupture. Shifting from the personal to the collective in this way is problematic for several reasons, not least because personal agency is easier to achieve than collective agency. But there is clearly a complex process going on here between the personal and the collective in the ways that the Joy Division myth was created and used by a group of young men to articulate their personal experiences of trauma and lift those experiences to the level of history.

This chapter is, in many ways, reconciliation with my initial irritation with a particular use of Joy Division to express trauma. Through Morley and the other male mythologizers of the band, a much more nuanced and powerful narrative emerges of how trauma can be addressed, articulated, overcome and can even create a new kind of hauntological history. But I also want to hold onto that irritation: it was real and by putting it into a memoir I have given it historical agency. The points at which I disidentify with the Joy Division myth allow other stories to be told.

Paying too much close anxious attention to Joy Division

My initial irritation came from a feeling that the turn to Joy Division transformed a specific traumatic event into a 'solitary, solipsistic experience' (Nevarez 2011) by somebody not directly involved in it. If this is lifted to the level of history or collective memory, arguably, the turn to the Joy Division myth might produce an overly or inappropriately traumatized response to events. The invocation of Joy Division in the wake of the bombing of the MEN Arena in May 2017, for example, served to unite the city in collective grieving but also, arguably overpersonalized the events. *Late, Late Show* host, James Corden responded to the bombing by referring to Manchester culture from football to music, citing Joy

Division in particular, before referring to the people of Manchester as 'Strong, proud, caring people with community at its core' (*Rolling Stone* 2017). It is not difficult to understand this as a performance of trauma in which the reference to Joy Division works as shorthand for a city that is familiar with both trauma and its survival. Susannah Radstone (2010: 29–32) suggests that such overpersonalization of history prevents other productive kinds of engagement with events in the public sphere. David Wilkinson (2016) has also argued that there are different narratives to be told about post-punk, which emphasize pleasure rather than trauma.

Wilkinson's argument, in particular, is a way of opening up the gendered dimensions of the Joy Division myth as cited by O'Brien earlier. The Joy Division myth tells male stories and tells them compellingly and poignantly. As Mark Fisher states: 'There was an odd universality available to Joy Division's devotees (provided you were male of course)' (2005). Fisher's K-Punk blog (from which this comes) is cited by Mathers as crucial to his conceptualization of the hauntology of Joy Division. That Fisher is aware that this is a male discourse is telling. He quotes liberally from Deborah Curtis's (Ian Curtis's widow) memoir *Touching From a Distance* (1995), highlighting how she was written out of Joy Division mythology. The Jon Savage quotations cited earlier come from his foreword to *Touching From a Distance*; a strange paratext that encloses the memoir's female disavowal of the myth in the very myth that it is challenging. There is clearly a sense in which the myth is silencing female interventions in it.

Fisher's K-Punk blog post also provides the most poignant coda to the Joy Division myth. It was adapted for a chapter in his collection *Ghosts Of My Life: Writings on Depression, Hauntology and Lost Futures* (2014). The book offers theoretical readings of culture through Fisher's personal experiences. Fisher's writing has much in common with the imaginative historicism of Morley. Like Morley, Fisher uses Joy Division to narrate his own anxieties: 'That is why Joy Division can be a very dangerous drug for young men' (2014: 59). Unlike Morley, though, Fisher did not write himself a liveable future out of his close anxious attention to Joy Division. As Curtis was for Fisher, hearing his voice for the first time in 1982, 'always-already dead' (2014: 52), so Fisher is for me, reading his writing on Joy Division for the first time in 2018. Fisher killed himself in 2017; and, like Morley with Curtis, I find myself reading his words not just as a critical engagement with emotional collapse but as an actual emotional collapse. His claim that 'suicide remains one of the most common sources of death for young males' (2014: 63) reads like a cry for help. Fisher positions male mental illness within the culture of laddism of the last two decades – the personal is lifted to the historical. In all the close anxious attention that is being paid to Joy Division we need to be alert to what stories are being lifted into history and where we identify and disidentify with them.

References

Crosthwaite, P. (2014), 'Trauma and Degeneration: Joy Division and Pop Criticism's Imaginative Historicism'. Available online: https://www.research.ed.ac.uk/portal/files/19018394/Crosthwaite_Pop_Criticism_chapter (accessed 15 September 2018).

Curtis, D. (1995), *Touching from a Distance*, London: Faber and Faber.

de Waal, E. (2011), *The Hare with the Amber Eyes*, London: Vintage.

Fisher, M. (2005), 'Joy Division: Nihil Rebound'. Available online: http://k-punk.abstractdynamics.org/archives/004725.html (accessed 15 July 2018).

Fisher, M. (2014), *Ghosts Of My Life: Writings on Depression, Hauntology and Lost Futures*, Arlesford: Zero.

Foucault, M. (1975), 'Tales of Murder', in M. Foucault, *I Pierre Riviere, Having Slaughtered my Mother, my Sister and my Brother…* , Harmondsworth: Penguin.

Haslam, D. (1999), *Manchester, England*, London: Fourth Estate.

Mathers, I. (n.d.), '"I Exist on the Best Terms I Can" Joy Division's *Closer* and Hauntology'. Available online: http://www.pd.org/Perforations/perf29/im1.html (accessed 12 September 2018).

McGarr, B. (2012), *Not a Guide to Manchester*, Stroud: The History Press.

Miller, N. K. (2002), *But Enough About Me: Why We Read Other People's Lives*, New York: Columbia University Press.

Morley, P. (1980), 'The Myth Gets Stronger', *New Musical Express*, 22 May. Available online: https://www.nme.com/blogs/nme-blogs/paul-morley-on-ian-curtis-the-myth-gets-stronger-768641 (accessed 21 July 2018).

Morley, P. (2000), *Nothing*, London: Faber and Faber.

Morley, P. (2006), 'A Northern Soul', *Observer*, 21 May. Available online: https://www.theguardian.com/music/2006/may/21/popandrock3 (accessed 20 August 2018).

Morley, P. (2013), *Earthbound: The Bakerloo Line*, London: Penguin.

Morley, P. (2016), *Joy Division, Piece by Piece*, London: Plexus.

Nevarez, L. (2011), 'How Joy Division Came to Sound like Manchester'. Available online: http://pages.vassar.edu/musicalurbanism/2011/07/13/how-joy-division-came-to-sound-like-manchester (accessed 6 July 2018).

O'Brien, L. (2018), 'Small Town Girl'. Available online: http://www.lucyobrien.co.uk/blog (accessed 2 September 2018).

Radstone, S. (2010), 'Reconceiving Binaries: The Limits of Memory', in L. Burke, S. Faulkner and J. Aulich (eds), *The Politics of Cultural Memory*, 26–47, Newcastle: Cambridge Scholars Press.

Reynolds, S. (2005), *Rip It Up and Start Again*, London: Faber and Faber.

Reynolds, S. (2018), 'Writing about Music: Then, Now and Tomorrow', *Writing the Noise*, University of Reading, 6 September.

Rolling Stone (2017), 'Watch James Corden's Emotional Reaction to the Manchester Bombing at Ariana Grande Show'. Available online: https://www.rollingstone.com/tv/tv-news/watch-james-cordens-emotional-reaction-to-the-manchester-bombing-at-ariana-grande-show-111849 (accessed 20 September 2018).

Savage, J. (1995), 'Foreword', in D. Curtis, *Touching from a Distance*, 9–11, London: Faber and Faber.

Stanley, L. (1992), *The Auto/Biographical I: The Theory and Practice of Feminist Auto/Biography*, Manchester and New York: Manchester University Press.

Wilkinson, D. (2016), *Post-Punk, Politics and Pleasure in Britain*, London: Palgrave.

3

Portrait of the artist as an indie star: Kristin Hersh and the memoir of process

Fraser Mann

Since early fame as the guiding creative force behind Rhode Island indie band Throwing Muses, Kristin Hersh has been a slippery and innovative artistic figure who has pushed boundaries and blurred disciplinary lines. Hersh's work combines musical composition, abstract lyricism, memoir and the visual arts. Her performances swing between spoken word and music and her subject matter addresses American landscape, mental health, family life, loss and, above all, the artistic process required to shape and communicate such myriad experience.

In November 2016 I watched Kristin Hersh perform songs to promote the release of her album *Wyatt at the Coyote Palace* in The Crescent Community Venue in York, UK. The partisan audience fell very quiet as this stalwart of alternative rock music sat down on a slightly too tall stool and plugged in her electric guitar. After tuning up she looked up and said, 'My friend told me last week that you should never start a show with something new, the crowd won't like it'. She then proceeded to do just that; hammering through a new song packed with oblique and opaque references to her New Orleans home. The trademark shifts in tempo and tone were certainly familiar but the music was undoubtedly new. As the song reached its conclusion, a small smile appeared on Hersh's face. 'Sorry about that,' she said, 'I'm still figuring out how to do this shit'. She then read a short passage of prose and dared the audience to make connections with the new song. This was a show about process. This is not to say that her songs lacked polish or professionalism, more that this was the work of an artist who was self-consciously examining her own role and her own creative activities. It was an exhilarating performance and this is a reading of Hersh as that artist in process.

Despite its ostensible status as memoir, Hersh's 2010 publication *Paradoxical Undressing* (published as *Rat Girl* in the US) bears close resemblance to the traditions of the *künstlerroman*. The artist's coming of age is most famously explored in Joyce's *Portrait of the Artist as a Young Man* (2000); a text in which the young protagonist forms an artistic identity shaped by experience, conflict and a wild array of interactions. Hersh's memoir explores similar territory and this analysis examines the ways that exterior and interior forces shape Hersh's creative practice and artistic identity. The memoir depicts the seismic twelve months during which, as an eighteen-year-old, she is diagnosed as bipolar, has her band signed by 4AD and discovers that she is pregnant. As the year in question unfolds, the teenage Hersh narrates her bohemian life in Rhode Island and Boston. Hersh writes about a loose community of artists, junkies, teachers and music industry workers. These figures help to form Hersh as songwriter and performer. Her bandmates (including half-sister and fellow indie superstar Tanya Donnelly) offer friendship and ballast to Hersh, while an unlikely union is formed with Golden Age Hollywood star Betty Hutton. Rhode Island and Boston's indie scenes are replete with a cast of fellow artists, scenesters and reassuringly odd fans. Hersh's wild and unpredictable creativity finds relative stability and direction in the form of record label 4AD's visionary leader Ivo Watts-Russell.

Hersh's unique relationship with sound is informed by her synaesthesia, bipolar disorder and pregnancy. Her visceral depictions of sonic performance evoke the claustrophobic energy of indie venues. These consciously creative locales sit alongside the pastoral openness of Rhode Island, the urban energy of Boston and the liminal depths of the Atlantic Ocean. The combination of these spatial configurations and the communities that inhabit them produce artistic practice. In turn, artistic practice helps to further develop Hersh's experiences. The memoir explores Hersh's creative process and the ambiguous role of the musical practitioner. This is an open-ended account of the artist in process. Hersh the performer says, 'I am still working out how to so this shit', and Hersh the writer repeats this. Process leads to creativity and creativity brings us back to process.

Paradoxical Undressing is a bricolage of diary entries, snippets of lyrics and more impressionistic memories of Hersh's younger childhood. Together, these create a temporal tension in which relational textual voices and modes communicate links and contradictions between experience, narrative and creativity. Like her performances, Hersh's focus here is on process. Her text resists teleology and closure. Sidonie Smith (1995: 19) argues that the contemporary 'autobiographical subject' engages in 'multiple stages simultaneously' and is 'called to heterogeneous recitations of identity'. Crucially, 'these multiple calls never align perfectly [and] create spaces or gaps, ruptures, unstable boundaries, incursions, limits and transgressions' (Smith 1995: 19). This is the mode at play in *Paradoxical Undressing*. Hersh as narrator exists in the visible sutures in her story. Textual artifice and patchworks of narrative provide opportunities to analyse fluid constructions of self. The text has no authoritative pivot and no one voice dominates. Susanna Egan (1999: 3) describes autobiographical voices that 'foreground the processes and present time of their own construction' and 'exchanges that authenticate presence but only in the fragile moment'. These are not memoirs written by an omnipotent self looking back and making sense. They are, Egan argues, more interested in communicating 'the strategies of their own composition' and so 'stake no claim for a unified or coherent identity' (1999: 8). *Paradoxical Undressing* offers just this. It is a text in which curatorship takes centre stage. The brief foreword to the text is the only part of the memoir that is written by a present-day Hersh, and in it she candidly discusses the process of reworking diary entries into a new shape. The diaries themselves are 'full of holes' (2010: i) and reading each page is 'oddly like crawling in a window' (2010: ii). Hersh also comments on the ways that fragments of her song lyrics 'reflect on a moment and its reverberations' (2010: ii). Songs, Hersh writes, 'don't commit to linear time – they whiz around all your memories ... they tell the future and they tell the past' (2010: ii). This is chiefly a process of textual ambiguity and paradox. Hersh is the curator of her life's materials. She is in charge of organizing a construction of self. Her role as artist is evident in the material and in the organization of material. This is both literary product and literary process.

Paradoxical Undressing is structured around music and musicality. Hersh's songwriting dominates the text with fragments of lyrical abstraction dropping in at moments that suggest their genesis. Hersh's music-making is a visceral and overpowering corporeal experience which ascribes sound and noise a frenetic agency. Her descriptions of live performance are impressionistic, destabilizing and unbearably loud. During a performance early in the text, for example, Hersh rubs tiger balm into her eyes in an attempt to 'fuzzify all the faces in the room' and leave her equipment a 'soft blur' (2010: 38). Her deliberate sensory impairment means that she can give herself up to the 'pounding noise' (2010: 40). The band's sound is hallucinatory, textural and multi-sensory. Songs are 'liquefied' and 'murdered perfectly with finesse' (2010: 45); while Hersh's identity is subsumed her subjectivity vanishes. She writes that 'the creepy, goofy mess that is our sound is finally playing itself – song tattoos glow all over me, I'm looking and seeing nothing, and I'm nowhere. Nowhere at all' (2010: 47). On lyrical composition she adds that 'before I know it, inflatable words fill my rib cage, move into my mouth, I gag on them and they fly out, say whatever they want, yell and scream themselves' (2010: 47). Hersh is not the creator at this moment; she is a corporeal conduit for sound and abstraction. Her songwriting is open-ended and the creative object itself appears to have an agency and power that battles with its creator. Songs are never complete; they are always reshaping in performance and in memories of those performances. Text, language and art are locked in struggle. Hersh's authorial power is almost entirely absent. She is, to use Watson and Smith's term (1998: 39), engaged in a process of 'negotiating strangeness'. Music's unpredictable abstractions and temporal fluidity are an organizational force on the text. Sonic experience jostles with memory and with the constructed self.

It would be overly simplistic, as Simon Reynolds and Joy Press (1996: 372) note, to 'hem in her songs' as a 'document of a specific individual with a specific mental disorder'. However, Hersh does describe her unique relationship with sound in terms of her experiences of synaesthesia and bipolar disorder. In hospital recovering from the road accident that triggers the former condition, Hersh describes sounds that begin as 'industrial noise' and 'a wash of ocean waves, layered with humming tones and wind chimes' (2010: 76). Over the coming days this cacophony begins 'organising ... into discernible parts' and 'melodies' (2010: 76–7). Hersh's brain is 'making sense of something, turning this sonic haunting into vocabulary with which I was familiar' (2010: 77). As with her performances, sound moves beyond auditory objectivity and achieves colour, texture and a 'visual pattern' (2010: 77). The sounds are 'gentle swathes of sound-light' and 'beats have a shape that appear and then disappear' (2010: 78). Ultimately, these organized noises become Throwing Muses songs. Hersh teaches them to the band but insists that this is not 'a journey from chaos to song ... the song just walks into the room fully formed' (2010: 78). Music 'lives across time as an overarching impression of sensory input' (2010: 78). This memoir's form, therefore, in all of its temporal elasticity, owes as much to music's shifting agency as it does to Hersh's open and fluid narrative composition. It is as if music leads Hersh the musician and Hersh the musician leads Hersh the writer. This loose causality self-consciously reveals the text's own narrative processes.

Hersh's relationship with sound darkens as the text enters its central section. Her diary entries are starker, shorter and increasingly abstract as she suffers from a breakdown, later diagnosed as a manic bipolar episode. Hersh has consistently maintained that simplistic conclusions regarding mental health and creativity are all too easy to jump to. Speaking to Sam Shepherd (2010), for example, she makes clear that she doesn't believe there is 'any validity to the idea that a mind would have to be broken in order to make sense'. Hersh asserts that she has had to 'learn to separate the music for the bipolar disorder' and the 'glaring light and dark shadows' that it produces. In a *Guardian* interview with Gareth Grundy (2010), Hersh goes further and says that she has always 'hated the connection between mental illness and art'. Hersh dismisses such discussion as cliché and rejects outright that you have 'to be sick in order to create beauty or confused to create truth'. The harrowing sections of the text in which Hersh attempts to communicate the rapid nature of her breakdown certainly support this. Thus far in the text, Hersh's relationship with sound has been productive and broadly symbiotic. However, as her health deteriorates, sound becomes malevolent, menacing and frightening. Rather than learning the songs and making them familiar, Hersh's hands 'can't play all the parts at once'. The sounds are 'brutal', 'horrifying', 'fractured, disjointed and harsh' (2010: 129). Multiple sounds are 'crashing into one another' and 'are flung into me through the sick orgasm of colour' (2010: 128). The frightening instability in Hersh's consciousness is a barrier to her artistic process.

Hersh's ill health is communicated through formal textual experiments and a palpable shift in tone. Felicity Nussbaum (1998: 165) contends that 'the minute particulars of an interiority' are best communicated in diary form. 'By eschewing narrative codes and opting for discontinuity and repetition ... diaries and journals ... avoid assigning meaning or a hierarchy of values' (1998: 165). As already established, this text is a diary at several removes. Hersh the author curates and edits Hersh the teenage diary writer. Nevertheless, this particular section of *Paradoxical Undressing* opts for a stylistic and visual form that marks it as distinct from the rest of the text. Each diary entry is short and truncated. The open spaces on each page are a void; they are oppressive emptiness. Minimal syntax and grammar replace more familiar prosaic shapes. Hersh's song lyrics share equal space with the diary entries. Whereas previously the poetic abstractions have sat in contrast to the linear narration of memory, at this stage of the text they merge. Lyrics and memories are only distinguished through italicization as the text gives itself up to figurative experimentation. Her illness is described as an elusive 'snake' that 'fades to static and disappears' or as a 'wolf ... growing dirty and sick, gaunt and broken' (2010: 141). When the illness reaches its nadir, the sounds 'play on erratically, torn sails on a ship' and a fragile Hersh details how she uses a 'razor blade' to 'cut the songs out' (2010: 143). Hersh's relationship with art and with her own creative process is constantly in flux. Her songwriting has the potential for happy productivity but also for violence and harm.

Hersh's creativity and relationship with sound fluctuate once more when she discovers later in the text that she is pregnant. She seeks permission from her amiable yet verbose psychiatrist 'Dr Syllable' to discontinue her medication and focus on the new rhythms of her body. The exterior agency of music and sound now fade; the 'white noise … whispered then fell – a pregnancy casualty' (2010: 233). The power held by sound takes a 'backseat to the Body Monster, letting it drive for a while' (2010: 233). Typical of a figure so attuned to musicality, Hersh's developing pregnancy is understood in these terms. The 'baby's heartbeat' is 'unconcerned with the universe' and in its rhythm Hersh finds a peace she has 'only ever associated with music' (2010: 233). Once more, there is an interesting link here between the form employed in *Paradoxical Undressing* and the manner in which Hersh's reworked diary entries communicate her formation as an artistic figure. Egan argues that the self-conscious construction of self in memoir is driven by the 'emphatic presence of the body' (1999: 5) and that the 'crises that generate autobiography … begin with the body' (1999: 7). Susan McClary (2002: xvii) argues that, in writing about music, there is a focus on 'the experience of the body as it performs music' and on music's 'uncanny ability to help us experience our bodies' (2002: 23). Toril Moi (2005: 65), when defining what she terms the 'lived body', argues that 'the body … does not carry its meaning on its surface. It is not a thing, but a situation'. The 'situation' is fluid and resists Cartesian dualities. Moi states that 'lived experience … will shape our experience of the body' (2005: 66) and that, in turn, 'the body-in-the-world that we are is an embodied intentional relationship with the world' (2005: 67). Hersh's understanding of self and the manner in which this self engages with the world comes out of such embodiment. Her creativity depends upon careful and attentive openness to sensory and corporeal experience. Her body drives her psyche and her textual selfhood follows this same path. This notion is evident in Hersh's descriptions of performance late on in her pregnancy. In addition to awareness of her newly 'active body part' and 'dancing gut', Hersh interprets performance through the response of the 'tiny heels' and 'little fists' that she can feel 'pound away' and 'push against' (2010: 243) her abdomen. The vanishing subjectivity in the early stages of the text is no longer viable. Now she 'no longer disappears' because 'mothers shouldn't disappear … they need to be present' (2010: 243).

Thus far, it appears that art and creativity are a solipsistic process and that Hersh is prone to turning further and further inwards. However, such a conclusion ignores the social and spatial constructions at work in the text. Hersh's art comes out of engagement with a broad and humane cultural community and with the physical and geographical spaces of Rhode Island and Boston. She navigates the personal, social and spatial in ways that break down distinctions between them. Her love for swimming brings together an intensely embodied experience with an aesthetic love of the Atlantic Ocean. Hersh is an island person but the ocean provides a liminal blurring at its edge rather than hard and defined borders. *Paradoxical Undressing* explores space in ambiguous ways. It is both lived and constructed; past and present.

As a narrative voice, Hersh is always alert to the space around her. The text is full of creative enclaves that exude bohemian spirit and subversive non-conformity. The Rhode Island home of a long-deceased and semi-mythic 'old man' (2010: 1) named Napoleon now houses a 'loosely associated group' (2010: 2) of creative and disaffected subjects whose lives exist outside of the mainstream. Touring musicians, painters, 'bored kids' and 'the lonely and lost' shelter here with the absent owner elevated to 'a kind of saint' (2010: 2). The opening pages of *Paradoxical Undressing* offer homage to this unruly bunch. Hersh's humour and affectionate caricaturing depict scenes of happy squalor and absurdist dialogue. Painters and musicians argue over the 'gaggle of lost souls' that haunt Napoleon's place with 'Manny the drummer' (2010: 3) so spooked he asks for a 'Narragansett medicine woman' to 'smudge the place with sage' (2010: 4). Hersh is self-deprecating about her own trade and cultural identity, insisting that 'musicians are sorta ridiculous', lack in 'normal hair' and wear an expression that is 'perpetually stunned' (2010: 4). Painters, meanwhile, 'dress like it's 1955', with clothes that they 'spatter … on purpose so everyone can tell they're painters' (2010: 5). In Boston, Hersh and her band live in a neighbourhood in which 'blue collar old people' (2010: 183) outnumber artists. Their neighbours are less concerned with indie aesthetics than 'town meetings where they discuss issues like litter and barking dogs' (2010: 183). In response, Hersh and her bandmates close in on each other and form a tight protective unit. Their house is a ramshackle utopia of artistic endeavour. Bassist Leslie's room is described as a 'Zen den … dimly lit and empty, nothing but a futon and a sewing machine' (2010: 183). Her religious devotion to her craft never seems to produce finished products, but this does not matter. It is 'the act of sewing that's important to her' (2010: 184). Also along for the ride is Vicky the Painter, a creative ally from Rhode Island. Vicky's space is exquisitely disordered with 'old movie posters and records … crooked on her walls [and] toys and paintings strewn around the floor' (2010: 184). The absence of a window is made up for 'tenfold with Day-Glo psychedelia' (2010: 184). Vicky's artistic process 'makes sense of chaos but also makes chaos' (2010: 184). In among the clutter and debris it is easy to miss the significance of this paradoxical claim. Art is open-ended; it is never a finished product. It sorts the chaos into further chaos and this notion drives Hersh's own creative self. Her cultural communities are chaotic and disordered. Her writing adds shape, but then those shapes too become chaotic. Like Leslie's sewing, the finished product is unimportant. This is art concerned with process.

Hersh frequently comes back to the chaotic spatial nature of Rhode Island Throwing Muses gigs. These cramped and sweaty spaces are well known to anyone who spent large chunks of the 1980s and 1990s squashed into small and intimate back rooms watching a favourite local band. Hersh playfully explores the manner in which gig space is organized on quasi-tribal lines. Moving from front to back, she sees the 'overtly enthusiastic', 'goth chicks who knit', 'neohippies', 'junkies', 'painters' and 'psychos' (2010: 31). Each group is lovingly portrayed in an affectionate paragraph full of wry observations. The neohippies, for example, 'all have the same hair, the same voice and the same clothes'; they 'dance like goofballs' (2010: 31). The junkies, meanwhile, are 'precious' to Hersh. They are a 'ghostly group' who she adds to the guest list because 'they don't have shit' (2010: 31). The tone shifts when the performances move to the edgier environs of Boston. There is a greater focus on competition and bands treat one another with suspicion. Hersh dismisses such behaviour as simply 'people [who] care about bullshit' (2010: 189). Still, the spaces themselves are gloriously dishevelled and the band takes great pleasure from the mysterious codes they suspect lie beneath the surface of the ostensibly prosaic graffiti. The vulgarities and occasional profundities are 'notes passed to faceless friends'; even the ubiquitous 'fuck you' which appears on 'every wall' (2010: 235).

The gig spaces and the atmosphere that accompanies performance are examples of what Bennett and Peterson term 'music scenes' and define as 'situations where performers, support facilities and fans come together to collectively create music for their own enjoyment' (2004: 3). The key issue here is that the creative act is its own reward. There is little sense that this is an activity designed to elicit profit or develop status. Hersh's egalitarian relationship with her audience and the affectionate manner in which she describes them suggest a commonality of purpose and a sense of community. Art in this instance is intensely social. Bennett and Peterson go to add some specific analysis regarding 'local scenes' (2004: 3). They examine the relationship between 'local music-making processes and the everyday life of specific communities' and find a 'focused social activity' in which a local community engage in 'collectively distinguishing themselves from others by using music and other cultural signs' (2004: 7). This is what Hersh's text depicts in great and loving detail. The cultural and artistic community that surrounds her is varied and heterogeneous, but united by its bohemianism. This is a cultural community that enables a two-way creative process. It exists as a result of the production and performance of music, but that existence leads to the performance and production of further music. For Hersh, the social aspect of her role as artist is as fluctuating and amorphous as that which she attributes to her body and psyche.

Large parts of *Paradoxical Undressing* are given over to the closeness that Hersh shares with her colleagues in Throwing Muses. The love and affection that unites these four musicians is held together by a loose manifesto of two 'bullshit principles' (2010: 42). The first point asks for a physical and emotional empathy in which the band does not distinguish 'toothache' from 'happiness [that] should seep out of pores, and clouds of jealousy and all the different kinds of love and disappointment [that] float around us' (2010: 43). Emotions have a physical presence evident in their texture and agency. Being alert to this is 'the kindest way to live on planet earth' (2010: 43). The second point calls for a minor but consistent level of inebriation. The band should always be 'kinda buzzed, enough to let go' (2010: 43). Hersh associates such a state with being 'light, non-judgemental, truthful' (2010: 43). The result of powerful empathy and a commitment to being a 'little tipsy' (2010: 44) is a set of creative colleagues who share a friendship around which Hersh's fluctuating life can organize itself. Her bandmates are a constant. They are the one presence and influence on Hersh's artistic process that alters very little. Even when the band relocates from the relatively provincial Rhode Island to urban Boston, they remain constant, funny and endearingly kind. They are Hersh's 'allies' and make 'everything clean and good' (2010: 183). Art may be chaotic, but friendship, it seems, is reassuringly simple.

At this particular cultural moment, Boston is home to a lively and increasingly high-profile scene that will go on to spawn indie luminaries such as the Pixies, Breeders, Belly and The Lemonheads. As such, the city's music scene is a site of creativity and innovation. Inevitably, though, it is also the site of aggressive aspiration and the vulture-like presence of the recording industry's amoral executives. Hersh divides local bands into two camps; those whose 'ambition' is 'an embarrassing tap dance' and those who 'make noises for noise's sake' (2010: 189). The former are 'uptight and self-conscious' while the latter are 'slamming joy and desperation, lethargy and force' (2010: 189). As with her own band, Hersh values emotional range and flux. The ability to communicate this musically suggests an ability to be alive to it in others. Empathy and emotional pluralism equal artistic authenticity. These bands – what Hersh terms the 'subculture's subculture' (2010: 189) – provide creative community and cultural influence. Hersh describes the manner in which 'the bands are in the audience until it's their turn to play' and that 'no-one seems to headline, bands just pile up, watching each other and cheering when somebody throws another log on the fire of *real* music' (2010: 189). Hersh wants to make and experience music that gets 'lower and dirtier', music that makes her 'hungry for a body depth or a mind mess' (2010: 190). Again, there is a melding of mind and body here. The scene is a receptive and productive mass of music and art.

Of course, this tangled mess of creative opportunity is undermined by the record industry's singular and simplistic attempts to monetize it. The industry, as Hersh sees it, is one that 'performs the questionable service of telling people what to think while reaching into their pockets for cash' (2010: 195). They are 'the fashion industry, not the music industry', unaware that 'music is timeless [and] fashion ephemeral' (2010: 195). Hersh draws an aesthetic line between superficial products that are 'scary chemical candy' and beauty that is 'valuable' in its ability to 'allow substance to shift styles' (2010: 195). The music industry is interested in static and sellable 'entertainment' rather than music that exists 'in the moment' (2010: 195) before morphing and moving on. Hersh reserves particular vitriol for 'the coke guys, the VIPs with orange tans and tinted glasses' (2010: 195–6). These are executives 'far removed from anything musical' (2010: 196). The tone adopted for one such 'legendary, brilliant man' (2010: 196) is marked by its hostility. He is 'dying one piece at a time, [his] money holding up what's left of [his] corpse' (2010: 196). Hersh equates creativity with life force, whereas this figure only represents moribund commerce. Despite the fact that he assures the band that he is ready to begin 'answering our prayers, fulfilling our dreams' (2010: 196), Hersh knows that this transaction will only hinder their artistic process. The creative decisions are taken away from the band and the record company 'tell you how your record will sound' (2010: 197). More significantly, 'your record is essentially their record' (2010: 197). Fluctuating and plural art is now reduced to a singular commodity and, as a result, 'your songs are gone' (2010: 197). The medium that should provide the income and listenership required to bolster a creative life is in fact a hindrance. Aligning with an executive like this means abandoning creative agency.

As with so much else in this text, however, the opposition between art's authenticity and the industry's shallow greed is more complex than it first appears. As a student at her father's university, Hersh forms an unlikely friendship with the actor Betty Hutton. A Hollywood star during the 1940s and 1950s, Hutton provides mentorship and advice. The text's fragmented make-up and temporal fluidity demonstrate the lasting influence that Hutton has on Hersh. Alongside the prose lie snippets of Throwing Muses' 2010 composition 'Elizabeth June', a song written in tribute to Hutton after her death that same year. Hersh's father, a philosophy professor known as 'dude' by colleagues and students alike, introduces the pair as Hersh is 'too young to make friends' and Betty 'too old' (2010: 16). Hersh is told that Betty overcame a 'fatherless, poverty-stricken childhood in Denver' to become a 'rich, famous movie star in Hollywood' (2010: 16). She is a 'shiny beast' and a 'warm heart in a cold world' (2010: 17). Hersh is unsure as to whether Betty's tale is true but, ever alert to narrative, she 'doesn't care if it's true or not' because 'she loves the story too much' (2010: 16). Betty's advice and influence on Hersh's artistic formation is very different from other characters in the text. She sees little wrong with the manner in which her era of film-making told stories of 'beautiful people living beautiful lives' (2010: 250). The key is that the stories are 'hyperreal' and 'a reality that should have been' (2010: 250). Betty sees artifice and knowingly celebrates it as an artist should. She tells Hersh that her audience will always see a 'caricature', regardless of how 'real' (2010: 250) the music is. The 'persona' and 'the personality' (2010: 251) are not separate entities. They are all part of a 'process of building up and tearing down' and of 'construction and destruction' (2010: 251). The artistic self is incomplete and changeable. Artifice and surface image are as much a part of her creative practice as the authenticity she is so desperate to maintain and communicate. It is important to find a way to make peace with this supposed dichotomy.

Of equal significance in helping Hersh to find a way to make progress in an industry she despises is 4AD head Ivo Watts-Russell. Hersh uses a chapter of the text to document their initial telephone conversations. These are funny and rambling exchanges in which they discuss names, their shared experiences of flu, Ivo's boil ('like a veruca and a carbuncle combined' (2010: 221)) and the fact that he is a fan of Throwing Muses' 'integrity'. Ivo is 'open' and entertaining; his English accent and 'childlike' honesty mean that she pictures 'a six year old with a bowler hat' (2010: 221) on the other end of the telephone. Despite his repeated apologies for 'not signing American bands' (2010: 220), a contract arrives in the post that merely offers to 'fund, release and work on one record, then see how we all feel' (2010: 222). The simplicity and modesty in this offer sit at a significant distance from the bombast and empty discourse offered by the other record companies. The deal is open-ended and is an opportunity for Hersh and her bandmates to experiment with their fluctuating sound. Ivo, Hersh decides, is a 'misguided angel' (2010: 222) and a kindred creative spirit.

Recording the album proves to be a testing experience, though, and the confines of the 'too nice' (2010: 305) studio are a stifling space. Fatigue and the search for a temporarily elusive creative energy take over and the very notion of recording songs becomes a 'stupid idea' (2010: 305). The paradoxical nature of the recording industry has infiltrated this most open of labels. It takes another phone call from Ivo to clear the creative hurdle. His oblique anecdote regarding an 'old man with a cauliflower ear' and the 'filthy London pigeons' that are 'all over him' (2010: 306) taps into the creative centre of this text. It combines spatiality with a visceral corporeality. It is strange and funny and contains no conclusions.

This is the tone in which Hersh thrives as an artist. Sounds, visions and ideas that are without a fixedness or linearity are her muse. As the album's recording is completed, Hersh reflects on the process and the manner in which it allows her to embrace duality and opposition. Music represents the 'ability to navigate a pristine or polluted terrain' and recognizes that 'light and dark are two different moods a mind shines on the subject matter at hand' (2010: 311). Hersh's songwriting and her role as an artist are focused on a full engagement with complexity and paradox. This is why the open and unfinished nature of her aesthetic is so central in the ways that she constructs her autobiographical self. Hersh is an artist who is constructed by the intensely interior as much as she is by the overtly social. Her private world and that of her friends and community bleed into one another. 'All humans embody this dichotomy', she argues, 'and music's just what that sounds like' (2010: 311). All of this comes back to Hersh's claim during that performance in York. Art is about admitting that you are 'still figuring out how to do this shit'.

References

Bennett, A. and R. Peterson (2004), *Music Scenes: Local, Translocal & Virtual*, Nashville, TN: University of Vanderbilt Press.

Egan, S. (1999), *Mirror Talk: Genres of Crisis in Contemporary Autobiography*, Chapel Hill, NC: University of North Carolina Press.

Grundy, G. (2010), 'Kristin Hersh: "I let bipolar disorder colour my early songs"', *The Guardian*, 25 July. Available online: https://www.theguardian.com/music/2010/jul/25/kristin-hersh-crooked-paradoxical-undressing (accessed 27 July 2018).

Hersh, K. (2010), *Paradoxical Undressing*, London: Atlantic Books.

Joyce, J. (2000), *Portrait of the Artist as a Young Man*, London: Penguin Books.

McClary, S. (2002), *Feminine Endings: Music, Gender & Sexuality*, Minneapolis, MN: University of Minnesota Press.

Moi, T. (2005), *Sex, Gender and the Body*, Oxford: Oxford University Press.

Nussbaum, F. (1998), 'The Politics of Subjectivity and The Ideology of Genre', in J. Watson and S. Smith (eds), *Women, Autobiography, Theory: A Reader*, Madison, WI: University of Wisconsin Press.

Reynolds, S. and J. Press (1996), *The Sex Revolts: Gender, Rebellion and Rock 'n' Roll*, Cambridge, MA: University of Harvard Press.

Shepherd, S. (2010), 'Interview: Kristin Hersh', *Music OMH*, 3 August. Available online: https://www.musicomh.com/features/interviews/interview-kristin-hersh (accessed 27 July 2018).

Smith, S. (1995), 'Performativity, Autobiographical Practice, Resistance', *a/b: Auto/Biography Studies*, 10 (1): 17–33.

Watson, J. and S. Smith (1998), 'Situating Subjectivity in Women's Autobiographical Practices', in J. Watson and S. Smith (eds), *Women, Autobiography, Theory: A Reader*, Madison, WI: University of Wisconsin Press.

4

Poet is priest: Julian H. Cope's subversive biography

Nathan Wiseman-Trowse

Since disbanding Liverpudlian psych post-punkers The Teardrop Explodes in 1982, front-man Julian Cope has sustained a long and varied career. At the time of writing, Cope's discography extends to thirty solo albums plus numerous collaborations and band set-ups such as Queen Elizabeth, Black Sheep and Brain Donor. Alongside his musical career, he has also become well regarded as a writer and has been published across a number of styles and formats. Cope's first long-form foray into the literary world came with his memoir *Head-On: Memories of the Liverpool Punk Scene and the Story of The Teardrop Explodes (1976–82)* (1994). Since then he has consistently written alongside his musical output and, almost a quarter of a century into his literary career, Cope's writing tends to fall into three categories: memoir, Neolithic European culture and music criticism. Commencing with *Head-On*, Cope's approaches to memoir and autobiography are extended by his second volume *Repossessed* (published with *Head-On* included as *Repossessed/Head-On* (1999)) that continue to detail his solo career up to the end of the 1980s. His work on pre-Roman Neolithic European culture – particularly its monumental archaeology – is contained primarily in two volumes: *The Modern Antiquarian* (1998) and *The Megalithic European* (2004). Thirdly, Cope's books on music include *Krautrocksampler* (1995), *Japrocksampler* (2007) and a collection of his 'Album of the Month' reviews originally posted on his Head Heritage (2018) website entitled *Copendium* (2012). One potential fourth strand to Cope's written output is suggested by his first novel, *One Three One* (2014a), although currently this remains his only published example of fiction.

The variety of books written by Cope (augmented by a number of poems and short prose pieces found in the liner notes of his recordings) is evidence of a widely divergent set of interests and methodologies. Certainly, Cope does not seem to be afraid of attempting new artistic forms as his career progresses. Yet, over the span of almost twenty years of literary production, a certain homology appears through Cope's recurrent fascination with the liminal territory between objective reality and subjective experience. Whether it is memoir, gazetteer, rock sampler or novel, Cope returns again and again to a hazy middle ground somewhere between the *thing that is* and the *thing that can be*. Fact and fiction interweave throughout all of Cope's books and, while it might be easy to suggest that the most notable factor in his writing is his own self-mythologization, this would be to underplay the role of its place within a broader project. Certainly, since Cope's shift across the *Peggy Suicide* (1991) and *Jehovahkill* (1992a) albums towards a more environmental, spiritual and antiquarian focus, an evolving body of work – performed, recorded and written – has charted the intersections between creative practice and shamanistic ritual. Indeed, Cope's literary awakening coincides with this change in preoccupations. Even at the start of his writing career with his first autobiography, the factual is never the most urgent object of attention. Through his writing – and in a manner loosely tethered to his recording career – Julian Cope has crafted a body of work with a purpose that understands the role of the rock performer as a modern incarnation of a shamanistic priest-class. As Cope puts it in the final pages of *Repossessed*:

> I had a beautiful vestigial Vision, not turned full on, more like a current of truthful gas that coursed through me. It said to me that I had a path: you are a practical choice for the Saying of Some Stuff because you've already had an existentialist career for 10 years. In another 10 Righteous years, the public can judge you against your first un-Righteous 10 years. If the Righteous-trip is in any way True, comparisons between the two periods will be as night is to day. Therefore you are useful to others. (1999: 197)

Ten years after that 'Vision', Cope had published his first four books and set out a template that, regardless of the form, melded the observable with the perceivable. Through that hyperreal miasma, Cope seems to be searching (not always successfully – that is part of the point, after all) for a way to access something else beyond the mundane and the everyday. The process benefits both him and those who engage with his work.

To start with Cope's two autobiographies, his foreword to *Head-On* immediately betrays a hint of the discourse that will prove central to his wider work:

> Only a month into the writing of Head-On, my dear friend and brother, Pete De Freitas, was killed on his motorbike at Rugely, Staffs, on his way from London to Liverpool. ... His death shattered me and appears to have precipitated the complete change in direction which my life then took.
>
> Since 1989, the whole world has changed. But I've re-read this book and it's clear as I'll ever get about that stuff. And it's not washing around in my brain anymore, which is a Major-League Vibe! So here 'tis! (1994)

Not only does Cope acknowledge the shift in his life and work towards the more politically, ecologically and spiritually engaged artist that he would become during this period, but his very tone suggests a way of reading what is to come. The term 'Major-League Vibe' seems incongruous coming from someone born in Monmouthshire, raised in Staffordshire and fed through the Liverpool post-punk scene. Yet this awkward juxtaposition, evoking both a 1950s and a 1960s American sensibility simultaneously, is just one of many euphemisms and pieces of slang borrowed from the countercultural discourse of the last seventy years. Cope's writing is littered with them. He writes, for example, 'I was a stinking sameclotheseveryday bullshitting bad-attitude Peter Noone teenangel dustbust my o – so personal life Aled Jones acid-nobody. I fucking sucked the runniest shit and I was beautiful' (1994: 64), or 'Earlier on, Dorian and I went to Sellafield to see how the Greedheads control our view of this Mo Fo. Ha!' (1998: 251). Or, more expansively:

> Dammit, fellow motherfuckers, I love The New Lou Reeds, and I care about this Stephen DK guy one helluva lot. I'll admit that even I find his songwriting often haphazard and patchy, and his three long-playing statements so far released are unlikely to set the world on fire however much I hassle your reluctant asses to go out and buy his work. (2012: 489)

Cope's adoption of a lexicon borrowed and adapted from a range of post-war youth countercultures and their associated music, films, literature and art places him firmly, and somewhat self-consciously, within a particular lineage; that of the hipster artist. The awkward self-consciousness that places often-archaic Americanisms against Cope's general Midlands/Liverpudlian vernacular adds to their power. He deliberately marks out his strangeness and his distance from 'straight' culture and, consequently, his place within a tradition of mystic-performers. To distort a title from Cope's *Jehovahkill* album, he is the poet as priest.

As Paul de Man suggests, autobiography suggests a level of authenticity above that of fiction, yet such suppositions may be illusory:

Autobiography seems to depend on actual and potentially verifiable events in a less ambivalent way than fiction does. It seems to belong to a simpler mode of referentiality, of representation, and of diegesis. It may contain lots of phantasms and dreams, but these deviations from reality remain rooted in a single subject whose identity is defined by the uncontested readability of his proper name … is the illusion of reference not a correlation of the structure of the figure, that is to say no longer clearly and simply a referent at all but something more akin to a fiction which then, however, in its own turn, acquires a degree of referential productivity? (1979: 920–1)

Whilst it is not the intention of this work to question the veracity of Cope's memoirs, de Man's assertion does show how the mode of autobiography shapes our understanding of the subject as much as it reports upon the events of the subject's life. That is to say that, while this may be a point generally true of autobiography, Cope seems particularly conscious of the way in which he structures his narratives to shape readers' experiences through his own stylization. *Head-On* and *Repossessed* are not fictionalized, at least as far as this author is aware, but the style suggests stylization and a heightened sense of event distilled through a discourse that adds layers of meaning. That discourse, a loose coalition of rock 'n' roll hipster talk and often-scatological British slang, not only provides a heightened sense of events but also helps to shape the way in which Cope himself is understood, at least as far as Cope wants his readers to see him. Cope writes passages that make a number of connections transcending the events that they are describing: 'The Two-Car Garage Band arrived Callyless and unafraid in a Japan just waiting to be weirded out … Now I arrived with my black-clad cohorts and my super crew, with one intention: to get satisfaction. To rock beyond our Role. To gorge ourselves – not to nibble Nippon, but to leap right on' (1999: 142). The 'Two-Car Garage Band' not only refers to Cope's band assembled for the *Saint Julian* (1987) and *My Nation Underground* (1988) albums, it signals the act as part of a continuum of garage rock augmented by a self-knowingly ironic English suburban take on that idea. The 'black-clad cohorts' makes connections to an adlib featured on 'Reynard in Tokyo' (1989), a live recording of 'Reynard the Fox' (1984). The reference to 'satisfaction' both seems to imply '(I Can't Get No) Satisfaction' by The Rolling Stones (Jagger and Richards 1965) and the 'satisfaction' to be demanded from a duel. This conflation of sexual terminology with connections to American blues idioms and a more archaic European sensibility sum up Cope's aesthetic in much the same way as the 'Two-Car Garage Band' does. Finally (clumsy pun on 'nibble' and 'Nippon' aside), the use of 'right on' suggests a layer of affirmation expressed once again through hip slang and rock vernacular, as in 'right on, man'.

Cope's conflation of vernacular styles does much to place him within a lineage that incorporates a classic rock historiography primarily influenced by American popular music and culture as well as a more parochial Englishness. Indeed, the latter goes some way to stopping the former from appearing ludicrous, given how out-dated much of his slang seems to be, providing just enough detached irony to allow us to forgive him. Cope's balancing act situates him as a rock 'n' roller while simultaneously allowing for the potential ludicrousness of such a position. This has been Cope's strategy throughout the latter half of his career. The motivations for such an approach seem to have their roots in Cope's understanding of the rock performer as a divine trickster/shaman figure. Indications of this abound throughout his work, but one notable instance might be the 'Yggdrasil' customized microphone stand initially used through Cope's more commercially successful solo phase in the late 1980s. The microphone stand features foot bars towards the base and a revolving angled upper half that allows Cope to clamber on to it and then swing around on top as he performs. When Cope auctioned the stand to raise funds for charity in the early 1990s the object was described as the 'Yggdrasil mic stand', referencing the elemental tree that connects the nine worlds of Norse mythology. The point is well established by the time Cope is lecturing on the links between Odin and the contemporary rock performer at the British Museum in 2001.

Both *Head-On* and *Repossessed* share a stylistic homology that is very much Cope's own. It is also evident in his writings on his *Head Heritage* website, particularly the 'Address Drudion' (2014b) and 'Unsung' pages. But it is at the other end of his literary career, when Cope moves into fiction, that the stylization of memoir and autobiography are more apparent. *One Three One*, his first novel, concerns a trip made by a faded rock performer named Rock Section to Sardinia to uncover the truth about a series of events centred around the 1990 FIFA World Cup tournament. Cope's novel is a sometimes dizzyingly confusing conflation of time and space that features a series of transcendent mystical journeys via the mysterious stone portals scattered across Sardinia's landscape. However, it is also a road trip novel with a title that references the *Strada Satale* (State Highway) 131 connecting Porto Torres in the north and Cagliari in the south. The road trip acts as a means to both explore Section's connection to the events of 1990, particularly his own kidnap and torture at the hands of Judge Barry Herzog, as well as placing the faded rock performer back into the same mystical lineage propositioned elsewhere in Cope's work.

The significance of *One Three One*, apart from being Cope's first foray into literary fiction, is how similarly it plays out aspects of his autobiography. Section's depiction is a thinly veiled version of Cope without, perhaps, the artistic and spiritual awakening that he went through at the end of the 1980s. Instead, Section's best years are behind him. His flirtation with pop stardom is an increasingly distant memory. But the Sardinian landscape and its Neolithic doorways to the past provide a means for Section (via the narcotic effects of ephedra) to connect with a mythic and mystic understanding of himself that reshapes aspects of contemporary popular culture such as the rock star, the football hooligan or UK rave culture. The novel opens with Section losing control of his bowels on the plane to Sardinia; an event recalling the state of Cope's own leather trousers worn on Teardrop Explodes tours (Cope 1999). Within seven lines of the opening of the novel, Cope is referencing Al Jourgensen of the band Ministry, another figure appearing in Cope's memoirs. In an interview with Cope for *The Quietus* following the publication of *One Three One*, the comedian Stewart Lee observes that 'in *131* there are so many different Copes that, as he does via the many guises of his musical and literary careers, he almost becomes anonymous. *131* finds Cope engaged in a staged Socratic dialogue with various possible versions of his past and future selves' (Lee 2014).

It is possible to take the position that Cope is using his variety of literary guises, linked also to his many musical incarnations, as a way to explore a sort of thematic landscape, regardless of the particular form that presents it. Instead of debating memoir, music criticism, antiquarian writing or fiction as being separate endeavours, Cope maps out a broader unity. It is not difficult to see how, in his memoirs, Cope relates to Rock Section in *One Three One*, but how does his more 'factual' (for want of a better word) writing relate? How can we understand Cope's music writing and antiquarian work as manifestations of the same themes? His antiquarian writing provides some clues. *The Modern Antiquarian*, and to a lesser extent *The Megalithic European*, continue to bridge the divide between *that which is* and *that which can be*. Both books are divided into two sections; initial essays exploring specific facets of Neolithic culture followed by a second section that acts as a gazetteer to the monuments and sites themselves. Cope is clearly keen to discuss not only his subject but also to actively encourage readers to see these sites for themselves in an informed manner. The gazetteer sections provide historical information about the sites, but also contain commentaries from Cope on his own visits to and impressions of the monuments. For example, upon visiting the Cumbrian stone circle Long Meg and her Daughters, Cope provides plenty of useful factual detail while also reflecting upon his own subjective impressions of that visit as a form of meta-commentary:

> It's hard to write. We've been here at Long Meg for over two hours now and what with the curiousness that took me over, my hands are no longer sensible with the pen ... A day at Long Meg is a righteous experience – I scour the horizon, I check our Meg's three-faced beauty, and I smile a lot. (1998: 253)

Each entry in the gazetteer part of *The Modern Antiquarian* features similar reflections and this makes it difficult to disentangle Cope from the subject matter of the sites themselves. Yet while his own experiences of the stones shape their depiction, the gazetteer format includes maps, directions and Ordnance Survey coordinates that act as an invitation to move beyond the page into and through the landscape itself. Ultimately, these features help to develop subjective responses to that landscape. In this way Cope's antiquarian writings act as potential portals in much the same fashion as *One Three One*'s Neolithic doorways do for Rock Section. Further, Cope's impressions meld the autobiographical with the factual and the subjective with the objective in much the same way as his memoir and fiction do.

Cope's writing on music betrays the same approach. *Krautrocksampler*, *Japrocksampler* and *Copendium* are ostensibly collections of criticism that are largely centred on marginalized or alternate histories of popular music. They achieve a balance between objective description and subjective impression in a way that is central to all three books. Again, Cope chooses to bifurcate his 'samplers' between extended essays and gazetteers of selected music. These recordings get the same treatment as the Neolithic sites in the antiquarian writings, with Cope acting both as informant and as a listening guide. In *Copendium*, particularly, Cope's own experience of the albums surveyed is central to his project. Cope's essay on Nico's *The Marble Index* (1968), for example, contains a lot of historical information about the making of the album, its themes and its reception. However, Cope also discusses the album's place in his own life and goes further in situating Nico and her art within his own broader project: 'This review is dedicated to Nico in her many roles: as the Artist, as the Muse and as the Norn tending the well at the foot of Yggdrasil, while simultaneously playing the role of Groah the goddess informing Odin as the traveller Svibdag.

Hail Nico, enduring, hail Nico, forever becoming' (2012: 48). This is music criticism as a reflection upon subjective experience. It is a means to introduce and provide context by fusing documentary and phenomenology. As such (and this is perhaps the attraction for Cope's fans), whatever form his writing takes is a means of engaging exterior and interior states and worlds. The writing assumes an aspect of ritual in which Cope is a guide who has ventured before the reader. He is capable of showing the way, even if readers' experiences are wildly divergent from his own and each other's. Cope is keen to erode the dominance of authenticity, be that through factual observations of the world around him or through the discourses of rock music. As he suggests in the introduction to *Japrocksampler*:

> But what greater oxymoron is there than the phrase 'authentic rock 'n' roll'? From the mid-1950s onwards, rock 'n' roll's screaming genius was its ability to pose as Saturday night entertainment for most of post-war Christendom, whilst simultaneously heathenizing all and sundry with its ardent beat and screaming electric overload. But authentic? If there's anything less authentic than 'a wop bop a loobop, a lop bam boom', then I'd love to hear it. When Little Richard pulled that arbitrary sucker out of the air, you can be damn sure he wasn't about to take a jet plane to the African country of his ancestors' birth in order to authenticate the tribal provenances of his Ur-holler … HE was its provenance, motherfucker! And every rocker who conscientiously mouthed that same 'a wop bop a loobop' gobbledegook mystical formula, from John Lennon to the MC5's Rob Tyner, unconsciously affirmed what we all unconsciously knew all along … that Little Richard was a God, a divinity, a shaman blasted from the Underworld to howl his song before Hell's trapdoor swept him off his feet as the Great Goddess yanked his skinny ass back down there … C'mere you! (2007: 12)

By extension Cope, given his parallel career as a rock musician, situates himself in a similar space where rock music and its pantomime of authenticity – its sonic overload and its linguistic strangeness – become tools to engage with something beyond the mundane.

While the focus of this work is on Julian Cope's writing, his literary career has to be understood within the broader *oeuvre* of his artistic output. Given the breadth and depth of Cope's work in his forty-year career thus far, two examples will suffice as illustrations of the way in which his literary approaches manifest themselves in other mediums. The first example relates to his recorded music and specifically his use of nonsensical verbalization as a practice within rock discourse. In 1984 Cope and his band recorded a session for David (Kid)

Jensen's BBC Radio 1 show that included the track '24a Velocity Crescent' (later appearing on the B-side of the 'Greatness and Perfection of Love' single in the same year and the *Floored Genius 2* compilation in 1993). The track consists of three verses consisting largely of gibberish and broken words over a chaotic sprawl of noise from the band interspersed by brief passages of break-neck drums, guitar and bass. In the final 'verse' Cope proclaims 'In-A-Gadda-Da-Vida, When the Music's Over, White Rabbit, Mass in F Minor', lines which reference Iron Butterfly, The Doors, Jefferson Airplane and The Virgin Prunes respectively. The song concludes with Cope's final line, 'rock 'n' roll, that's where I'm coming from'. The speed and noise of the musical accompaniment coupled with Cope's glossolalic interjections are within the lineage of psychedelic rock. The track's nonsensical approach is its very point. It is a modern incarnation of Little Richard's own 'Ur-holler'. It points to both a contrived absurdity and a deeper inarticulable truth. Cope's own linguistic stylization in his writing is an attempt to continue this process by fusing the factual and the ineffable.

Such stylization also manifests itself at times through the visual accompaniment to his music. Two maps are included in Cope's work; one in the first *Floored Genius* compilation (1992b) and the second included with 1996's *Interpreter* album. The former, entitled 'A New Description of the Tamworth Mound', depicts the landscape around Tamworth where Cope grew up. The hand-painted map not only illustrates the geography of the region but is overlaid with sites of significance to the Cope story thus far: Alvecote Priory 'where Joss and I played cricket as children' (Cope 1984), the sites of the photo shoots for the *Fried* (1984) and *Saint Julian* (1987) album covers and so forth. Here Cope is embarking upon a form of psychogeography. In doing so, he fuses manifest landscape with his own mythologized narrative and flits between autobiographical detail and the stories of his songs. That he should take a similar approach in subsequent writing is very much in keeping with broader preoccupations throughout his career.

It is perhaps this psychogeographical state that best explains what Julian Cope is attempting across his writing and through his broader output. As Merlin Coverley puts it:

> Psychogeography seeks to overcome the processes of 'banalisation' by which the everyday experience of our surroundings becomes one of drab monotony … [Psychogeographical] writers and works … all share a perception of the city as a site of mystery and seek to reveal the true nature that lies beneath the flux of the everyday. (2006: 13)

While psychogeography is often associated with urban spaces and fusing the material city with immaterial subjective experiences, Cope's writing suggests a psychogeography linked to landscape in a much broader sense. Whether this be through his reimagining of physical landscape such as Tamworth, Sardinia, post-war Germany or the Avebury Neolithic complex, or his reimagining of musical 'landscape', or indeed the landscape of his autobiography, the tensions between fact and fiction provide mechanisms for Cope to aim for something less tangible. Cope's shamanistic practice as a conduit and a guide has a transformative potential; one that can be found in the libidinous and ridiculous scream of rock 'n' roll as much as it can be found in the myth-structures of European antiquity. As such, one might choose not to see the variety of Cope's writing as a series of dalliances with various literary forms. Rather, Cope's project is to harness the power of self-mythologization and its place within discourses of music and belief across almost everything that he creates. It is in the strangeness, the absurdity, the babble and confusion of Cope's narratives that the doorways potentially open, where the poet is priest.

References

Cope, J. (1984), 'Reynard the Fox', *Fried* [CD], London: Mercury Records.
Cope, J. (1987), *Saint Julian* [CD], London: Island Records.
Cope, J. (1988), *My Nation Underground* [CD], London: Island Records.
Cope, J. (1989), 'Reynard in Tokyo', *5 O'Clock World* [Vinyl], London: Island Records.
Cope, J. (1991), *Peggy Suicide* [CD], London: Island Records.
Cope, J. (1992a), *Jehovahkill* [CD], London: Island Records.
Cope, J. (1992b), *Floored Genius: The Best of Julian Cope and The Teardrop Explodes 1979-91* [CD], London: Island Records.
Cope, J. (1993), *Floored Genius 2: Best of the BBC Sessions 1983-1991* [CD], London: Nighttracks Records.
Cope, J. (1994), *Head-On: Memories of the Liverpool Punk-Scene and the Story of The Teardrop Explodes; 1976-82*, London: Magog Books.
Cope, J. (1995), *Krautrocksampler: One Head's Guide to the Great Kosmische Musik – 1968 Onwards*, London: Head Heritage.
Cope, J. (1996), *Interpreter* [CD], London: Echo Records.
Cope, J. (1998), *The Modern Antiquarian: A Pre-Millennial Odyssey Through Megalithic Britain Including a Gazetteer to over 300 Prehistoric Sites*, London: Thorsons.

Cope, J. (1999), *Repossessed: Shamanic Depressions in Tamworth and London (1983–89) / Head-On: Memories of the Liverpool Punk-Scene and the Story of The Teardrop Explodes (1976–82)*, London: Harper Collins.

Cope, J. (2004), *The Megalithic European: The 21st Century Traveller in Prehistoric Europe*, London: Element.

Cope, J. (2007), *Japrocksampler: How the Post-War Japanese Blew their Minds on Rock 'n' Roll*, London: Bloomsbury.

Cope, J. (2012), *Copendium: An Expedition into the Rock 'n' Roll Underworld*, London: Faber and Faber.

Cope, J. (2014a), *One Three One: A Time-Shifting Gnostic Hooligan Road Novel*, London: Faber & Faber.

Cope, J. (2014b), 'Address Drudion', *Head Heritage*. Available online: http://www.headheritage.co.uk/addressdrudion/ (accessed 16 January 2018).

Cope, J. (2018), Unsung: 'Julian Cope's Album of the Month', *Head Heritage*. Available online: http://www.headheritage.co.uk/unsung/albumofthemonth/ (accessed 16 January 2018).

Coverley, M. (2006), *Psychogeography*, Harpenden: Pocket Essentials.

de Man, P. (1979), 'Autobiography as De-facement', *MLN*, 94 (5): 919–30.

Jagger, M. and K. Richards (1965), '(I Can't Get No) Satisfaction' [Sound Recording] Performed by The Rolling Stones, London: Decca.

Lee, S. (2014), 'A Journey to Avebury: Stewart Lee Interviews Julian Cope', *The Quietus*. Available online: http://thequietus.com/articles/15594-julian-cope-stewart-lee-interview (accessed 3 March 2017).

Nico (1968), *The Marble Index* [Vinyl], New York: Elektra.

5

Grace Jones: Cyborg memoirist

Janine Bradbury

In her landmark essay 'A Cyborg Manifesto', Donna Haraway ([1991] 2010: 150) deploys the metaphor of 'a hybrid of machine and organism' to undermine monolithic constructions of Western (American) identity predicated on race, gender and other arbitrary markers of difference. Haraway's cyborg, or 'cybernetic organism' (2010: 149), emblemizes our potential to challenge, destabilize and confuse seemingly 'natural' binary oppositions between human/animal, animal-human/machine and physical/non-physical in ways that hold enormous potential for the future of feminist politics (2010: 151–3). Perhaps no figure better represents a configuration of the cyborg aesthetic and a blurring of these boundaries than the singer, performer, muse, model and actress Grace Jones. Whether channelling a wild, caged animal on the cover of Jean-Paul Goude's *Jungle Fever* (1982), emerging out of a mechanized underground lair crafted in the shape of her own head in a Citroën CX2 advertisement (1985) or appearing as a molten, amorphous entity in the video for 'Corporate Cannibal' ([2008] 2010), Jones persistently breaches these boundaries. Over the course of a career spanning half a century, and like the cyborg Haraway envisages, Jones has consistently challenged hegemonic narratives of race, gender and locale.

In her 'own' words, Grace Jones is 'black, but not black; woman, but not woman; American, but Jamaican; African, but science fiction' (Jones 2015: 82). With her androgynous style, fiery reputation and closely cropped hair, she is renowned for 'breaking certain' (if not all) 'laws about how [she] was meant to behave and look, as a model, a girl, a daughter, an American, a West Indian, a human being' (2015: 82). Through a commitment to collaborative practice with producers (Tom Moulton, Sly and Robbie, Tricky and Brian Eno among others) and visual artists (her ex-partner Jean-Paul Goude, Helmut Newton and Keith Haring, for instance), Jones offers an aesthetic and sound that represents a cyborgic bridge between 'worlds ambiguously natural and crafted', between 'machine and organism', and between 'the territories of production, reproduction, and imagination' (Haraway [1991] 2010: 150). Her greatest hits embrace a polyphonic bricolage of genres ranging from reggae and dub on the track 'My Jamaican Guy' (1982) to disco and bossa nova in 'La Vie en Rose' (1977). Her live performances and audio recordings reflect a vocal and tonal dexterity that is utterly compelling. As Steven Shaviro (2010: 29) writes of 'Slave to the Rhythm' (1985), this track is a 'strange hybrid' which, sung 'without any warmth or soul', 'simultaneously embraces … Kraftwork-style roboticism on the one hand, and African-derived rhythmic multiplicity on the other'. And yet her acoustic live performances of John Newton's hymn 'Amazing Grace' (as featured in Sophie Fiennes's recent documentary *Bloodlight and Bami* (2017)) can only be described as pure, unadulterated, sonorous gospel testimony. Importantly, in her revision and adaptation of prior modes of expression (with her cover versions of Broadway musical songs on her debut album *Portfolio* [1977], for instance, or her reappropriation of a black masculine aesthetic), Jones participates in the distinctly black cultural mode of 'signifyin(g)' (Gates [1988] 2014: 85), a trope through which black writers, performers and artists 'repeat, revise, reverse, or transform what has come before' (Caponi 1999: 22). Whether in the studio with Sly and Robbie or featured in her former partner Jean-Paul Goude's manipulated images, assemblages and collages, Grace Jones is a hybrid of subject and object, embodied performance and synthetic production, 'a creature of social reality as well as a creature of fiction' (Haraway [1991] 2010: 149). She is a polysemic, post-human cultural icon who, like the cyborg itself, is transgressive, mutable and resists definition.

In this chapter, I read Jones's autobiographical text *I'll Never Write My Memoirs* (2015) as an artefact that contributes to this post-human mythogenesis. My consideration of the text is informed by the audio-visual materials that comprise her 'star image' (Dyer 1998: 34), but is focused primarily on narrative voice and form by reading Jones's book as part of a black autobiographical tradition, specifically the narratives of enslaved and formerly enslaved people. It is important to note, as Joanne M. Braxton (1989: 18) quite rightly argues, critical discussions of black autobiography have disproportionately focused on the stories of men despite a rich concurrent tradition of black female autobiographical writing during slavery and beyond. *I'll Never Write My Memoirs* fits into 'a tradition within a tradition' of black women's life writing by individuals including Harriet Jacobs and later Audre Lorde, and Maya Angelou who 'operat[e] within the dominant, familiar, and essential masculinist modes of autobiography', 'reshap[ing] and redefin[ing] their inherited formulae' (Braxton 2009: 128). Drawing comparisons between Jones's work, Haraway's manifesto and canonical slave narratives authored by men and women, I make a case for reading Grace Jones not simply as 'a cyborg feminist', a figure who 'argue[s] that "we" do not want any more natural matrix of unity and that no construction is whole' (Haraway [1991] 2010: 157), but as a 'cyborg memoirist' who uses the black autobiographical form to advance this agenda.

Jones toys with what Leigh Gilmore (1994: 42) describes as 'the technologies of autobiography ... those legalistic, literary, social, and ecclesiastical discourses of truth and identity through which the subject of autobiography is produced' in order to fragment and complicate questions of self rather than to cement them. When we read her text as part of a black American autobiographical tradition and as a black Atlantic text that draws upon Afrofuturist tendencies, we can better understand how this process occurs. Experimenting with the limits and potential of writing the self, Jones plays with notions of temporality, spatiality, perspective and authenticity to challenge stereotypical notions of femininity, blackness and age. My work here is both an exercise in and meditation on Gilmore's philosophy of 'autobiographics' (1994: 42) both as 'a reading practice' (which I perform) and a process 'of self-representation' (that Jones partakes in), which is 'concerned with interruptions and eruptions [and] with resistance and contradiction as strategies of self-representation' in women's life writing. And so in keeping with this practice, my reading of Jones's memoir pays particular attention to what Eve Kosofsky Sedgwick might describe as the 'open mesh of possibilities, gaps, overlaps, dissonances, resonances, lapses, and excesses of meanings when the constituent elements of anyone's gender, of anyone's sexuality aren't made (or *can't* be made) to signify monolithically' (1994: 8). In other words, I am interested in the ways that Jones 'queers' the autobiographical genre by reclaiming it as cyborgic territory where she refuses to 'set the record straight' (Jones 2015: ix). Moreover, I actively seek to uncover the 'resistance' that is generated via a comparative reading of Haraway's and Jones's work, uncovering tensions and 'dissonances' between the two texts, particularly with regard to discourses surrounding motherhood and maternity.

Haraway's cyborg is suspicious of the very idea of origin: 'the cyborg has no origin story in the Western sense', is suspicious of 'original unity', 'original stor[ies]' ([1991] 2010: 151), and 'original wholeness' ([1991] 2010: 167). The African-American autobiographical form, rooted in the slave narrative tradition, is also mindful of the limitations of tracing origins even as it simultaneously attempts to substantiate and verify the conditions through which most people of colour came to *be* in the Americas – slavery. But while the slave narrative attempts to craft an origin story by way of validating the experiences of people of colour, Jones's work utilizes narratives of origin to resist being read in any objective, singular or substantive way. For instance, as James Olney (1984: 50–1) explains, a portrait of the author and 'an appendix or appendices composed of documentary material' are two conventional paratextual features of slave narratives. The *Narrative of the Life and Adventures of Henry Bibb, an American Slave, Written by Himself* ([1849] 2000), for instance, includes a 'Report' on the veracity of his claims which details his 'subject[ion] to a rigorous examination' as regards 'Facts – dates – persons – and localities.' Jones on the other hand, renouncing the need for authentication, includes a preface where she boldly states 'I don't care if you don't believe me' (2015: ix). Moreover, in a fascinating reversal of the legalistic discourses used to legitimate the enforced labour of people of colour in the Americas, Jones includes a rider as her appendix, a document in which she defines and sets the conditions of her own labour. Her equivalent of an 'author portrait' (the cover images on the hardback edition) is in some ways in keeping with images associated with the black autobiographical tradition of the nineteenth century and appeal to the sensitivities of white readers. While the front cover image is certainly 'cheekier' than Bibb's, it is, in comparison to the images associated with her star image, modest – her flesh is mostly covered. While the back cover features an image of Jones topless, she demurely covers her chest with her hands (a quasi-Venus Pudica), and gazes into the distance – a classic image of passivity. Even though many (although not all) of the images of Jones that fans are familiar with (Goude's covers to the albums *Slave to the Rhythm* [Jones 1985] and *Nightclubbing* [Jones 1981], for instance) evoke a kind of, to borrow from bell hooks (2015: 116), 'rebellious desire, an oppositional gaze', Jones does not look directly at camera in either image on the cover of her book. As hooks (2015: 115) reflects, 'There is power in looking', for black looks are 'seen as confrontational, as gestures of resistance, challenges to authority'; 'white slaveholders (men, women, and children) punished enslaved black people for looking', and 'slaves were denied their right to gaze' (2015: 115). Although on initial consideration Jones appears to be abdicating her power in refusing to look her reader in the eye, she is actually adopting a key strategy of the signifyin(g) trickster of African mythology (see Gates [1988] 2014) who misleads and misguides. She warns us in her preface, 'It's up to you whether you go inside. If you do go under the covers, don't be outraged at what you find. It's your fault for lifting the covers' (2015: x). And, indeed, the anecdotes and reflections Jones divulges between the 'safe' covers of the book are at times obscenely provocative.

Jones also signifies on the opening lines of canonical slave narratives that explore the origin of the subject. Olney (1984: 52) observes that the phrase 'I was born' often appears in the opening line of slave narratives to 'attest to the real existence of a narrator, the sense being that the status of the narrative will be continually called into doubt, so it cannot even begin, until the narrator's real existence is firmly established'. The first chapters of the autobiographies of Henry Bibb, Henry Box Brown, William Wells Brown, Mary Prince and Frederick Douglass (and many others) all begin with those same three words, which serve to complement paratextual materials such as 'photographs, portraits, signatures, [and] authenticating letters' that all make the same claim: 'this man [or person] exists' (Olney 1984: 52). Jones also opens her first chapter with those memorable three words, signifyin(g) on this tradition:

> 'I was born about forty-five miles from the city of Richmond, in Louisa County, in the year 1815.' (H. B. Brown [1851] 1999)
> 'I was born May 1815, of a slave mother, in Shelby County, Kentucky, and was claimed as the property of David White Esq.' (Bibb [1849] 2000)
> 'I was born in Tuckahoe, near Hillsborough, and about twelve miles from Easton, in Talbot county, Maryland.' (Douglass [1845] 1999)
> 'I was born in Lexington, Ky.' (W. W. Brown [1849] 1996)
> 'I was born at Brackish-Pond, in Bermuda, on a farm belonging to Mr. Charles Myners.' (Prince [1831] 2000)
> 'I was born.
> It happened one day, when I least expected it, on an island measuring only 4,411 square miles, a teeming mountainous land of wood and water among a chain of islands in the center of the Caribbean Sea at the western edge of the Atlantic Ocean.' (Jones 2015: 1)

Jones complicates the specifically autobiographical tradition syntactically, by separating out the existential statement ('I was born') from the geographical information that traditionally follows it within the sentence with a full stop and line break, and also by conveying that geographical information in a way that lyrically locates it in the broader diasporic context of the black Atlantic rather than in a regionalized locale. The signifyin(g) opening of Jones's memoir thus serves to distance the autobiographical subject from any single point of origin in keeping with Haraway's manifesto. Jones was born, yes, but in the first few lines she does not explain when or where exactly, rendering her a 'floating signifier' (Haraway [1991] 2010: 153). She is devoid of referent, even if only momentarily. This again serves to undermine the notion that Jones can be authenticated in any substantial way.

In keeping with Haraway's vision of the cyborg, Jones also defies attempts to locate any authentic or authoritative origin of meaning in the text through her use of a co-author. Although the title appears ironic, in that it would seem that Jones did indeed opt to write her memoir after all, we must remember that *I'll Never Write My Memoirs* is an 'as-told-to' autobiography produced in partnership with music journalist Paul Morley. In this sense, Jones signifies on the slave narrative tradition of including a caveat about authorship. Henry Box Brown, William Wells Brown, Henry Bibb, Harriet Jacobs all have the phrase 'Written by Himself' or 'Written by Herself' in the title, even when an amanuensis is involved, while Mary Prince's text is 'Related by Herself'. While it is certainly not uncommon for a contemporary celebrity autobiography to be produced in the way that Jones's book is, the interracial dynamic between Jones and Morley evokes the slave-amanuensis relationship that facilitated the publication of eighteenth- and nineteenth-century slave narratives. It also transgresses the boundaries of 'propriety' that usually characterized these arrangements in the nineteenth century. Generally speaking, black women authors of slave narratives such as Harriet Jacobs, Mary Prince and Mattie Jackson all had white female amanuenses or editors (see Bohls [2013: 78–82] on Prince's relationship with Susannah Strickland; Gunning [1996: 135–7] on Jacobs's and Lydia Maria Child's arrangements, and Moody [2001: 103–27] on Jackson's connections with Dr L. S. Thompson). Even though, as Olney (1984: 50) notes, historically an amanuensis might offer a testimonial verifying that 'the narrative is a "plain, unvarnished tale" and that naught "has been set down in malice, nothing exaggerated, nothing drawn from the imagination"', as Vincent Carretta (2011: 54) observes of the antebellum African-American literary tradition, 'As-told-to narratives present the reader with the obvious problem of trying to identify the authentic black voice behind the words transcribed by his or her amanuensis.' In Jones's case, the use of Morley as 'amanuensis/editor/author' (Olney 1984: 50) means that authenticity of Jones's project is called into question. This, however, is no bad thing given that Jones's star image is one that balks at the idea of a verifiable and objective authenticity. A cyborgic persona that resists a definitive point of origin can only thrive on the possibility of multivalent interpretation. And so Morley's position as a 'collaborator on this book' (Jones 2015: 284) is not meant to validate Jones's memoirs; instead it serves to fracture, disrupt and undermine our elevation of Jones to the status of what Roland Barthes (1977: 146–7) describes as an 'Author-God' who offers a 'single "theological" meaning' to the text. Certainly, Jones's choice to embrace Morley's involvement raises alarm bells for any critic, thinker and activist wary of the ways that white men have historically exploited the labour of women of colour. But his ghosting of the memoir, while problematic in many ways, also renders any 'claim to "decipher" [the] text' (Barthes 1977: 147) – including my own – moot. Jones ensures that the ghost of the amanuensis is metamorphosed into the spirit of the collaborator and this disrupts the dynamic of oppressor/oppressed and subject/object that historically characterizes white/black cultural production.

Haraway's conceptualization of the cyborg as one who 'does not mark time on an oedipal calendar' ([1991] 2010: 150) also resonates with the representation of time in the narratives of formerly enslaved people. It is not unusual for the black subject to exist outside of time due to the fact that enslaved people rarely knew the exact date of their birth because slave 'patriarchs' and masters did not share this information. As Frederick Douglass writes in the second, third and fourth sentences of his autobiography: 'I have no accurate knowledge of my age, never having seen any authentic record containing it. By far the larger part of the slaves know as little of their ages as horses know of theirs … I do not remember to have ever met a slave who could tell of his birthday' (Douglass [1845] 1999).

While Douglass does not know his age, or at least withholds this information in order to emphasize the ways in which black people have been dehumanized by white enslavers, Jones deliberately withholds this information in her memoir in order to dehumanize her account, or rather to amplify the post-human and cyborgic elements of her memoir. She refuses to disclose her precise age, preferring instead to 'keep the mystery' (2015: 3). For Jones, time is not chronological or empirical: 'Time … is an energy. I'm another energy, and the two energies wrap around each other' (2015: 3). She doesn't see time as 'past, present, and future' (2015: 368) and claims that she hasn't aged because 'I don't believe in time, I don't believe in age, I don't believe in getting older' (2015: 370). This is because, like Haraway's cyborg, Jones lives in 'a world without genesis, but maybe also a world without end' ([1991] 2010: 150). This is reflected in the structure of her memoir. Although the text follows the conventional trajectory of the autobiographical form beginning with Jones's birth and ending in the contemporary moment, the book's structure elides a true beginning and a definitive end. The final chapter promotes future endeavours and firmly signals outside of the text with its concluding line, 'it's time for something else to happen' (Jones 2015: 380). Additionally, the book's preface is entitled 'Before' and is positioned before the book's first chapter and Jones's presence in the text does not begin with her birth, but with reference to her memories of the womb.

Jones's *in utero* origin narrative not only imaginatively recovers the unknown specifics of one's birth as emphasized in Douglass's narrative, but is one of several ways that Jones, in the nascent cyborgic tradition, signifies on Christian imagery in order to upset Western grand narratives about who we are. 'In retelling origin stories,' Haraway argues, 'cyborg authors subvert the central myths of origin of Western culture' for '[w]e have all been colonized by those origin myths, with their longing for fulfilment in apocalypse' ([1991] 2010: 175); and indeed, *I'll Never Write My Memoirs* signifies on the idea of creation, deliverance and apocalypse. Jones's own dawn alludes to the book of Genesis where 'In the beginning' God created 'light' and 'divided the light from the darkness' (Gen. 1–5). In Jones's Genesis, however, we see a spatial inversion of these realms: the light is not an exterior space (the 'heaven and earth' that God created and opened out for man) but is instead located within the literal dark, in the distinctly female space of the womb itself, the space in which she 'had been floating for so long' (Jones 2015: 1). For Jones 'Inside, [her mother] there was the light' and to be born is to 'enter the darkness' (2015: 1). Here, Jones not only toys with the Old Testament creation story with its imagery of light and dark, but resignifies Jesus's description of himself as having 'come a light into the world' (John 12.46), who leads 'children of the light' who 'believe in the light' (John 12.36). Jones believes in the light, but it is distinctly maternal and matrilineal rather than patriarchal and religious. Jones's narrative persona, like Haraway's cyborg, thus resists an engagement with patriarchal and ecclesiastical markers of time and reverses the notion of teleological delivery or, rather, Christian deliverance from the darkness into the light. She is delivered into the darkness.

Haraway ([1991] 2010: 150) argues that the cyborg is an 'incarnation ... outside salvation history' and Jones rejects the very notion of salvation in her defiance of revelation and apocalypse: 'I didn't start to doubt God, or faith, or the belief. I never had a distinct moment when I turned on the religion that had been tightly wound around me squeezing the freedom out of me. I didn't have a moment of revelation, that it was all nonsense, or dangerous, or superstitious' (Jones 2015: 35). For Jones, her religious upbringing binds her in ways that are conveyed through gendered imagery, 'squeezing her' corset-like (2015: 35), and restricting her freedom. Moreover, her non-acceptance of

Christianity is, like her, not bound by time or definable in a single 'moment' (2015: 35). Her rejection of the premise of 'revelation', a term etymologically synonymous with Haraway's 'apocalypse' (OED Online 2018) is indicative of a dismissal of the very possibility or necessity of salvation itself. Jones does not need saving, for, in her opinion, there is nothing to be saved from. For Jones there will be no delivery from evil or hell, for the transcendent and mystical realms of heaven and hell are located in profane, secular and material places. Port Antonio in Jamaica, for example, is 'a fucked-up heaven, which suits me' (Jones 2015: 191) and Studio 54 is a 'kind of heaven or a kind of hell, or both' (2015: 160). Perhaps Jones undermines these Judeo-Christian narratives by way of rebelling against the strictly religious father figures in her life – specifically her step-grandfather, the tyrannical Mas P, and her father, a Pentecostal minister. Again, this echoes a central trope of the slave narrative through which authors, such as Douglass ([1845] 1999) condemn 'the corrupt, slaveholding, women-whipping, cradle-plundering, partial and hypocritical Christianity of this land'. In its signifyin(g) biblical allusions and narrative structure, then, Jones's memoir speaks to and plays out some of Haraway's theoretical suggestions for how one might subvert hegemonic ontological narratives about who we are, where we are and why we are.

In a sense, Jones's cyborg memoir, in its play with time, structure and narrative linearity, facilitates her manipulation of what Michael Hanchard (2001: 253) describes as 'racial time' or 'the inequalities of temporality that result from power relations between dominant and subordinate groups'. Time, Hanchard argues, 'when linked to relations of dominance and subordination, is another social construct that marks inequality between social groups' (2001: 253). Under slavery, slave owners controlled the relationship that enslaved people had to time (how it was spent and what it could yield) and in the mid-twentieth century 'to be black in the United States meant that one had to wait for nearly everything' (Hanchard 2001: 263) except, I would add, incarceration and death, which continue to hurtle into the life trajectories of black people with alarming and disproportionate velocity. If time is something that historically has impeded people of colour, both within the United States and throughout diasporic communities, such as those in Jones's home nation of Jamaica, to reject time is an immensely political act. Jones exercises a sense of 'temporal freedom', which is not only a freedom from 'racial time' but an alignment with 'world-time', which 'transcends the life of an individual' (Hanchard 2001: 265). Perhaps it is more akin to what Haraway ([1991] 2008: 150) describes as our own 'mythic' time.

This is conveyed, in part, by combining cyborgic descriptions of regeneration with references to black African history:

> If I am from another era, everywhere I look, at the electric sheep all around me, it all seems to indicate that we are still inside that era. There is no new era, only the one I am still part of being stored and restored.
>
> … Even death won't stop me …. You can find images of me from centuries ago. Faces that look like mine carved in wood from ancient Egypt, Roman times, the Igbo tribe of southern Nigeria, and sixteenth-century Jamaica, fierce enough to turn people pale, to shrink their hearts. I have been around for a long time, heart pounding, ready to pounce on my prey, blurring borders, speaking my mind, believing that the world is full of visible and invisible forces, crossing the water, tripping, grieving, loving, hunting, conquering, seducing, fighting, dreaming, laughing, and I always will be.
>
> … I will be ready for the afterlife, for my bones to be buried in the mountains of Jamaica, or the canals of Venice, or the dark side of the moon, or under the ground in the cites I've lived and loved. (Jones 2015: 369)

On the one hand, Jones resembles James Cameron's *Terminator* ([1984] 2001), a death-defying figure who cannot be stopped, a creation that emerges out of the same 1980s zeitgeist as Jones's own cyborg aesthetic when, as Graham Thompson (2007: 26) highlights, '[a]nxieties about the human body and its place in a society increasingly dominated by science and technology spill out into American culture'. And yet Jones not only emblemizes regeneration but reincarnation. She transcends periodization. Her prose echoes pan-African lyricism in works such as Langston Hughes's 'The Negro Speaks of Rivers' ([1921] 2003) and Nikki Giovanni's 'Ego Tripping' (1968) in ways that connect the black Atlantic experience to 'world time'. Crucially, Jones's rendition of these tropes are infused with allusions to science fiction (Philip K. Dick's *Do Androids Dream of Electric Sheep?* [1968] 2007) as well as technological references to the storage of data. In this sense, *I'll Never Write* can be read as an Afrofuturist text that, as Mark Dery explains, 'treat[s] African-American themes and addresses African-American concerns in the context of twentieth-century technoculture' (1994: 180). Of course, as a Jamaican-born, French-speaking resident of the United States and the diasporic metropoles of Paris and London, Jones complicates Dery's definition of Afrofuturism as African-American. But in this extract, she certainly provides a narratological link between pan-Africanism and cyborg imagery. As Kodwo Eshun (2003: 293) explains, Afrofuturism is also concerned with 'the dimension of the predictive, the projected, the proleptic, the envisioned, the virtual, the anticipatory and the future conditional' as well as a pan-African 'liberationist idyll of African archaism'. In this spirit, Jones's regenerative imagery reaches across the middle passage, across the black Atlantic diaspora, and across time and space from ancient Egypt and Rome to Nigeria, to colonial Jamaica, up and out into space, to the moon and back down underground. And it is 'proleptic', 'projective', visionary and forward-looking in its invitation into the future. However, Jones's cyborg is also infused with powers that hint at 'invisible forces' such as hoodoo mysticism, and at a primal power that hints at racial essentialism. And so Jones both defies embodied, earthly, time-bound human experiences, and indulges in a racialized discourse that, for better or worse, has been misread as embodied and essentially black. In this sense, Jones doesn't altogether epitomize a post-human ideology as promoted by Haraway. In many ways she advocates and endorses readings of blackness and femininity as embodied and biological. This is one of the ways in which her text jars with 'A Cyborg Manifesto'.

A further complication of the cyborg aesthetic occurs with Jones's embrace, rather than 'suspicion', of birthing and reproduction, which she uses to provide a narrative arc and a semblance of cohesion to her story. The centrality of motherhood in the text chimes with slave narratives authored by black mothers (for instance, Harriet Jacobs's narrative), which amplify this trope by way of condemning the inhumanity of a system in which black women are vulnerable to rape, children are enslaved and which routinely separates children from their mothers. Although Haraway ([1991] 2010: 181) argues (albeit it symbolically) that 'cyborgs … are suspicious of the reproductive matrix and of most birthing', Jones finds the reproductive matrix and birthing to be fulfilling and enjoyable. For instance, even though narratologically Jones's recollection of her own birth is unconventional, the graphic description of her own birth is celebratory and defiant in tone; she arrives 'feetfirst', 'kicking', 'sticky with fury, soaked to the skin', 'neck full extended' (2015: 1). Midway through the text, Jones recounts how much she enjoyed her pregnancy and the relative ease with which she gives birth to her son Paulo; even though she remembers the sensation of her unborn child moving inside her as 'alien', she is a self-proclaimed 'jungle mother' (2015: 219) who 'instinctively felt [childbirth] would be a powerful, positive thing … the most natural thing in the world' (2015: 216). And, towards the close of the memoir, in the chapter 'Grand', Jones draws her text to a close with her memories of becoming a grandmother to her granddaughter Athena, reflecting 'I never really had a grandmother, not in any traditional, nurturing sense. Athena made me feel grand. I definitely wanted to be Grandma' (2015: 374). To describe Jones as merely cyborgic is to overlook her embracing of motherhood as natural and normative, and – perhaps – a biological imperative.

Crucially, as central as this reproductive imagery is to the memoir, Jones does disrupt expectations of what motherhood can and should be. While Jones indulges rhetoric around 'natural birth' (2015: 223), she rejects patriarchal expectations about how a mother should behave and what a mother should do. For instance, she discusses the ease with which she blends the historically separate realms of domestic motherhood and work by breastfeeding Paulo in the studio while recording *Warm Leatherette* (2015: 223). Jones also recounts writing 'Nipple to the Bottle' (1985), a song rife with maternal imagery after an argument with Goude, whom she infantilizes by comparing him to a breastfeeding child in the lyrics. In her focus on her relationship with Athena, Jones also upsets the historically potent image of the plump, asexual, black mammy who fits 'into a pattern of representatives of African-American women taking care of white children and preferring them to their own' (Wallace-Saunders 2008: 13). Her grandchild Athena is ostensibly white and somehow, like Jones herself, ghostly, horrific and ethereal:

> I shouldn't really say it, but it was like a *Rosemary's Baby* moment. She had these deep purple eyes, and this little spray of red hair, and her skin was so white ... it was almost transparent. She was like Elizabeth I in wrinkled miniature. Her blue-purple eyes locked right on mine. It was an extraordinary moment. (Jones 2015: 373)

Athena's whiteness is made 'strange' ('purple eyes', 'transparent skin') rather than normative and given (Dyer 1997: 10). And in a fascinating reversal of historical racial power relations, Jones rejects her ancestral 'position' as the colonial subject of the monarch associated with the establishment of empire; instead she is the grandmother of Elizabeth I.

The most revelatory fusion of cyborg and maternal imagery within the memoir is evident in Jones's discussion of Goude's iconic cover for *Slave to the Rhythm* (1985). The cover features Jones appearing to scream furiously through a graphically hyper-extended jaw, while looking directly at the camera. A fragment of Kodak safety film protrudes from her hard-angled afro, representing Jones's strong identification as photographic object, but also her status as transgressive photographic subject (she cannot be captured 'on film', she tears it up, wears it, controls it, owns it). The Kodak safety film also symbolizes her temperament – her apparent destruction of safety film metaphorically suggests that she balks at attempts to protect her, and safety film was introduced because the alternatives, like Jones herself, can be highly flammable, combustible and difficult to work with (see *Chronology*). Jones's dark brown skin is featured against a white background which itself consists of shards of shattered glass or plastic. The frequency of her black screams, emblemized in the form of the long play grooves appearing across the cover (specifically across her mouth and hair), are such that whiteness cannot contain them. Despite the post-human aesthetic here, in her memoir Jones suggests that the cover is Goude's tribute to the mother of his child and captures the 'expression as I gave my final push before our son appeared, my mouth stretched as wide as it could' (2015: 220); Goude 'extended the last, big scream, the final push, the birth moment, made my mouth impossibly open' (2015: 220). In this sense, one of the most iconic cyborgic images of Jones's music career could be interpreted as an essentializing commentary on maternity, childbirth and what Barbara Creed might describe as one of the many 'faces' of the 'monstrous-feminine' (1993: 3). It is also a moment where Goude takes a moment of black female creativity and production (in the form of giving birth to human life) and co-opts it as an emblem for his own generative, technological capacity as artist, photographer and curator of the star image of 'Grace Jones'.

To conclude (and for future consideration), it is worth highlighting that Haraway makes much of the ways that 'women of colour' use language, literacy and, indeed, life writing in her manifesto. For her, '"women of colour" might be understood as a cyborg identity, a potent subjectivity synthesized from fusions of outsider identities and in the complex political-historical layerings of her "biomythography"' (Haraway [1991] 2010: 174). And, indeed, *I'll Never Write my Memoirs*, is in some ways a 'biomythography' or as Audre Lorde, who coined the term, defines it, 'fiction ... a piece of art, not merely a retelling of things that happened to me' (Jay [1983] 2004: 110) (see also Lorde 1982 and Weekes 2006: 324). It blends and layers myth, cultural history, lyricism and art in ways that the contemporary 'music memoir' form amplifies and facilitates. But Jones engages with the 'complex political-historical layerings' of her narrative, specifically discourses of racial and gendered essentialism that have characterized stereotypes of black diasporic subjects (such as the mammy), in ways that really test the supposed limitations of a 'natural matrix of unity' in Haraway's work. While Jones as visual artist and subject confuses the binary oppositions between human/animal, animal-human/machine and physical/non-physical in the ways that Haraway advocates and indeed uses the [black] autobiographical form as a way of resisting straightforward readings of identity, in its engagement with the themes of reproduction and maternity, Jones's texts ultimately complicate, rather than merely complement, a reading of 'A Cyborg Manifesto'.

References

Barthes, R. (1977), *Image, Music, Text*, trans. S. Heath, London: Fontana Press.

Bibb, H. ([1849] 2000), 'Narrative of the Life and Adventures of Henry Bibb, An American Slave, Written by Himself: Electronic Edition', *Documenting the American South*. Available online: https://docsouth.unc.edu/neh/bibb/bibb.html (accessed 26 July 2018).

The Bible: Authorised King James Version (2008), ed. R. Carroll and S. Prickett, Oxford: Oxford University Press.

Bohls, E. A. (2013), *Romantic Literature and Postcolonial Studies*, Edinburgh: Edinburgh University Press.

Braxton, J. M. (1989), *Black Women Writing Autobiography: A Tradition Within a Tradition*, Philadelphia, PA: Temple University Press.

Braxton, J. M. (2009), 'Autobiography and African American Women's Literature', in A. Mitchell and D. K. Taylor (eds), *The Cambridge Companion to African American Women's Literature*, 128–49, Cambridge: Cambridge University Press.

Brown, H. B. ([1851] 1999), 'Narrative of the Life of Henry Box Brown, Written by Himself: Electronic Edition', *Documenting the American South*. Available online: https://docsouth.unc.edu/neh/brownbox/brownbox.html (accessed 26 July 2018).

Brown, W. W. ([1849] 1996), 'Narrative of William W. Brown, an American Slave. Written by Himself: Electronic Edition', *Documenting the American South*. Available online: https://docsouth.unc.edu/fpn/brownw/brown.html (accessed 26 July 2018).

Caponi, G. D. (1999), 'Introduction: The Case for an African American Aesthetic', in D. G. Caponi (ed.), *Signifyin(g), Sanctifyin' & Slam Dunking: A Reader in African American Expressive Culture*, Amherst: University of Massachusetts Press.

Carretta, V. (2011), 'The Emergence of an African American Literary Canon 1760-1820', in M. Graham and J. W. Ward, Jr. (eds), *The Cambridge History of African American Literature*, 52–65, Cambridge: Cambridge University Press.

Chronology of Motion Picture Film: 1889-1939 (2018). Available online: https://www.kodak.com/bd/en/motion/about/chronology_of_film/index.htm (accessed 27 July 2018).

Creed, B. ([1993] 2007), *The Monstrous Feminine: Film, Feminism, Psychoanalysis*, London: Routledge.

Dery, M. (1994), 'Black to the Future: Interviews with Samuel R. Delany, Greg Tate, and Tricia Rose', in M. Dery (ed.), *Flame Wars: The Discourse of Cyberculture*, 179–222, Durham, MD: Duke University Press.

Dick, P. K. ([1968] 2007), *Do Androids Dream of Electric Sheep?*, London: Gollancz.

Douglass, F. ([1845] 1999), 'Narrative of the Life of Frederick Douglass, an American Slave. Written by Himself: Electronic Edition', *Documenting the American South*.

Available online: https://docsouth.unc.edu/neh/douglass/douglass.html (accessed 26 July 2018).

Dyer, R. ([1997] 2008), *White*, Abingdon: Routledge.

Dyer, R. (1998), *Stars*, new edn, London: BFI.

Eschun, K. (2003), 'Further Considerations on Afrofuturism', *DR: The New Centennial Review*, 3 (2): 287–302. Available online: https://muse-jhu-edu.yorksj.idm.oclc.org/article/48294 (accessed 27 July 2018).

Gates, Jr. H. L. ([1988] 2014), *The Signifying Monkey: A Theory of African-American Literary Criticism*, 25th anniversary edn, Oxford: Oxford University Press.

Gilmore, L. (1994), *Autobiographics: A Feminist Theory of Women's Self-Representation*, Ithaca, NY: Cornell University Press.

Giovanni, N. (1968), 'Ego Tripping (there may be a reason why)', *Poets.Org*. Available online: https://www.poets.org/poetsorg/poem/ego-tripping-there-may-be-reason-why (accessed 27 July 2018).

Goude, J. and H. Hayes (1982), *Jungle Fever/Jean-Paul Goude*, ed. H. Hayes, London: Quartet.

Gunning, S. (1996), 'Reading and Redemption in Incidents in the Life of a Slave Girl', in D. M. Garfield and R. Zafar (eds), *Harriet Jacobs and Incidents in the Life of a Slave Girl: New Critical Essays*, 131–56, Cambridge: University of Cambridge Press.

Grace Jones: Bloodlight and Bami (2017), [DVD] Dir. Sophie Fiennes, London: Spirit Entertainment Limited.

Grace Jones Citroen CX 2 advertisement ([1985] 2006) [You Tube]. Available online: https://www.youtube.com/watch?v=1L2Qm1Sux9I (accessed 26 July 2018).

Grace Jones - Corporate Cannibal ([2008] 2010) [You Tube]. Available online: https://www.youtube.com/watch?v=Cc61C-VsTko (accessed 26 July 2018).

Hanchard, M. (2001), 'Afro-Modernity: Temporality, Politics, and the African Diaspora', *Public Culture*, 11 (1): 245–68. Available online: https://doi.org/10.1215/08992363-11-1-245 (accessed 26 July 2018).

Haraway, D. J. ([1991] 2010), 'A Cyborg Manifesto: Science, Technology, and Socialist-Feminism in the Late Twentieth Century', in *Simians, Cyborgs, and Women: The Reinvention of Nature*, 149–82, Abingdon: Routledge.

hooks, b. (2015), *Black Looks: Race and Representation*, 2nd edn, London: Routledge.

Hughes, L. ([1921] 2003), 'The Negro Speaks of Rivers', in H. L. Gates Jr, et al. (eds), *The Norton Anthology of African American Literature*, 1291, 2nd edn, London: W. W. Norton.

Jackson, M. J. ([1886] 1999), 'The Story of Mattie J. Jackson; Her Parentage – Experience of Eighteen Years in Slavery – Incidents During the War – Her Escape from Slavery. A True Story: Electronic Edition', *Documenting the American South*. Available online: https://docsouth.unc.edu/neh/jacksonm/jackson.html (accessed 26 July 2018).

Jacobs, H. ([1861] 2003), 'Incidents in the Life of a Slave Girl. Written by Herself: Electronic Edition', in L. M. Child (ed.), *Documenting the American South*, 2nd edn.

Available online: https://docsouth.unc.edu/fpn/jacobs/jacobs.html (accessed 26 July 2018).

Jay, K. ([1983] 2004), 'Speaking the Unspeakable: Poet Audre Lorde', in J. W. Hall (ed.), *Conversations with Audre Lorde*, Jackson: University of Mississippi Press.

Jones, G. (1977), 'La Vie en Rose', *Portfolio* [Vinyl], New York: Island.

Jones, G. (1977), *Portfolio* [Vinyl], New York: Island.

Jones, G. (1980), *Warm Leatherette* [Vinyl], New York: Island.

Jones, G. (1981), *Nightclubbing* [Vinyl], New York: Island.

Jones, G. (1982), 'My Jamaican Guy', *Living My Life* [Vinyl], New York: Island.

Jones, G. (1982), 'Nipple to the Bottle', *Living My Life* [Vinyl], New York: Island.

Jones, G. (1985), *Slave to the Rhythm* [Vinyl], New York: Island.

Jones, G. (2015), *I'll Never Write My Memoirs*, London: Simon and Schuster.

Lorde, A. (1982), *Zami: A New Spelling of My Name*, New York: Crossing Press.

Moody, J. (2001), *Sentimental Confessions: Spiritual Narratives of Nineteenth-Century African American Women*, Athens: University of Georgia Press.

OED Online (2018), 'apocalypse, n.', Oxford University Press, June 2018. Available online: www.oed.com/view/Entry/9229 (accessed 27 July 2018).

Olney, J. (1984), '"I Was Born": Slave Narratives, Their Status as Autobiography and as Literature', *Callaloo*, 20 (Winter): 46–73. Available online: www.jstor.org/stable/2930678 (accessed 26 July 2018).

Prince, M. ([1831] 2000), 'The History of Mary Prince, a West Indian Slave. Related by Herself. With a Supplement by the Editor. To Which Is Added, the Narrative of Asa-Asa, a Captured African: Electronic Edition', 3rd edn, *Documenting the American South*. Available online: https://docsouth.unc.edu/neh/prince/prince.html (accessed 26 July 2018).

Sedgwick, E. K. (1994), *Tendencies*, Durham, MD: Duke University Press.

Shaviro, S. (2010), 'Post-Cinematic Affect: On Grace Jones, *Boarding Gate* and *Southland Tales*', *Film-Philosophy*, 14 (1): 1–102. Available online: https://doi-org.yorksj.idm.oclc.org/10.3366/film.2010.0001 (accessed 26 July 2018).

The Terminator ([1984] 2001), [DVD] Dir. James Cameron, Los Angeles: MGM.

Thompson, G. (2007), *American Culture in the 1980s*, Edinburgh: Edinburgh University Press.

Wallace-Saunders, K. (2008), *Mammy: A Century of Race, Gender, and Southern Memory*, Ann Arbor: University of Michigan.

Weekes, K. (2006), 'Othered Writers, Other Forms: Biomythography and Automythology', *Genre*, 39 (2): 329–46. Available online: https://doi.org/10.1215/00166928-39-2-329 (accessed 30 July 2018).

6

'Walking the Dead': Memory and self-reflexive intertextuality in late-style David Bowie

Kevin Holm-Hudson

From his earliest music, with influences as diverse as Anthony Newley and the Velvet Underground, intertextuality was always an important feature of David Bowie's work. 'I feel like an actor when I'm on stage, rather than a rock artist', Bowie told *Rolling Stone* in 1972. 'Sometimes I don't feel like a person at all ... I'm just a collection of other people's ideas' (Pegg 2016: 6). In 1973 he told TV interviewer Russell Harty, 'I'm a collector, and I've always just seemed to collect personalities and ideas' (Howard 2016). Bowie was open about his use of quotation and allusion, defying the conventional rock-critic discourse of individual 'authenticity'. In doing so he was one of the first rock artists to foreground intertextuality as a key element of his creative work.

According to Robert Hatten (1985: 69), intertextuality 'derives from the view of a literary work as a text whose richness of meaning results from its location in a potentially infinite network of other texts'. Hatten distinguishes between *stylistic* and *strategic* intertextuality. *Stylistic* intertextuality functions as a synecdoche for a style or genre; a pedal steel guitar, for example, may signify 'Nashville-sound' country music of the 1950s–60s or Hawaiian music, depending on context. In *strategic* intertextuality, reference is made by similarity to a specific work (or song); strategic intertextual links may be made by means of direct quotation or by 'family resemblance' – similarities in melodic contour, harmonic progression or timbre, for example. Strategic intertextuality was a key element of Bowie's glam era. One need only consider the Morse-code figure lifted from the Supremes' 'You Keep Me Hanging On' (1966) and the octave-leap reference to Harold Arlen's 'Over the Rainbow' (1939) in 'Starman' (1972), the Eddie Cochran/Duane Eddy guitar drawl in 'Hang on to Yourself' (1972) and the Bo Diddley/Yardbirds pastiche of 'The Jean Genie' (1972). Stylistic intertextuality is more broadly evident in the 'plastic soul' of *Young Americans* (1975), the Krautrock elements of *Station to Station* (1976) and the so-called 'Berlin trilogy' (*Low*, *'Heroes'* and *Lodger*, 1976–1979).

Beginning with 1993's *The Buddha of Suburbia*, Bowie's intertextuality took a reflexive turn. In subsequent albums he increasingly drew upon his own earlier work in a kind of late-career self-assessment, exploring a trove of musical memory until his death in 2016. This chapter explores Bowie's late-period self-referential intertextuality, beginning with *The Buddha of Suburbia* and continuing through his final album *Blackstar*. I draw upon Edward Said's writings on 'late style' (2007) to explore how Bowie at last dropped his performative mask by critically re-evaluating and recontextualizing his earlier music. For Said, 'late style' creative works are often notable for their 'intransigence, difficulty, and unresolved contradiction' (2007: 5); 'irreconcilable opposites are deliberately collapsed into each other, threatening complete senselessness' (2007: 159). While such stylistic contradictions may not always be self-consciously referential to an artist's earlier *oeuvre*, Bowie's late work does incorporate quite intentional self-referential elements as an extension of his postmodernist stance that he started to adapt in the early 1970s, resulting in a conflation of histories. As Lawrence Grossberg, commenting on postmodernity in post-1970s rock, observes: 'Both the future and the past appear increasingly irrelevant; history has collapsed into the present' (1984: 229).

The inevitable ageing of 'classic' rock artists challenges our conception of rock as 'youth culture'. Lou Reed's *Magic and Loss* (1992), Neil Young's *Prairie Wind* (2005) and much of the post-1990s work of Bob Dylan (Roberts 2016), for example, reflect on the mortality of the ageing rocker. Mick Jagger can now sing 'what a drag it is growing old' with the perspective of real experience so, to put a spin on Pete Townshend's famous lyric, what happens when the rock star doesn't die before he or she gets old? Said writes, 'There is … an inherent tension in late style that abjures mere bourgeois ageing and that insists on the increasing sense of *apartness* and *exile* and *anachronism*, which late style expresses and, more important, uses to formally sustain itself' (2007: 17, emphasis added). This not only negates the 'youth' ethos of rock but its sense of shared subculture or community.

After Bowie's death, his longtime keyboardist Mike Garson revealed that Bowie had allegedly had his time of death revealed to him by a psychic in the late 1970s. Garson told *Billboard* '[the psychic] told him he was going to die exactly when he died. … There are a lot of psychics who are out of their minds and full of it, but this one was real. David knew it and didn't doubt it for a second. He told me about [the reading] with certainty, accepted it and planned his future out based on that. He had 30, 40 years to plan out his life.' According to Garson's biographer Clifford Slapper, the psychic actually predicted Bowie's death 'within a 24 month range' (Graff 2018). While it is easy to question the veracity of such stories, one does find a pervasive overshadowing melancholy and themes of ageing and mortality in Bowie's late work, even as early as 1980 ('Ashes to Ashes' representing the death of Major Tom). Beginning in the late 1990s, such references become more plentiful. A few examples follow. He revived the introverted bookworm persona of 1969's 'Conversation Piece' in 2002's *Heathen*, casting it in the ruminations of an old man. In 1999's *'hours ... '*, the cover of which depicts an older Bowie holding a dead younger Bowie, *Pieta*-style, he sang that he had 'seven ways to die'. In 2001's unreleased *Toy* album – mostly a set of self-covers of songs written and originally recorded between 1964 and 1970 – he added a new song, 'Uncle Floyd', about a beloved children's cable-TV show remembered from his New York days in the late 1970s and early 1980s. (This song makes its way to 2002's *Heathen* as 'Slip Away'.) On his 2003 *Reality* album, he portrayed himself as 'The Loneliest Guy', even while asserting in another song that he'll 'Never Get Old'. The video for the final song on *Reality*, 'Bring Me the Disco King', finds Bowie encountering his own corpse in a dark forest. After *Reality*, and a subsequent silence lasting nearly ten years, Bowie surprisingly re-emerged in 2013 with a new song and video, 'Where Are We Now?', reflecting wistfully on his time in Berlin; the cover of its album *The Next Day* is a negation of the cover image from 1977's *'Heroes'* (the only album of Bowie's so-called 'Berlin trilogy' recorded entirely in Berlin), with Bowie's portrait nearly completely covered by a white square.

Said, describing Beethoven's late period, remarks that 'the artist ... abandons communication with the established social order of which he is a part and achieves a contradictory, alienated relationship with it. His late works constitute a form of exile' (2007: 8). The same can be said for Bowie's late work. Conflicted in his acceptance of his earlier personae, he nonetheless revisits them, reflects upon them, and references them.

The persistence of Major Tom

Tiffany Naiman (2015: 307), writing about the role of memory in Bowie's song and video 'Where Are We Now?', observes that memories are 'inherently temporal', but that, paradoxically, they also transcend time. 'Memory is the future already past, memory indicates lost access to an experience – but memory can also perform in the present and shape new experiences. Though grounded in the past, memory is not confined there, but reaches forward to be performed in the present.'

The recurrence of the 'Space Oddity/Major Tom' trope in Bowie's work is a notable example of memory transcending time. 'Space Oddity' (1969), the song that introduced the doomed astronaut Major Tom, was Bowie's first major hit after five years of fruitless striving for pop stardom. Moreover, the song loomed large over his career for another few years as subsequent singles and albums failed to capture the public's fancy. Not until the creation of Bowie's Ziggy Stardust persona in 1972 did the shadow of 'Space Oddity' recede – and even then it could be argued that Ziggy was a recycling of the song's outer-space tropes.

Bowie's regard for the success of 'Space Oddity' evolved over the years. In 1979 he re-recorded the song with a sparse, funereal arrangement, a strategically intertextual link to John Lennon's cathartic single 'Mother' (1970); on New Year's Eve 1979 he performed that version of the song on Thames Television's 'Kenny Everett Show' in a padded-cell set. In 1980's 'Ashes to Ashes', he essentially killed off Major Tom at last, labelling him a 'junkie' (thus further conflating the character with Bowie's own drug use in the 1970s) and reusing some of the previous year's padded-cell footage in its promotional video. Major Tom and Ziggy are perhaps referenced generically in 1985's 'Loving the Alien' but, by 1990, Bowie was determined to put both characters behind him. The *Sound and Vision* tour was intended to be his final performances of those songs. Bowie's band Tin Machine (1988–1992) went even further, attempting to counteract the perception of Bowie as 'star' front man altogether and recasting him as but one member of a fully democratic rock quartet. Nonetheless, by the mid-1990s, Bowie seemed to come to terms with his past personae and began playfully invoking them again in a rich tapestry of stylistically and strategically intertextual references extending from 'Buddha of Suburbia' (1993) through later songs such as 'Hallo Spaceboy' (1995), 'Like a Rocket Man' (2013) and culminating in 'Blackstar' (2016).

'Never born, so I'll never get old': the 'Buddha of Suburbia' video

The Buddha of Suburbia (1993), Bowie's 'soundtrack' album, inspired in part by the coming-of-age novel by Hanif Kureishi, seems to have triggered a different response to his past. Kureishi's novel (1990) concerns a mixed-race teenager named Karim who grows up a racial outsider in Bromley (the suburb of South London where Bowie grew up) and dreams of a glamorous life in central London which, despite its geographic proximity, is depicted as an exotic 'other world'. Bowie loved the book, recognizing his own youth in parts of the storyline and its setting, and agreed to contribute music for the BBC miniseries (O'Leary 2012).

The video for the title song 'Buddha of Suburbia' was filmed on location in Bromley. As the video was intended to promote the miniseries, scenes from the programme are intercut throughout the video. They depict Karim riding his bike, hanging out with friends in the schoolyard, attending concerts and so on. The footage of Bowie's performance interests us here. In the first verse, he is shown walking down a Bromley street dressed in black with a black trench coat and passing almost-identical nondescript suburban homes while smoking a cigarette. At the chorus, there is a change of setting and camera technique. Bowie is now shown standing in the middle of the street at an intersection. Leaning to one side and seemingly singing to the heavens as the camera pans around him clockwise, he pulls inward and changes direction just before the saxophone solo concludes the chorus. For the second verse, Bowie is seated on a round garden planter playing an acoustic twelve-string guitar. This provides the first (visual) signifier of nostalgia as it was Bowie's preferred instrument in his *Space Oddity–Hunky Dory* period and well into the Ziggy Stardust era. Yet, it is not heard at this point in the song; the guitar is merely a prop, albeit a powerfully symbolic one.

The song's pivotal moment occurs at 3:23. The transitional riff from 'Space Oddity' makes an altered appearance on electric guitar (the 1969 original had been on acoustic twelve-string). Bowie is depicted in the middle of the street at the intersection making 'air guitar' motions to the riff. The acoustic guitar has disappeared to 'go electric' in the mix. This is a clear 'episodic marker' – a musical gesture initiating a one-way change from one musical section to another (Tagg 2012: 518–20). Here, the gesture initiates the coda, fulfilling the earlier implicit key change from D major to E major. Example 1 shows the original 'Space Oddity' riff and its altered appearance in 'Buddha of Suburbia'. The opening interval, shown in brackets, is altered, but the whole-step ascent of the last three chords is the same, as is the rhythm.

As the song continues, further strategic intertextual references to Bowie's 1970 song 'All the Madmen' make their appearances. The song's opening and closing words – 'Day after day' and the Dada-inspired chant 'Zane Zane

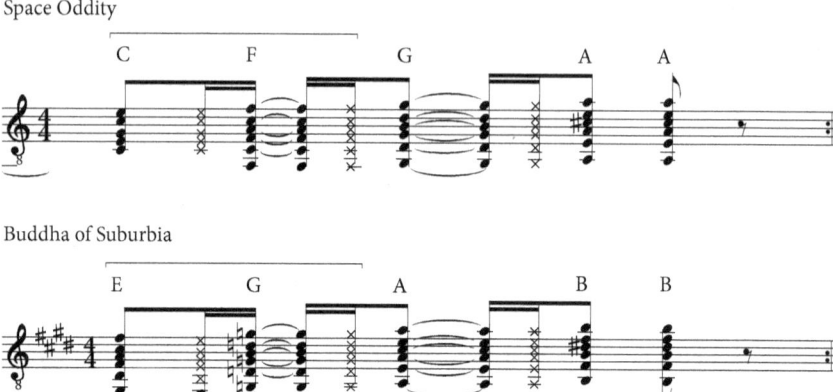

Example 1. Bowie's 'Space Oddity' riff, in original form and as transformed in 'Buddha of Suburbia'.

Zane, Ouvrez le chien' – appear in the coda. The electroshock and lobotomy connotations of the original 'day after day' line are transformed in this context to the 'inherent valorisation of repetition' of suburbia (Grossberg 1984: 229). When Bowie sings 'Zane Zane Zane, Ouvrez le chien' a second time (4:14), he rolls his eyes at the seeming in-joke. The strategic incursions from 'Space Oddity' and 'All the Madmen' – songs recorded nearly a quarter-century previously – invoke the past while also, in retrospect, signalling the reflexive turn Bowie's intertextual practice would take, thus exemplifying Said's assertion that late style works exist 'beyond their own time, ahead of it in terms of daring and startling newness, later than they describe a return or homecoming to realms forgotten or left behind by the relentless advancement of history' (2007: 135).

Self-covering and memory: *Toy*, 'Conversation Piece' and 'Uncle Floyd'/'Slip Away'

During the '*hours ...*' tour in 1999, Bowie began adding new versions of some of his earliest material from the 1960s to his sets. Eventually he had the idea to re-record some of these songs, dating from 1964 to 1970. These recordings, along with three new songs ('Uncle Floyd', 'Afraid' and 'Toy (Your Turn to Drive)'), were to become an album called *Toy* slated for a mid-2001 release. However, disputes with Bowie's label, Virgin, thwarted this plan and Bowie left to set up his own label, ISO. 'Afraid' and 'Uncle Floyd' (retitled 'Slip Away') were subsequently released on Bowie's 2002 release *Heathen*, and three of the re-made songs – 'Baby Loves That Way', 'Shadow Man' and 'You've Got a Habit of Leaving' – saw release as *Heathen* B-sides. 'Conversation Piece', another product of the *Toy* sessions, found its way to become a bonus track on some editions of *Heathen*. Eventually, a version of the *Toy* album was leaked to the internet in 2011; there was no comment about the release from Bowie or his representatives. Collectively, the *Toy* songs provide an opportunity to study Bowie's 'self-covers'. Generally, rock artists will re-record material to regain control of the mechanical rights to a song (as, for example, Little Richard's re-recordings of his early hits). Often in such instances an effort is made to recapture or duplicate the sound of the original recordings. This was not the case with *Toy*. Bowie's new versions are mostly complete rearrangements, his vocals effectively an old man's commentary on his youth.

'Conversation Piece' dates from 1969. Recorded during the *Space Oddity* sessions, it was left off the album and eventually released in March 1970 as the B-side to 'The Prettiest Star', the unsuccessful follow-up single to 'Space Oddity'. Not until *Space Oddity*'s CD reissue in 1990 was the song included as a bonus track. In its earnest melancholy and country-inflected setting it evokes Neil Young, another of Bowie's early influences ('Kooks', from 1971's *Hunky Dory* album, is a stylistic tribute to Young in his 'After the Gold Rush' period; Bowie also covered 'I've Been Waiting for You', from Young's 1969 eponymous solo debut, for his 2002 album *Heathen*). As Chris O'Leary (2016) notes, the lyrics belie the song's title – this is a song about isolation and introversion: 'it captures well the curse of urban anonymity – its title is a cruel joke, the "conversation" only going on in the singer's head'. Comparing the two versions, they are in the same key with the same modulation before the third verse; they are also nearly the same tempo (58 beats per minute for the *Toy* version compared to the original version's 62 beats per minute). However, the drums in the *Toy* recording are in a half-time groove, giving it a funereal feel. The older Bowie also sings an octave lower, sounding more reflective in his melancholy. O'Leary (2016) finds that this different performance gives the song a different meaning. In its earlier incarnation it reads almost like a suicide note, the final verse and chorus implying that its protagonist may have hurled himself off a bridge into the river; the *Toy* version, he writes, is 'sung by a man in his winter years, blankly cataloging the last room in which he'll ever live' (O'Leary 2015a: 117). In the same way that the conversations of a young man are different from those of someone older (and presumably wiser), youthful impetuousness and passion are replaced over the years by weariness and resignation.

If nostalgic memory gave rise to the impulse to re-record early material for the *Toy* album, then it also inspired one of the new songs, 'Uncle Floyd'. *Uncle Floyd* was a low-budget children's show hosted by Floyd Vivino that began broadcasting on a New Jersey UHF station in 1974. The show attracted a cult following for its corny unrehearsed skits and puppet characters such as the ventriloquist dummy Oogie and the skeleton character Bones Boy. The show was briefly picked up for syndication in 1982 ('once a time they nearly may have been/Bones and Oogie on a million screens') but was not successful in its prime-time format and returned to local New Jersey channels and then to cable. The show lasted until 1992 and Bowie learned about it from John Lennon. He watched it regularly during his time in New York in 1979–1980, even attending a live taping of the show in 1981 (O'Leary 2014). As he began revisiting his youthful material for the *Toy* project, Bowie wrote a new song about the Uncle Floyd show. Producer Mark Plati recalled, '"Uncle Floyd" was a moody track which began its life with a semi out-of-tune piano and some grainy synth strings which sounded like they were pulled off of an old 78 rpm record. Both sounds gave the effect of someone playing in a basement of some small, sad, lonely house' (Plati 2000).

Bowie also added the Stylophone pocket synthesizer to the mix, an instrument invented in 1967 by Brian Jarvis and marketed as a 'toy synthesizer'. Rather than using physical keys, the design of the Stylophone featured touch-sensitive pads that were played with a stylus ('History – Dubreq', n.d.); Bowie can be seen playing the Stylophone in a live performance of 'Slip Away' recorded in Paris in 2002, at 5:00 into the video ('Slip Away'). He famously had used the instrument in 'Space Oddity' (1969); its inclusion in 'Uncle Floyd' (and, later, 'Slip Away') intertextually references that song, as do the single, reverbed electric guitar notes heard in the introduction to 'Slip Away' (O'Leary 2014). The evocation of old technology (an 'out-of-tune piano', 78 rpm records) provides stylistic intertextual cues to set the mood of memory frozen in time; 'down in space it's always 1982', as Bowie sings, 1982 being the year of both *Uncle Floyd*'s syndication and Bowie's commercial breakthrough with 'Let's Dance' (O'Leary 2014). Bowie's voice is also processed in the choruses, double-tracked and modified by Leslie speakers to give his voice a tremulous warble, a stylistic intertextual reference and tribute to his late friend and fellow *Uncle Floyd* fan John Lennon.

In comparing 'Uncle Floyd' with its remake 'Slip Away', O'Leary correctly notes that 'the biggest revision [in "Slip Away"] was to bring up the chorus to hit right after the second verse, and dispensing with the guitar solo. You can see why Bowie and Visconti did it – why hold back your biggest hook until four minutes into the track? – but the move ruined the glorious slow arc of "Uncle Floyd"' (2014). Of course, this formal reordering also brings the song into pop-song-form conformity – two verses, chorus, verse and chorus. But there was another subtle irregularity to 'Uncle Floyd': the opening four chords of the first and second verses (F, E7, Edim, F) are reversed in the third verse, reharmonizing the melody (F, Edim, E7, F). It is unclear if this change was intentional, or in what way this harmonic change might reflect the negation of time and space conveyed by the lyrics ('Oogie knew there's never ever time / Some of us will always stay behind'). Nonetheless, the errant progression was 'corrected' for 'Slip Away', and O'Leary (2014) asserts that the more conventional 'Slip Away' remake is analogous to the syndicators' efforts to make *The Uncle Floyd Show* more commercially mainstream.

'That's what it sounds like when you're dead': 'Bring Me the Disco King'

2003's *Reality* album closed with one of Bowie's most hypnotic and evocative songs: 'Bring Me the Disco King'. The lyrics conjure images of 'killing time in the Seventies', 'hot cash days' with orgies of a 'river of perfumed limbs' and of 'good-time girls', all of which look back on Bowie's younger decadent years. All the same, there are flashes of uncertainty and even hints of betrayal as Bowie sings, 'You promised me the ending would be clear / You'd let me know when the time was now'.

Like 1973's 'Aladdin Sane', the song features a lengthy, jazz-inflected piano solo by Mike Garson (who played on both recordings). Unlike 'Aladdin Sane', however, vocals do not return after the solo – the piano has the last word. Examples 2 and 3 show comparative formal diagrams for 'Aladdin Sane' and 'Bring Me the Disco King', respectively. Both songs avoid polished predictability. 'Aladdin Sane' adds one-measure extensions to formal units, resulting in occasional nine-bar verses and choruses, whereas 'Bring Me the Disco King' avoids repeating the exact return of previously heard and expected sections (compare the varying 'verse – chorus' structures throughout the song).

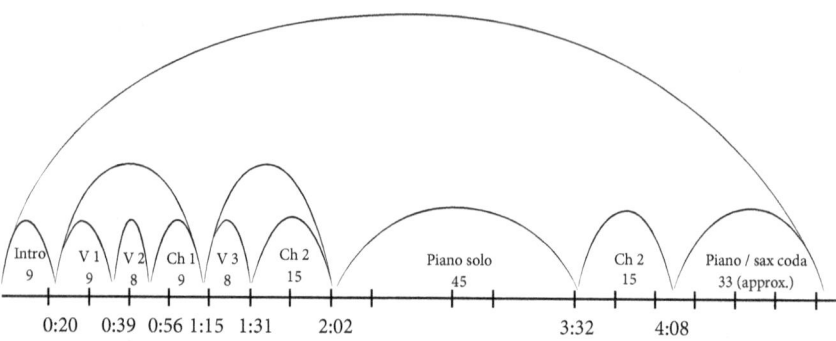

Intro & Verse 1:9 measures (2+2+2+3)
Chorus 1: 9 measures (3 + 2 + 4)
Chorus 2: 15 measures (3 + 2 + 6 + 4)
Piano solo: 45 measures (two-chord shuttle progression, with one measure appended to end)

Example 2. David Bowie, 'Aladdin Sane', formal chart.

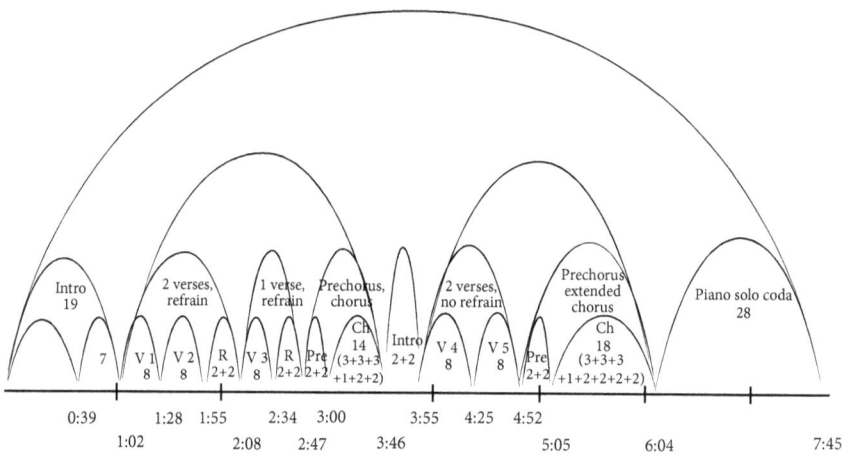

V: Verse
R: Refrain
Pre: Prechorus
Ch: Chorus

Example 3. David Bowie, 'Bring Me the Disco King'.

'Bring Me the Disco King', like a demo, has an unfinished fragmentary quality. Instrumentally, there is only Garson's digital piano and Matt Chamberlain's drum loop (originating from the 2001 *Heathen* sessions, where it had been tracked for an entirely different song) – no bass or other instruments. Working against this is the lushness of Bowie's vocal, triple- and even quadruple-tracked in jazz-inflected close-harmony clusters.

In comparing 'Aladdin Sane' with 'Bring Me the Disco King', it helps to contextualize both songs within their respective albums. Both songs resist commercial formulas. The *Aladdin Sane* album was originally conceived as a 'Ziggy Stardust in America' project (O'Leary 2015b: 258). Its themes of psychological disturbance play out among a cavalcade of American musical styles, including distorted references to doo-wop ('Drive-In Saturday'), Bo Diddley ('Panic in Detroit') and Chicago blues ('The Jean Genie'). The title track is a nightmarish vision of afterhours-club jazz, with Garson's manic piano solo including fragmentary references to George Gershwin's 'Rhapsody in Blue' and The Champs' 'Tequila' (1958) and with Bowie singing lines from The Drifters' 'On Broadway' (1963) among the din. 'Bring Me the Disco King' provides a hypnotic, uneasy close to the *Reality* album, which is less about pastiche and more about songwriting craft. If *Aladdin Sane* draws upon intertextual references to Bowie's roots in early rock and R&B, *Reality* is more self-reflective, with 'Bring Me the Disco King' harkening back musically and lyrically to the *Aladdin Sane* era in particular. Here the unsettling mood is provided by the contrast between Bowie's meticulously crafted and polished vocals with the relentless mechanism of the drum loop. The 'unfinished' quality of the track – the sensation that one is listening to a demo – gives the song a curiously confessional quality, even if Bowie is characteristically guarded in his imagery. The 'unpolished' track is in keeping with Said's observations of late style, as Bowie ransacks his trove of memories from a long (and decadent) career. As Example 3 shows, even the form of the song is unconventional; choruses are not the same length, refrains appear and then vanish from their expected places of return. The drum track never stops until the song's abrupt ending. It is the heartbeat (or, as a form of rhythmic technology, a pacemaker) that eventually gives out. After the video for the song included in the press kit for the *Reality* release, Bowie remarks, 'That's the sound of death. That's what it sounds like when you're dead' (*Bring Me the Disco King* 2003).

'The moment you know': past and present collisions in 'Where Are We Now?'

Bowie's return-to-the-public single 'Where Are We Now?' (2013) turns to Berlin as a locus for the singer's thoughts and memories. The distance of years is physically paralleled by Bowie's residence in New York at the time of the video's release. Places are important markers for memory. Kevin McCarron (1995), writing on the distinction between 'pilgrims' and 'tourists' in rock fandom, notes that 'pilgrim' sites are memorials that arise spontaneously, often a response to the death of a rock artist and the place of death (examples include the house where Queen singer Freddie Mercury died or the intersection where T. Rex's Marc Bolan died in a car crash). It is possible to view the Berlin footage of the 'Where Are We Now' video through a 'pilgrim' lens; Berlin is the location where Bowie was at last able to put the drug-addled and paranoid *Aladdin Sane/Station to Station* Bowie behind him and re-emerge with 'a new career in a new town', to borrow the title of one of his *Low* instrumentals. Tiffany Naiman (2015: 314) finds that 'Where Are We Now' superimposes temporalities, 'having the audience continuously experience separate epochs spliced with others, which blurs our sense of time, and allows for the creation of new meaning'. She asserts that the 'video is not nostalgic for Berlin of 1977, rather it is fixated on the moment of change in the 1990s when the wall was demolished and global capitalism encroached upon a city that had been divided' (Naiman 2015: 315). Daryl Perrins (2015: 332) concurs, noting that catching the 'train from Potsdamer Platz' would not have been possible during the Cold War period as Potsdamer Platz station was located in no-man's land. Likewise, Bowie's image of '20,000 people' crossing Bösebrücke with 'fingers ... crossed just in case' is a reference to Bösebrücke's status as the first border crossing to open on 9 November 1989 (Naiman 2015: 332).

The theme of memory in 'Where Are We Now?' is more complex than might appear on first view. First, we are not seeing images from Bowie's Berlin, but rather from a different time in Berlin's past, the time when the dismantling of the wall forever changed the Berlin that Bowie remembered. Second, the loss of Bowie's Berlin soon changes to other, more personal forms of loss, as Bowie is later seen in video director Tony Oursler's studio wearing a 'Song of Norway' t-shirt referring to the musical for which the dancer and actress Hermione Farthingale left Bowie in 1969.

'Something happened on the day he died': interpreting *Blackstar*

Like the video for 'Where Are We Now?', the ten-minute short film of 'Blackstar' was also released without prior announcement in advance of the album on 19

November 2015. At the time, no mention was made of a forthcoming album; indeed, given its length it seemed to be an independent work. *Blackstar* and the video for 'Lazarus' were released on Bowie's sixty-ninth birthday, a date just two days before his death. Given the timing of the release and his demise, it was to be expected that fans would interpret the album and its videos as a last testament. The internet buzzed with rumours and interpretations of alleged messages in the lyrics, the music, the videos and the cover art. The video director Johan Renck offers few clues: 'Most things like this are for the eyes of the beholder, you know? You make of it whatever you want. What I *can* say, on one side of things there is no deliberate, underlying, firm quest to have any references to past times' (cited in Joffe 2015, emphasis in original). In sharing ideas and images, Renck reports that Bowie told him, 'The one thing I think is important is to not go into any second guessing or analyzing what these images mean, because they're between you and me. People are going to go head over heels to try to break it down and figure it down across the spectrum, and there's no point in even engaging that' (2015).

An exhaustive survey of fan interpretations of *Blackstar* is beyond the scope of this article. Nonetheless, there are numerous self-referential intertextual elements. The astronaut's corpse depicted in the opening shot of 'Blackstar', for example, is widely interpreted to be that of Major Tom; after releasing himself adrift in 'Space Oddity' and being depicted 'strung out in heaven's high' in 'Ashes to Ashes', he is at last depicted in his final resting place on a distant planet in the shadow of a black star. The spasmodic dancing in the 'Blackstar' attic sequence, attributed by Renck to the old *Popeye* cartoons of Max Fleischer (Lynch 2015), is also found in the 1980 video for 'Fashion'. In both the 'Blackstar' and 'Lazarus' videos, Bowie is also portrayed as the blinded 'Button Eyes' character; this connects with the video for 'Jump They Say' (1993), in which at the exact midpoint ('at the center of it all'?) Bowie is pictured on a hospital gurney with bandaged eyes (Boyce 2016). Finally, in the 'Lazarus' video, Bowie is also seen wearing the form-fitting outfit in which he was depicted drawing a Kabbalistic Tree of Life in the *Station to Station* cover art, in 1976.

The rumours concerning the imagery in *The Last Day* and *Blackstar* are comparable to the 'Paul is Dead' rumours concerning Paul McCartney's alleged demise during The Beatles' heyday. While some of the purported symbolism perceived by fans and shared on the internet is likely coincidental, other elements – such as those listed above – are more difficult to attribute to mere coincidence. Bowie himself was never very forthcoming about the meanings in his music and videos, allowing his fans to discover and construct meaning for themselves.

'A dying man who can't die': *Lazarus*

Concurrent with the recording of *Blackstar*, Bowie was also developing a musical theatre project. *Lazarus* is loosely based on Walter Tevis's novel *The Man Who Fell to Earth* (which inspired Nicolas Roeg's 1976 movie of the same name, Bowie's major film debut). Against a backdrop of songs that go back as far as 1970 ('The Man Who Sold the World'), Thomas Jerome Newton – Bowie's alien character from *The Man Who Fell to Earth* – is revisited later in his life. He describes himself as 'a dying man who can't die' (Bowie and Walsh 2016: 28). In one telling passage, Valentine (a violent acquaintance, first portrayed in Bowie's 2013 song 'Valentine's Day') tells Newton, 'I've always thought there has to be something more beautiful than what we've been given down here. It's possible to rewrite this bad world and escape it' (Bowie and Walsh 2016: 60). Rewriting thus becomes a process of revising and rebuilding ever more elaborate worlds of imagination. Newton is tormented by ghosts of memory; people that are by all appearances real but who he insists are hallucinations of his mind. In the musical's dramatic climax, Newton is compelled by Valentine to stab one of the ghosts, a teenage girl. After he stabs her, Newton regains his composure and says:

> And I'm not of this world. And not yet marked by this place here. Not pinned down in this apartment – not divided into days and praying for my death – and bullied by this broken mind – and before all of this happened to me – and before the journey down here – to wake in the place I was born …. To be back there in that home – my sad past … rewritten now. (2016: 76)

As popular music scholar Simon Frith (1984: 59) asserts, 'Nostalgia works on feelings, not arguments.' Tormented by ghosts of people that are by all appearances real, Newton's world lacks the rationality he once knew as a scientist and inventor. Only by stabbing and delivering this ghost from her half-life can he in turn regain rest.

Perhaps the most emotional appeal to nostalgia in Bowie's late work is found in his posthumously released song 'No Plan' (2017). The video depicts an assemblage of televisions in a shop window (an homage to the TV installations of Nam June Paik, as well as to the multiple televisions Newton collected in *The Man Who Fell to Earth*) attracting a crowd as it spontaneously lights up and delivers what appears to be Bowie's message from the great beyond: 'Here, there's no music here / I'm lost in streams of sound'. The chord progressions for the verses in 'No Plan' and the verses in 'Buddha of Suburbia' are strikingly similar

(Example 4). Both songs share the same key (D major); both songs make use of a tonic pedal throughout the verse; the first two chords are identical (though voiced differently, the earlier song derived from guitar voicing and the later song presumably keyboard-based). In addition, although the third chord in each progression is not identical, both chords enable the chromatic lowering of the sixth scale degree from B-natural to B-flat (marked with brackets). The 'sigh'-like effect of the descending half-step – an affective convention dating back at least to the Renaissance (Haynes and Burgess 2016: 42–3) – is further enhanced in 'No Plan' by an additional half-step inner-voice descent from D to C-sharp as the verse ends on a D major seventh chord.

The similarity of the chord progressions in 'Buddha of Suburbia' and 'No Plan', despite the intervening years and differing instruments of origin, exemplifies Said's description of late style as 'a sense of recapitulation and return for a long artistic trajectory' (2007: 159) and neatly frames Bowie's late-period agenda of self-referential strategic intertextuality. In his late work, Bowie seemed to be tying up loose ends not only musically but thematically. Tropes ranging from the Legendary Stardust Cowboy ('I Took a Trip on a Gemini Spacecraft', *Heathen*, 2002) to Anthony Burgess ('Girl Loves Me', *Blackstar*, 2016) swung back into his *oeuvre*.

In concluding by examining the role of memory in Bowie's work, it should be recalled that, early in his career, Bowie was something of a singer-songwriter, albeit an unconventional one when compared to 1970s contemporaries such as

Example 4. Harmonic progressions in 'Buddha of Suburbia' and 'No Plan' compared.

James Taylor or Joni Mitchell (Neil Young was certainly one of his early models). Even though he was later to tell interviewer Terry Gross that 'it's all artifice' (Gross 2016), Bowie nevertheless returned to a singer-songwriter mode on his own terms later in his area. Singer-songwriters draw from memory, which may be shared explicitly (Taylor's 'Fire and Rain') or indirectly (much of Mitchell's work). Bowie is much more circumspect about drawing from memory, as his previous memories are often themselves previously constructed identities: Major Tom, Ziggy Stardust, Aladdin Sane, Halloween Jack, Plastic Soul Man, The Thin White Duke. It is in these late songs that we may see Bowie, comfortable with a smaller, faithful audience, making music for his own satisfaction and for the satisfaction of revisiting old memories. It is as if he is flipping idly through a scrapbook to see what memories come forth from the pictures we encounter after many years have intervened.

References

Bowie, D. and E. Walsh (2016), *Lazarus*, London: Nick Hern Books.
Boyce, N. (2016), 'Strangers When We Meet: David Bowie, Mortality, and Metamorphosis', *The Lancet*, 387 (10018). Available online: http://www.thelancet.com/journals/lancet/article/PIIS0140-6736(16)00226-9/fulltext (accessed 9 January 2018).
'Bring Me the Disco King' (2003), [Video] Dir. Steven Lippman, USA: Flip Productions. Available online: https://www.youtube.com/watch?v=H7D4R4YnpN0 (accessed 8 January 2018).
Bring Me the Disco King (2003), [Music Video] Dir. Steven Lippman, USA: SME.
'Buddha of Suburbia' (1993), [Video] Dir. Roger Michell, UK: Virgin. Available online: https://www.youtube.com/watch?v=48d4irOHhLY (accessed 9 January 2018).
Frith, S. (1984), 'Rock and the Politics of Memory', *Social Text*, 9/10 (Summer): 59–69.
Graff, G. (2018), 'David Bowie Was Told All About His Death Years Earlier, Says Keyboardist Mike Garson', *Billboard*, 2 February. Available online: https://www.billboard.com/articles/columns/rock/8097937/new-david-bowie-biography-mike-garson (accessed 15 February 2018).
Gross, T. (2016), 'David Bowie on the Ziggy Stardust Years: "We Were Creating the 21st Century in 1971"'. Available online: https://www.npr.org/2016/01/11/462653510/david-bowie-on-the-ziggy-stardust-years-we-were-creating-the-21st-century-in-197 (accessed 22 February 2018).
Grossberg, L. (1984), 'Another Boring Day in Paradise: Rock and Roll and the Empowerment of Everyday Life', *Popular Music*, 4: 225–58.

Hatten, R. (1985), 'The Place of Intertextuality in Music Studies', *American Journal of Semiotics*, 3 (4): 69–77.

Haynes, B. and G. Burgess (2016), *The Pathetick Musician: Moving an Audience in the Age of Eloquence*, New York: Oxford University Press.

'History – Dubreq' (n.d.). Available online: https://dubreq.com/history/ (accessed 3 January 2018).

Howard, T. (2016), 'Starman! The Story of Bowie's Ziggy Stardust', *NME*, 11 January. Available online: http://www.nme.com/blogs/nme-blogs/star-man-the-story-of-bowies-ziggy-stardust-763290 (accessed 30 January 2017).

Joffe, J. (2015), 'Behind "Blackstar": An Interview with Johan Renck, the Director of David Bowie's Ten-Minute Short Film', *Vice*, 19 November. Available online: https://noisey.vice.com/en_us/article/david-bowie-blackstar-video-johan-renck-director-interview (accessed 6 March 2017).

Kureishi, H. (1990), *The Buddha of Suburbia*, New York: Penguin Books.

Lynch, J. (2015), 'David Bowie's "Blackstar" Single / Short Film Debuts, Director Explains "Popeye" Influence', *Billboard*, 19 November. Available online: https://www.billboard.com/articles/news/6770048/david-bowie-blackstar-video-debut-popeye (accessed 9 January 2018).

McCarron, K. (1995), 'Pilgrims or Tourists? Rock Music and "Shrines" in England', *Critical Survey*, 7 (2): 165–71.

Naiman, T. (2015), 'When Are We Now? Walls and Memory in David Bowie's Berlins', in T. Cinque, C. Moore and S. Redmond (eds), *Enchanting David Bowie: Space Time Body Memory*, 305–21, New York: Bloomsbury.

'No Plan' (2017), [Video] Dir. Mark Romanek, USA: Satellite Films. Available online: https://www.youtube.com/watch?v=xIgdid8dsC8 (accessed 9 January 2018).

O'Leary, C. (2012), 'The Buddha of Suburbia'. Available online: https://bowiesongs.wordpress.com/2012/11/27/the-buddha-of-suburbia (accessed 22 February 2018).

O'Leary, C. (2014), 'Uncle Floyd – Slip Away'. Available online: https://bowiesongs.wordpress.com/?s=Uncle+Floyd (accessed 8 January 2018).

O'Leary, C. (2015a), 'Bring Me the Disco King'. Available online: https://bowiesongs.wordpress.com/?s=Bring+Me+the+Disco+King (accessed 9 November 2017).

O'Leary, C. (2015b), *Rebel Rebel: All the Songs of David Bowie from '64 to '76*, Winchester, UK: Zero Books.

O'Leary, C. (2016), 'Conversation Piece'. Available online: https://bowiesongs.wordpress.com/2016/01/26/reissues-conversation-piece/ (accessed 8 January 2018).

Pegg, N. (2016), *The Complete David Bowie*, London: Titan Books.

Perrins, D. (2015), '"You never knew that, that I could do that": Bowie, Video Art and the Search for Potsdamer Platz', in T. Cinque, C. Moore and S. Redmond (eds), *Enchanting David Bowie: Space Time Body Memory*, 323–36, New York: Bloomsbury.

Plati, M. (2000), 'Chronology of *Toy* in the Voyeur'. Available online: http://mark-plati.com/toy.html (accessed 3 January 2018).

Roberts, R. (2016), 'Celebrating the Late Career Work of Nobel Prize Winner Bob Dylan, When He Started Getting Obsessed With Death', *Los Angeles Times*, 13 October. Available online: http://www.latimes.com/entertainment/music/la-et-ms-bob-dylan-nobel-late-albums-20161013-snap-story.html (accessed 29 December 2017).

Said, E. W. (2007), *On Late Style: Music and Literature Against the Grain*, New York: Vintage Books.

'Slip Away' (2002), [Video] France: Arte TV Music Planet Special. Available online: https://www.youtube.com/watch?v=FQrJE56oU7I (accessed 22 February 2018).

Tagg, P. (2012), *Music's Meanings: A Modern Musicology for Non-Musos*, Larchmont, NY: Mass Media Music Scholars' Press.

7

Memory, graffiti and The Libertines: A walk down 'Up the Bracket Alley'

Benjamin Halligan

I had wanted to visit 'Up the Bracket Alley' (see Figure 7.1) since it had become something of an unofficial heritage site. The 'alley' itself is an unremarkable concrete stretch between Grove Passage and Hare Row (see Figure 7.2), off Cambridge Heath Road in Bethnal Green in the East London borough of Tower Hamlets. The alley doesn't appear on all maps, is difficult to find and possibly even dangerous to visit. But nearby graffiti for 'Up the Bracket Alley' pointed me in the right direction. In fact, it's graffiti that has renamed this stretch, an alley that once serviced the garden exits of the houses that are now rundown shops, takeaways and fly-by-night small businesses.

Figure 7.1 Up the Bracket Alley in 2012.

By way of visitor information: our alley has one entrance, one exit, high walls either side, barbed wire across some of these walls, and is barely lit. The lone walker is easy to spot as he or she enters, easy to cut off either way, and presumably quickly relieved of their effects, with objections readily dispelled through utilization of the hard brick walls. There's a Victorian underpass in which to divide the spoils and nearby main roads are ideal for the getaway. If mugged before closing time, the nearest pub from which to seek assistance is The Hare, at 505 Cambridge Heath Road.

I made this trip and took these photographs in 2012 (see Figure 7.4). At that point, the idolized 'indie' rock group The Libertines were seemingly long over. The group had finally imploded around 2004 and, those eight years later, would have seemed in danger of being forgotten altogether as music and cultural scenes moved on. (The group was to reform in 2014.) Was the passion that they had aroused and orchestrated in their fans and followers, between 1997 and 2004, in danger of being forgotten too? Not entirely, it seems. 'Up the Bracket Alley' was where fans and followers had gone to write about a group that lived on in their memories, to memorialize that passion, or to demonstrate that they would not let these feelings go. Roger Sargent's 2011 documentary on The Libertines, *There Are No*

Figure 7.2 Grove Passage becomes Up the Bracket Alley.

Innocent Bystanders, includes a sequence in which Bârat visits the alley. He reads the inscriptions and suppresses seemingly powerful and conflicting emotions.

This alley was the location for the external shots of the 2002 promo video for the second single by The Libertines, 'Up the Bracket', directed by Gina Birch (formerly of The Raincoats). The video opens in Grove Passage/Hare Row with Carl Bârat, Pete Doherty, Gary Powell and John Hassell casually approaching and delivering the song while ribbing each other (see Figures 7.3 and 7.5). The video moves on to incorporate shots of the rusting gasworks on the old canal just around the corner as the group ambles by.

Figure 7.3 From 'Up the Bracket' (opening sequence, Grove Passage/Hare Row, 2002).

Figure 7.4 The location in April 2012.

Figure 7.5 From 'Up the Bracket' (opening sequence).

The Libertines' early career was brief and explosive. In the manner of punk, they seemed to suddenly up-end models of musical taste, fandom and stardom (and distribution and marketing). For a while, the London quartet were wildly popular and their popularity was founded, in part, via ideas of familiarity and access. They were disconcertingly available in the early days. They were prone to play in a friend's living room or on a carpark roof at a moment's notice. They moved through squats and pub-crawls and dives and drug dens. They swept their ragtag army of fans, associates and scenesters in their wake – often with the whole rabble pursued by paparazzi and police. Doherty recalled, seemingly of 2003, still 'doing little terrorist gigs, literally playing in crack houses around Kilburn – little dives, and a few half-decent clubs; didn't really make any money, but just getting these songs out' (quoted in Honniball 2008: 12). The chief 'interpreters' of The Libertines around this time – Hedi Slimane (2005), Anthony Thornton and Roger Sargent (2006), Fabio Paleari (2007) – understood that the fans were of central importance. A scene and a look, not stardom, came under their scrutiny. This included shabby rooms and crash pads, discarded clothes, beer and cigarette debris and ripped furniture. They made use of junk-shop oddities like old flags and army uniforms, while impromptu graffiti offered a liminal written record. All of this was interspaced with the singers and scrums of fans and formed part of their rendering of the group and its circles in *London Birth of a Cult* (Slimane 2005), *The Libertines: Bound Together* (Thornton and Sargent 2006) and *I Won't Give Up* (Paleari and Montgomery 2007). Interlopers with agendas sought to gain access to the centre (particularly at the point at which Doherty began a relationship with model Kate Moss) and, as with documentary-maker Max Carlish for *Stalking Pete Doherty* (2005), found attempts rebuffed, even violently.

The music was the sound of this chaos. This is evident in their boisterous debut album, *Up the Bracket* (2002); a record produced by Mick Jones, formerly of The Clash. But the music rarely incorporated punk's rebarbative nature. Instead it was unapologetically romantic and sentimental. It looked to the 'doomed' First World War poets and London post-war bohemian culture for inspiration. Libertines graphics (posters and flyers, album and single covers, websites, tattoos) often incorporated faded British Empire detritus – particularly threadbare or partly shredded Union Jack flags that, as with Vivienne Westwood's and Alexander McQueen's occasional use of the same, seemed to hark back to the ending of the 'glory days' of British culture as a global exemplar. The back-and-forth dueting between the two bandleaders, Doherty and Bârat, added a frisson of intimate friendship and kinship among outcasts to the mix. Thus, Doherty makes for a case study for Hawkins's model of the 'British pop dandy' whose 'out-of-key phrasing and unhinged pitching work as an obvious marker of authenticity' (2009: 111) and offers a favourable comparison to more conventionally delivered (and conceptualized, produced and presented) popular singers of this time. Live, The Libertines veered between impassioned brilliance, cresting along on the collective emotions of the moment, and a near-inability to deliver their own music. In the latter case, the songs would effectively collapse, or fail to gel, or even be missed off altogether from the intended or misremembered or lost set list. Jones's recording of 'Skag & Bone Man' (seemingly live, in the studio; a B-side on the *I Get Along* EP) captures this. The song ends so prematurely, after one minute, that it prompts a bemused exchange to the effect that the group had forgotten to play a substantial part of it – 'We fucked it all up; we missed half the song out.' The physical and mental condition of the group members, or the karma of the moment, seemed to directly impact on The Libertines. The gigs, from a musical perspective at least, got progressively worse. A trend developed for audience members to smuggle in emergency marine flares and ignite them mid-song, filling the venue with smoke while the group played on and security scrambled to find and eject the culprits. Gigs tended to end unexpectedly (and frequently after enormously delayed starts) with police raids and roadblocks, or via electricity shut offs by exasperated venue owners, or equipment failure, or even with hospitalization of band members (see Thomsen 2003) or the partial destruction of the venue (see *NME* 2004). Sometimes it was a mixture of all of these things. Such a carry-on lent itself to admiring word-of-mouth and mythologizing. (Although, as Berkers and Eeckelaer (2014) argue, there is a strongly gendered dimension to such approval, with concern or condemnation more the response from the mainstream news media to female performers who are seen to act in the same ways.)

The scene was simultaneously announced and reflected in 'Up the Bracket'. The band messing around near the old gasworks like kids playing truant from school, and then back to someone's house for a party with assorted characters sitting around or joining in the fun (see Figure 7.6). The *mise-en-scène* is a thrift shop bric-a-brac collage that locates the music and scene in a sense of English identity and culture. These move through 1960s appropriations of military uniform (as with The Beatles, Jimi Hendrix and Eric Clapton; see Press 2017) via the Libertines' Beefeater jackets, 1970s Glam (a Marc Bolan album is briefly glimpsed) and a number of 1980s indie styles (in the shambolic delivery and so obviously flunked lip-syncing).

English Heritage sanctions and announces 'Official' heritage locations in the United Kingdom with an iron Blue Plaque; something of a contentious matter in relation to popular music in particular (see Roberts and Coen 2013). Unofficial mock-up Blue Plaques (often plastic stickers) can sometimes be found in shop windows indicating previous uses of the building that are of historic interest or minor curiosity. However, in 'Up the Bracket Alley', marker pens and spray paint democratize and collectivize such an impulse. They lock such unofficial heritage celebrations into memories and sharp personal responses. They offer an alternative to committee-approved civic acknowledgements and branding. The providers of graffiti also mimic the video, which incorporated (fresh) Libertines graffiti on the alley walls.

Figure 7.6 Concert/party in the living room, from 'Up the Bracket'.

The graffiti writers directly inscribe the lyrics onto the alley. The music of this area (Bethnal Green was a haunt of The Libertines) is now written 'onto' this area, and so returned to it (see Figures 7.7, 7.9, 7.10, 7.14, 7.15, 7.16 and 7.17). These working-class environs – shabby, yet in view of, albeit certainly not a part of, the Square Mile (glass skyscrapers, mass surveillance, headquarters and embassies, 'the Gherkin') were the essential canvas for The Libertines. In 2012, the ambience and weather and boozers and characters remained present and correct. Unlike Père Lachaise cemetery in Paris, with its much graffitied and 'vandalized' Jim Morrison headstone, there is no relic here: just the site for memories of the group (see Figures 7.11, 7.13 and 7.18).

'Up the Bracket' itself begins with a startling yell. It is a shouted, incoherent, territorial declaration (even if only sonically, and to the annoyance of those disturbed from their sleep) of the fond ownership of a particular area. It is the sort of cry usually made up into the sky in the small hours from just such a backstreet. With this, The Libertines stake their claim to the stomping ground. The visitor implicitly agrees; they are, after all, now sightseeing this alley on the grounds of this association. Disturbances in the night are part of the experience of these particular streets. Sinclair (1998) reads the area almost entirely with respect to the legacy (psychic and psychogeographical) of the London gangsters the Kray twins. 'Up the Bracket' seems to allude to this brutal past, too. The 'two shadow men on the Vallance Road', wrong-footed by a 'fuck off' gesture ('you see these two cold fingers?') by the singer when he is asked by them for the whereabouts of the song's addressee ('your': presumably the listener), set about delivering a beating.

The territory, mythology and scene were underwritten for this imagined community by a pseudo-theology. The picaresque times of The Libertines were also the journey of the ship Albion. Were you onboard or not? One mark of absolute allegiance for a fan was a tattoo (as with Miriam; see Figure 7.8), or even to tattoo over the signatures, signs and slogans written on their bodies by The Libertines, thus creating permanence on the graffitied body. Doherty's own writings, published in *The Books of Albion* (2007), covered the period in a jarringly oblique manner. For those able to decipher the handwriting, his concern was more with the evolving emotional narrative (friends, parties, slights, fillips) than the matter of gaining success with music releases or chart positions attained. This Albion sensibility conceded nothing to industry concerns. *The Books of Albion*, which consists of photographs of diary and scrapbook entries, begin in such a manner, too: 'A young man's journey over the last seven or eight years. In and out of consciousness, in and out of [HM Prison] Pentonville, in and out of several hearts, homes and hostels' (2007).

Figure 7.7 2 Cold Fingers: Libertines lyrics as graffiti on Up the Bracket Alley.

When success comes, it seems secondary to a heavily subjective and highly sentimental and occasionally idiosyncratic set of observations. Indeed, this was part of the problem for Doherty's handlers and colleagues. Acclaim did not temper or refine the liabilities of his old ways.

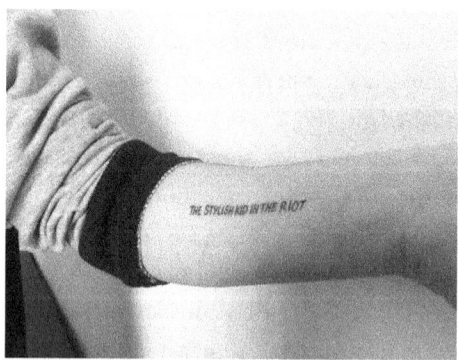

Figure 7.8 Miriam's tattoo adapts lyrics from 'Time for Heroes' by The Libertines (2003).

Miriam: *I was with my dearest friends, and I was doing some small stick and poke tattoos on them* [i.e. DIY tattoos, with a sewing needle]. *We'd recently reconnected with The Libertines and their music, and it was a night some time after their new album and reconciliation.*

It was a very nice evening, spent in excellent company, talking about our youth, and about The Libertines – and so I poked this tattoo on my own arm. I didn't even think too much before doing it. It seemed the perfect quote for me – nothing too romantic, or overdone. I think that having it stabbed on myself, by myself, on a Saturday night, makes it even more punk!

Anyways this past year also helped me making new memories over the teenage ones I had of The Libertines.

The first person I loved was a huge fan of Peter and Babyshambles so after it went down the drain between us I still loved Babyshambles but I couldn't listen to Peter's voice anymore. The only thing that stuck with me after that was my incredible admiration and love for Peter, for his songwriting and poetry, and his style in general. I just kinda got over The Libertines and Babyshambles when I was about 17, up until the new album came out [Anthems for Doomed Youth, 2015] *and it was like falling in love again.*

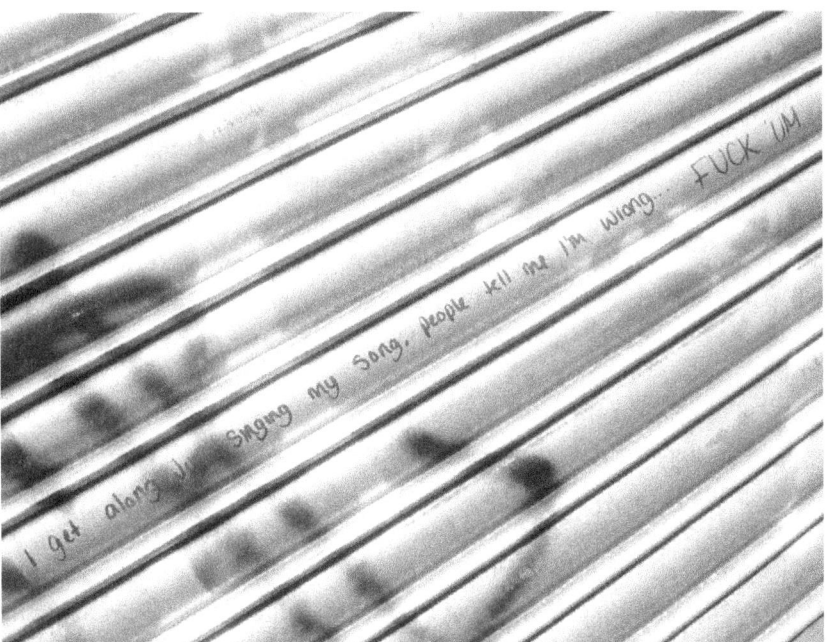

Figure 7.9 'I get along just singing my song people tell me I'm wrong … FUCK 'UM' (lyric).

Figure 7.10 'The Arcadian dream will never fall through. X. 13/2/12'; 'I lived my dreams today'; 'What became of the likely lads?' (lyrics).

So, invariably, the waters soon became too choppy for the good ship Albion. The album that followed their debut *Up The Bracket* (2002), *The Libertines* (2004), featured a cover picture of Bârat and Doherty, huddled together and tired and emotional. Both bare their Libertines tattoos from the 'freedom gig' in Chatham. This performance occurred only hours after Doherty's release from gaol for a stretch arising from his burglary of Bârat's flat. A flyer from the time (designed by Sophie Thunder; see Figure 7.12) embedded this setback into the unfolding story of the band itself. It even featured Doherty's prisoner number.

Incarceration was to become a feature of Doherty's time in the spotlight. The ambience of crime, hard drugs and violence enveloped the group and was to bring it crashing down. Both Doherty and Bârat established subsequent bands, post-Libertines. Doherty's Babyshambles has since spent more than a decade alternatively squandering and realizing potentials. In so doing, they delivered at least one genuinely unique album (*Down in Albion*, 2005, also produced by Mick Jones) and live experiences like few others. A concert for a very modestly sized audience in the Shrewsbury Music Hall (1 October 2005) started late and lasted near two and half hours. It had a band that featured Doherty's Pentonville

Figure 7.11 'The Arcadian dream has fallen though, BUT the Albion sails on course ... THANX SO MUCH! Betina & Bienie. 7/8/2011.'

cellmate The General. The group were at times in the audience and at others the audience were up on stage. It culminated with Doherty's arrest shortly after the Drug Squad had raided the venue.

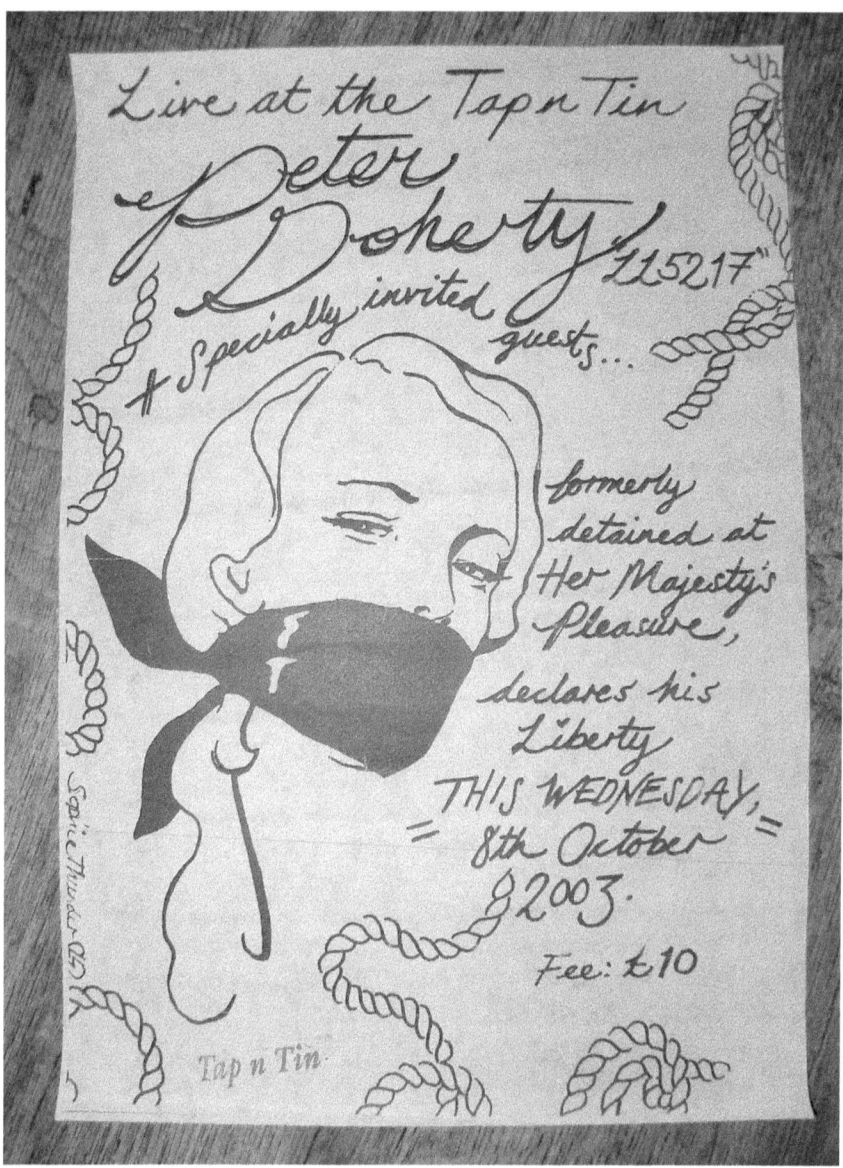

Figure 7.12 Sophie Thunder's design for the 2003 'Freedom Gig'.

In 2012, The Libertines were a memory. Those in the music industry who fêted The Libertines (the two leaders were, after all, white heterosexual boys with guitars) and were unable to cope with their erratic behaviour had turned to safer groups. (Heterosexual – although Doherty has spoken of his previous

Figure 7.13 'Pete Doherty is Innocent.'

career, imagined or otherwise, as a gay prostitute/amateur burglar (Ward 2005).) Such safer groups kept their habits private or actually turned up to play gigs. Or groups who did not weigh in so much, or at all, on affairs of state. Or groups who would not scare off potential advertisers, and who kept a distance from their constituents, too. Albion had retreated, and this alley had become the central node of a ramshackle heritage trail. Fans, seemingly from all over the world, would visit, graffiti the walls and metal shutters, and presumably take photographs, too. The messages are arresting. These are not the unimaginative scrawlings of the band's name or the fan's name, and who they are '4', but more considered responses and utterances (jostling with other strains of graffiti). The writers reproduce stretches of lyrics invariably loaded with emotional significance. They collectively curate something of a public archive concerning who The Libertines were and what they meant and continue to mean.

Formative cultural periods, even many years later, take on new guises and new roles and functions. The alley writing channels the lyrics and calls them back into existence, refusing to let the words go. In this respect, the words are not so much graffiti sloganeering but something more akin to the spiritualist trope of automatic writing. Such writing is conducted in a trance-like state without control over the movement of the writing hand, as if 'possessed by discarnate personalities or being taken over by secondary personalities' (Stevenson 1978: 327). The words seem to have been communicated from those on the other side of the grave.

Figure 7.14 'Thought you might like to know you broke my heart' (lyric).

Figure 7.15 'If you've lost your faith in love and music, the end won't be long' (lyric).

Figure 7.16 'Stylist kids in the riot' (lyric).

Figure 7.17 'I'm so clever but clever ain't wise' (lyric).

The alley becomes an imaginary meeting place for the group and their fans. It is a zone for the expression of collective memories. This isn't the kind of space that's created for group reformations and reunions, or committee-designated as heritage. And the determination of the alley as an autonomous zone for such expressions and for the persistence of fandom via small illegal acts must be considered to have been collectively made and maintained. The traces of the activities that distinguish an otherwise deeply unremarkable stretch of concrete are some way beyond the conceptions and practices of the nostalgia industry.

'Up the Bracket' ends with images of Doherty running away (see Figure 7.19). He moves down Grove Passage/Hare Row. There is a shot of a red graffitied 'Libertines' superimposed across them and the lyric, 'But we never get close / that's close enough now.' It's an obscure, but fitting, sentiment. The visitor is seeking communion with a place. They get close but cannot get close enough since time has moved on. After these considerations and my time in this spot, it seems an apt closing image to the old video: the exit from The Libertines, the ending of their music scene – a figure glimpsed in the alley, and no longer in reach. Doherty isn't here, and younger selves had, as of 2012, vanished, too. But this is the place of the meeting or overlapping of those disappearances.

Figure 7.18 'Time for Heroes [song title] – Pete you changed my life I love you more than you could imagine thank you.'

What's left, then, is the writing. There's something persuasive and self-validating about the activity of graffitiing. This isn't a case of thoughts on an internet forum or social media, or blog or online reviews or journalism – or just championing the music. Everyone seems to engage in those, with little or

Figure 7.19 From 'Up the Bracket' (closing sequence).

no opposition. To take the time to graffiti requires preparation (materials: pens/spray cans) and planning (discretion: it is a time-limited activity). What should be written? Does the writing memorialize a cultural scene, and enshrine or inscribe one's own feelings onto one of its places of pilgrimage? Does it revive and enliven that scene, and allow for the demand that the scene persists nonetheless – carried forward by and for those who visit? Or any calibration or continuity of these elements? The activity of writing allows for a material and communal sense of leaving a bit of oneself there. Those who note their coming from other countries on the alley walls will return home knowing that, for a while at least, their inscriptions are part of the tapestry left behind in distant Bethnal Green. As they exit the alley, they would share with all contributors the sense that part of them remains. The alley is changed by their visit. These acts of writing, and the writing itself, validate the music and the scene. It evidences the ways in which they continue to exert meaning and supports a collective emotional payload. Even as the years go by.

References

Babyshambles (2005), *Down in Albion*, LP: RTRADLP240.

Berkers, P. and M. Eeckelaer (2014), 'Rock and Roll or Rock and Fall? Gendered Framing of the Rock and Roll Lifestyles of Amy Winehouse and Pete Doherty in British Broadsheets', *Journal of Gender Studies*, 23 (1): 3–17.

Carlish, M. (2005), *Stalking Pete Doherty* (North One Television/Max Carlish; tx. Channel 4, 17 May).

Doherty, P. (2007), *The Books of Albion: The Collected Writings of Peter Doherty*, London: Orion.

Hawkins, S. (2009), *The British Pop Dandy: Masculinity, Popular Music and Culture*, Farnham, Surrey and Burlington, VT: Ashgate.

Honniball, S. (2008), *Beg, Steel or Borrow: The Official Babyshambles Story*, London: Cassell.
Libertines, The (2002), *Up the Bracket*, Rough Trade. LP: RTRADELP065.
Libertines, The (2002), *Up the Bracket/Boys in the Band*, 7" single: RTRADES064.
Libertines, The (2003), *I Get Along*, 12" EP: Rough Trade 2182300241.
Libertines, The (2004), *The Libertines*, Rough Trade. LP: RTADLP166.
NME [*New Musical Express*] (2004), 'Libertines Fans Riot at Secret Show', *New Musical Express*, 22 April. Available online: http://www.nme.com/news/music/the-libertines-332-1359349 (accessed 20 January 2018).
Paleari, F. and R. Montgomery (2007), *I Won't Give Up*, Bologna: Gradiche Damiani.
Press, C. (2017), '50 Years After *Sgt. Pepper*, The Beatles' Military Jackets Continue to Inspire', *Fashionista*, 14 June. Available online: https://fashionista.com/2017/06/sgt-pepper-beatles-suits-uniform-fashion (accessed 3 January 2018).
Roberts, L. and S. Cohen (2013), 'Unauthorising Popular Music Heritage: Outline of a Critical Framework', *International Journal of Heritage Studies*, 20 (3): 241–61.
Sargent, R. (2011), *There Are No Innocent Bystanders*, Pulse Films. DVD/Digital theatrical release.
Sinclair, I. (1998), *Lights Out for the Territory: 9 Excursions into the Secret History of London*, London: Granta Books.
Slimane, H. (2005), *London Birth of a Cult*, Göttingen: Steidl Verlag.
Stevenson, I. (1978), 'Some Comments on Automatic Writing', *Journal of the American Society for Psychical Research*, 72 (4): 315–32.
Thomsen, L. (2003), 'The Libertines: Freedom Gig, Tap 'n' Tin, Chatham, Kent'. *The Independent*, 9 October. Available online: http://www.independent.co.uk/arts-entertainment/music/reviews/the-libertines-freedom-gig-tapntin-chatham-kent-90641.html (accessed 10 January 2018).
Thornton, A. and R. Sargent (2006), *The Libertines: Bound Together*, London: Time Warner Books.
Ward, V. (2005), 'The Beautiful and the Damned'. *Vanity Fair*, December. Available online: https://www.vanityfair.com/news/2005/12/moss200512 (accessed 14 January 2018).

8

Reading lyrics, hearing prose: Morrissey's *Autobiography*

Laura Watson

On 17 October 2013, Penguin Classics published *Autobiography* by Morrissey. Steven Patrick Morrissey is best known as the vocalist and songwriter (alongside guitarist Johnny Marr) for the 1980s Manchester band The Smiths. Following the band's split in 1988, he embarked on an equally successful solo career. But from the moment he entered the spotlight as a miserabilist, acerbic popstar, empathizing with those on the margins and antagonizing the establishment, he has cultivated a persona that confronts traditional notions of what it means to be a popular musician. Since 2016, however, his politics (including a pro-Brexit stance) have been fiercely scrutinized – and in a move that alienated swathes of fans and eroded his authority as an ally of the marginalized, he endorsed the far-right party For Britain in April 2018 (Morrissey 2018a; 2018b).

In this chapter, I theorize that *Autobiography* marks a departure for how Morrissey constructs himself as an artist and casts new light on his musical output. Following introductory comments, I situate the 2013 book in the field of contemporary music memoirs. Subsequently, I investigate the relationship between this memoir and its author's activity as a recording artist, through an analysis that demonstrates how Morrissey's mode of lyrical expression influenced the text's themes and literary style. Secondarily, I trace how synergies operate between his musical catalogue and the book's audio-visual paratexts. Finally, given the rhetorical inflection of Morrissey's recent political pronouncements, I suggest that his memoir alerts audiences to his practice of re-appropriating song lyrics to serve new agendas. To date, scholars have cited *Autobiography* and its critical reception to support queer readings of Morrissey's recordings and performances. Dillane, Power and Devereux (2014: 149) observe that media scrutiny of the star's romantic relationships appeared 'within hours' of the book's publication. Similarly, a study of male homosocial desire in Morrissey's music incorporates brief reference to the memoir (Rukes 2017: 8). In addition to bringing a fresh perspective to queer interpretations of the singer's output, the book potentially develops how listeners understand other themes in his lyrics.

Via his Smiths' and solo output, Morrissey has articulated a counter-hegemonic social and political stance (Power, Dillane and Devereux 2016). Themes as varied as vegetarianism, anti-monarchism, opposition to Thatcherite policy in the 1980s, condemnation of US imperialism in the early 2000s and critiques of British class politics have informed his songs. Yet the cultish devotion he inspired in fans globally has – until recently – transcended the politics of a given era or locale. Nor are his lyrics always political; they plumb a pool of eclectic cultural references and are frequently autobiographical. Morrissey and his collaborators marry these lyrics with a highly polished pop sensibility – chiefly, a compelling vocal delivery to the fore of a catchy, guitar-driven, indie soundscape, the effect of which is amplified by the singer's stage presence in live contexts. Despite a tendency towards obfuscation and ambiguity of meaning (Devereux and Dillane 2011; Hawkins 2011), polysemic lyrics allows listeners to project private meaning onto this material, generating strong connections with it. *Autobiography* provides another platform for Morrissey to ponder issues explored in his songs. Reciprocally, it promises fans a more fleshed-out portrait of the persona sketched in the contours of his music and the media.

Autobiography as a contemporary music memoir

Before embarking on close reading, I seek to contextualize *Autobiography* in relation to the memoir phenomenon that has emerged in early twenty-first-century rock culture. I refer to rock as a shorthand for popular music understood to be 'serious, significant and legitimate', as Keir Keightley puts it (2001: 109). Conceptually speaking, rock is more usefully defined by these aesthetic criteria rather than a style or sound. To extend this argument, I suggest that rock culture is no longer even strictly the preserve of music, for it now encompasses a literary domain, too. Following Bob Dylan's *Chronicles, Vol. 1* in 2004 – not the first contemporary music memoir but a landmark text, nonetheless, owing to Dylan's canonic status – an abundance of books in this genre have appeared. That genre is the putative sole-authored music memoir, distinct from the ghost-written autobiography or co-authored life-story 'as told to' a professional journalist. While commercial considerations and editorial oversights still factor into these projects – especially as they are mostly the work of first-time literary authors – this does not diminish the status of these books as independent artistic statements. There are parallels here with how solo performers release albums that rely on a team of background collaborators. Producers, sound engineers, session musicians, backing singers and additional writers may all contribute to the process without their input thought to compromise the integrity of the 'solo' album. Memoirs can be considered a type of artistic output analogous to recordings, particularly when authors exploit literary gifts self-evident in their lyrics. As the recipient of the 2016 Nobel Prize for Literature, Dylan ranks as the most celebrated of such individuals. Comparable figures include Patti Smith (author of two memoirs and earlier poetry collections), Elvis Costello and Morrissey. British press reaction to Morrissey's memoir highlighted its writerly qualities: the *Telegraph* praised it as 'the best-written musical autobiography' since *Chronicles* (McCormick 2013), while Terry Eagleton (2013) proclaimed 'Morrissey is now out to demonstrate that he can write the kind of burnished prose no other singer on the planet could aspire to'. In a rare hostile review, the *Independent* advised the publishers to 'look at Patti Smith's *Just Kids* to see how it could and should be done' (Tonkin 2013).

A special issue of *Popular Music and Society* on 'Musical Autobiography' highlighted the growing importance of this genre, although the editors and contributors conceptualize 'musical autobiography' as encompassing 'a range of different media and genres' (Stein and Butler 2015: 118). Beyond the parameters of 'musical autobiography', this book can be categorized as a contemporary or new memoir, a genre of literary autobiography that has recently focused scholarly attention (DiBattista and Wittman 2014; Madden 2014; Smith and Watson 2010). Smith and Watson assert that the storyteller in the contemporary memoir 'becomes, in the act of narration, both the observing subject and the object of investigation, remembrance, and contemplation' (2010: 1). As the memoir renders the subject 'at once author and character' (DiBattista and Wittman 2014: 17), Morrissey assumes a dual identity in his book that the genre's constructedness presupposes. Madden remarks that new memoirs are 'written in ways that forefront the linguistic medium ... and the artifice of textual transformation' (2010: 223). Such qualities are perceptible here.

'Sister, I'm A Poet': from pop lyrics to literature

As early as 2011, Morrissey professed a desire to publish his memoir with Penguin Classics, an imprint usually reserved for fictional works of long-dead canonic authors (Michaels 2013). The link with Penguin Classics fiction hints at how the life-story text is a narrative construct; the product of a subjective process. It alludes to the distance between truth and how that is told, to the kinds of ambiguities that characterize Morrissey's lyrics. The singer's association with Penguin signalled a new investment in his literary persona. Morrisey has long resisted attempts to fix his identity, whether that relates to his artistic self, sexuality or nationality. His musical self, for example, 'is constantly renegotiated through the process of performance, appropriation, and representation' (Hawkins 2011: 73). *Autobiography* injects new energy into this process, enabling Morrissey to recalibrate his public identity to encompass author as well as pop star. Beyond his choice of publisher, the next step in that process was his participation in a book-signing at the Akademibokhandeln in Gothenburg, Sweden, on the day of publication. Ostensibly a low-key, mid-week event in a shopping centre, wholly appropriate for promoting a debut writer, this meet-and-greet seemed curated to portray Morrissey as a literary figure decoupled from the pop universe. Regardless, the event elicited the usual excitement from his fans (Crouch 2013). And while the memoir was not strictly his debut – he published two obscure, slim volumes on the New York Dolls and James Dean in the early 1980s (Morrissey 1981; 1983) – it was his first ambitious literary statement.

Morrissey's self-fashioning strategy of presenting himself as an author infuses the substance of *Autobiography*. 'When there is no matching of lives, and we live on a strict diet of the self, the most intimate bond can be with the words that we write' (2013: 96), he observes towards the end of a fourteen-page passage discussing his poetic awakening. Delving into the *oeuvre* of his literary idols, he quotes A. E. Housman, Hillaire Belloc, Oscar Wilde, W. H. Auden, Dorothy Parker, Stevie Smith, John Betjeman, Patrick McGill and Patrick Kavanagh (2013: 86–99). Beyond this sphere of late nineteenth-century and twentieth-century influence, he comments that the duple rhythm of Robert Herrick's seventeenth-century poetry sounds 'like two tapping feet responding to each other' (2013: 91). This passage acts as bricolage which, as I elaborate below, is a distinctive trait of Morrissey's output. Equally important, it also functions to curate Morrissey's lyrical legacy as a continuation of an Anglophone poetic tradition. Weaving his thoughts around this textual tapestry, he remembers: 'I have a sudden urge to write something down but this time they are words that must take a lead. Unless I can combine poetry with recorded noise, have I any right to be?' (2013: 90). Pronouncing his songs a form of poetry, the author implies that *Autobiography* should be read as a serious creative effort, too. Morrissey's subsequent foray into fiction in 2015 with *List of the Lost* confirmed the grand scale of his literary aspirations. Critics mauled his novel, however: the British press consensus was that the book was almost unsalvageable, centred on a ludicrous, narcissistic plot and expressed in hyperbolic prose (Clark 2015; Niven 2015). As a final indignity, it won the infamous *Literary Review* Bad Sex in Fiction Award in 2015.

Ironically, the novel's failure reminded readers of *Autobiography*'s strengths. Among these, it reignited debate about The Smiths. Naturally, the band is central to the discussion, not least their rancorous dissolution, which alone occupies fifty pages (Morrissey 2013: 302–51). Johnny Marr later gave his perspective in his 2016 memoir *Set the Boy Free* (2016). The guitarist claimed not to have read *Autobiography*, yet was writing in the shadow of Morrissey's intervention in The Smiths' lore. Via his book, the singer had taken the helm of the critical discourse, steering journalists and Marr towards a reappraisal of the band. The coexistence of these two books, I suggest, recreates in a literary format an essence of the band's aura: the Morrissey–Marr creative axis. An unintended legacy of this pair of memoirs is that they expose their authors' respective limitations and interdependence on one another in their former partnership. A *Pitchfork* columnist griped: 'Marr cannot express in words what he expresses in chords … you'd think he'd have learned his best work usually involves a writing partner' (Goddard 2016). Meanwhile, Morrissey's reminiscences of The Smiths and his later instrumental, compositional collaborators underline how he partly relies on others to realize his ideas musically. In that sense, *Autobiography* looks outwards, situating the singer in relation to his peers and provoking responses from them. Still, the release of the single 'Suedehead' in February 1988 marked Morrissey's induction as a solo artist, hence a focus on him as an individual is integral to the book, too.

Engaging as his perspective on The Smiths is, he undoubtedly lured other readers with revelations about his love life. After decades of gossip about his sexuality, the singer's insights into his private relationships validated the queer readings invited by lyrics to songs such as 'This Charming Man', 'Speedway' and 'All the Lazy Dykes', and by the singer's use of queering strategies on stage and in music videos (Dillane, Power and Devereux 2014; Rukes 2017). Synergies between his work as a musician and writer operate beyond queer discourses, though. *Autobiography* opens with scenes of childhood, pivoting between urban Manchester where

Morrissey was born and Dublin, home to his parents and where he spent many summers. Geographic and cultural displacement is captured in trivial details, too, such as 'Irish banter is lyrical against the Manchester blank astonishment' (2013: 8). These diasporic reflections echo the theme of 'Irish Blood, English Heart' (2004). The single trod familiar territory in attacking the monarchy as well as the Conservative and Labour parties, but further eviscerated British colonialism in Ireland, namely the seventeenth-century Cromwell invasion. Yet Morrissey remains ambivalent in this song, embracing a dichotomous national identity that originates in his ancestry ('Irish blood') but which is now English. The memoir similarly navigates the complexities of the immigrant experience, particularly the loosening of ties in subsequent generations, which the 2004 song captures. Morrissey writes that 'as each year passes my sister and I are less willing to leave Manchester. Ireland is our soaring past – ruddy and cheerful, yet somehow the past' (2013: 37). Evoking the lyrics' blood-heart imagery, he tracks the tide of family members flowing from Ireland to Britain. 'Nannie's cousin John Joe Rahilly will arrive from Dublin and will anchor himself around the house' (2013: 38–9). Visual paratexts surrounding these pages underline the song's metaphors. An image of an aunt is captioned: 'Rita, born one August 13th in Dublin, yet everywhere in the heart' (2013: 36). As Sutton (2015: 208) states, paratexts such as photographs contribute to popular musicians' memoirs by reinforcing their subjects' 'claims to authenticity'. Morrissey's choice of image and caption here effectively enables him to assert his heritage.

'Irish Blood, English Heart' appears on *You Are the Quarry*, an album that features a further tirade against imperialism in 'America Is Not the World'. This song skewers what Morrissey perceives as the straight, white, masculine hegemony of US politics and its geopolitical narcissism. His critiques of oppression are, however, partly undermined by lyrics that admit attachment to the superpower. Similarly, the memoir addresses the nuances of his sentiments towards his adopted US home. 'My country?' he wondered after the 9/11 attacks (2013: 356–7). Later, he condemns George W. Bush and Tony Blair as war criminals, and rails against US immigration policies in the book's closing pages (2013: 455–7). But basking in the aftermath of a gig in 2007, he reflects, 'America IS the world after all' (2013: 431). Such contradictions, as noted earlier, form part of his public disposition. Meanwhile, the song-title pun is typical of Morrissey's literary style; his book is peppered with arch references to his lyrics. Plenty are obvious, with heavy-handed typographical emphasis, but others depend on knowledge of the author's song catalogue.

Familiarity with The Smiths pays off in one of the book's most dramatic passages. In a gothic evocation of a disorienting nocturnal drive around Saddleworth Moor in 1989, Morrissey details how he and his companions encountered the ghost of a teenage boy (2013: 229–39). Referencing the crimes of Ian Brady and Myra Hindley, who murdered five children in Manchester during the 1960s and buried them in various locations around the moors, Morrissey writes that 'the bleak moor has seen them all out ... child-killers who murder and smile' (2013: 233). The Moors Murders had formed the subject of 'Suffer Little Children', the B-side to the 1984 Smiths' single 'How Soon Is Now?'. Crucial to the lyrics is a focus on victims whose bodies were never recovered. Specifically, in the second part of this song Morrissey adopts the ghostly persona of a child crying out to be found. Thirty years later, his memory of passing through that haunted landscape prompted him to write, 'I can scarcely imagine more terrible things as I stand here, as we are all silenced by the rising inferno of the wind. Do the wails of the gales drown out pitiful sobs? Might a roadside sack contain the remains of the sister of the murdered boy?' (2013: 234). Both 'Suffer Little Children' and this passage portray the imagined suffering of the murder victims, the ongoing torment endured by families who never learn the exact whereabouts of the children's resting places. This passage exemplifies again how the book develops topics Morrissey has explored as a lyricist. Beyond the thematic links, the poetic language triggers memories of the song. The cadence of the prose relocates the reader to Morrisey's soundscape. Slow internal rhyme generated by the long vowels in 'the wails of the gales drown out pitiful sobs' contrasts with the faster beat of 'contain the remains'. Connections between music and prose push beyond the horror of the subject matter.

Part of the reason the news story lodged itself in Morrisscy's consciousness was its proximity to his boyhood in 1960s Manchester. Those formative years in the city also inspired The Smiths song 'The Headmaster Ritual' (1985). Another track that the memoir illustrates in striking detail when it reproduces the military metaphors deployed in the lyrics. The song denounces the use of corporal punishment against schoolchildren, condemning Manchester schools without going as far as to identify St Mary's Secondary Modern School or its headmaster who beat Morrissey. Both the institution and principal are named in the book (Morrissey 2013: 55–63). The lyrics portray the principal as an army brute who terrorizes his charges – and that imagery of teachers as soldiers and abusers resurfaces on the page in 2013. Under the headmaster's regime as the singer remembers it, 'small hands crack under the powerful military might of

[his] excited slam. Undersized and freshly plucked from junior school, these boys are still children and are no match for the satanic attack launched by this heaving and burning artilleryman' (2013: 56). Morrissey's abhorrence of violence, above all when directed at those helpless to defend themselves, is further apparent on the 1985 album *Meat is Murder*. Comparing heifers to humans and the meat industry to a form of massacre, as he does on the title track, he amplifies this stance to extremes in the book by accusing agriculturalists of a 'Holocaust carnage inside every abattoir' (2013: 182). When expanding on the subjects behind 'The Headmaster Ritual' and 'Meat is Murder', the memoir reverberates with the songs' emotional force, persuading readers that the character projected on the page is consistent with the persona Morrissey has constructed for the stage.

In analysing the textual relationships between *Autobiography* and Morrissey/Smiths songs, two strands may be distinguished. The first is thematic connection between lyrics and life-story; how the memoir sparks musical reminiscences as traced in the above examples. The second strand, to develop points mentioned in these instances, pertains to how the prose stylistically echoes the Morrissey and Smiths catalogue. As a memoirist, Morrissey communicates in the distinctive stylized voice and vocabulary he has honed as a singer and songwriter. To grasp how that voice leaps off the page we need to hear it first. The sound of Morrissey's singing voice 'closely resembles his spoken voice' (Hawkins 2011: 310). It 'succumbs to the ordinariness of speech' through 'pitch slippage, straining and controlled exertion' (2011) – but the realism of Morrissey's delivery does not detract from how his words are 'meticulously selected' and precisely enunciated (Hawkins 2011: 316). To listen to that voice is to hear the natural rhythms of speech which, whether they lean towards the conversational or oratorical, impart carefully crafted ideas. The singer reproduces this rhetorical idiom in *Autobiography*, generating formal symbiosis in the sense that his prose, like his lyrics, can appear conversational and unfiltered. Under scrutiny, however, this text is revealed to be deliberately constructed.

'Stop Me If You Think You've Heard This One Before': bricolage in *Autobiography*

Morrissey's textual aesthetic migrates from an oral setting to the printed page, comparable to how Dylan's poetic idiom (its prolixity, stream of consciousness, density of cultural allusions and so on) translates from the folksong medium to prose in *Chronicles*. Unlike Dylan, though, Morrissey extensively repurposes lyrics to tell his life-story or provides biographical context to illuminate their original meaning. By drawing on this lexicon he engages in bricolage, which already informs his songwriting and visual aesthetic. Tracing in Morrissey's music a practice theorized by Claude Lévi-Strauss, Lee Brooks (2011: 267) discusses how he 'delve[s] into a toolbox of cultural references that is at once limitless yet apparently limited by an overwhelming connection to a particular remembrance of the past'. Prominent allusions include Oscar Wilde in his lyrics and James Dean in the 'Suedehead' music-video. The bricolage strategy in *Autobiography*, I argue, expands on the 'closed universe of cultural reference' (2011: 263) shaping these songs and videos. For example, the commentary on Wilde's poetry in the bricolage passage mentioned above reaffirms Morrissey's admiration of the writer. Bricolage functions on another level, too: Morrissey treats lyrical texts as malleable materials he can retool into prose. This powerfully plants the aural memory of songs in the topography of the printed word. It pervades the language of the book, sometimes independently of how the thematic content cues recollections of songs.

To demonstrate, I highlight a few instances of self-citations. 'My childhood is streets upon streets upon streets upon streets', reads the first sentence (Morrissey 2013: 3), elaborating on the title of 'On These Streets I Ran' (2006). Later, the memoirist recalls a teenage conversation that began '*Are you still ill?*' (Morrissey 2013: 139). Italics emphasize the title of The Smiths' 'Still Ill' (1984), while redirecting outwards the soul-searching 'I' of the second verse to 'you'. Another adolescent memory, of playing an extra on a television drama, prompts the author to describe his fleeting appearance on 'a punctured bicycle on a hillside desolate' (Morrissey 2013: 104). No typographical underscoring is necessary for even casual fans would recognize the opening to 'This Charming Man' (1984). The appropriation of band and solo lyrics from the well known to the obscure enlivens the lengthy account of Morrissey's legal disputes with his former bandmates over the payment of royalties. '*Lee/please/stand up and defend me*', he quips from 'In the Future When All Is Well' (2006) (Morrissey 2013: 333). Recognizing the damage to the group's interpersonal relationships following these protracted court cases, he writes: '*There is another world, there is a better world; well, there must be*, and even if the passing of time might mellow you into forgiveness, it doesn't mean you ever again want to be friends' (2013: 351). There, he segues seamlessly from 'Asleep' (1987) to prose. Later, he dismisses the notion of the band's reformation by channelling their song 'You've Got Everything Now'

(1984). 'I smile at the thoughts of a Smiths reunion, for I've got everything now', he rephrases it (Morrissey 2013: 415). I have enumerated just a few instances of song-lyric bricolage. Precise phrases first voiced in song are replayed on the printed page as literature.

Readers further encounter passages that sound rooted in his lyrics but elude definitive association. 'The louder they shout, the less the world wants to be like them. The louder they shout, the more they believe the world will respect them', Morrissey complains about US immigration officials (2013: 456). He draws the disconnection between the authority figures and those around them by repeating 'The louder they shout ... '. Without recourse to literal citation, these lines evoke the tension of 'The More You Ignore Me, the Closer I Get' (1994); they also tap into the chorus repetition of those title words. Beyond the linguistic bricolage and articulation of themes linking music and memoir, the book reproduces larger structural characteristics of Morrissey's songwriting craft. The Smiths' catalogue, for example, is marked by 'a defiant rejection of the formulaic predictability and structures found in pop songs'; this rejection is codified by the 'absence of middle sections, easily discernible choruses and instrumental passages' (Hawkins 2011: 71). Morrissey has utilized a similar idiosyncratic formal practice in his solo output; for instance, 'Speedway' (1994) exemplifies his aversion to the conventions of song pacing in how the track's 'verse fragment' opening cuts to the chorus almost immediately (Devereux and Dillane 2011: 198). *Autobiography* similarly disregards the norms of formal signposting in popular literature. A book of nearly five hundred pages, it lacks chapter divisions and begins by launching into a six-page paragraph. Nonetheless, like Morrissey's lyrics, it maintains narrative momentum.

Another point of contact between the book and Morrissey's solo recorded catalogue is that *Autobiography* bears the iconic styling of his album sleeves. The front cover recycles the photographic portrait of the singer's face as featured on the *Greatest Hits* artwork (2008), albeit in a blued-toned tint instead of the original sepia shade. Melissa Connor (2011: 144) argues that 'the repetitive use' of Morrissey's portrait on album covers is a Warholian device 'of turning the self into cultural entity'. The book's jacket design plus the inclusion of further portraits between the covers continues that Warholian project and is consistent with how his music is packaged. Moreover, the reuse of these tropes points towards a process of repetition intrinsic to Morrissey's aesthetic. Songs such as 'Panic' and 'There Is A Light That Never Goes Out' (1986) each reiterate a single line ad nauseam for the last minute of a short pop track. These songs are designed so that listeners internalize those words; likewise, echoes of lyrics in the memoir facilitate their deeper permeation into the cultural consciousness.

So far, I have analysed how *Autobiography*'s prose is intertextual and how its visual paratexts share the iconography of the author's album artwork. The book moves through personal, social and political themes Morrissey has already addressed on record. Snippets of lyrics sing out from a text inflected by a musical voice. But this book is not merely akin to a sound recording – in its audiobook format, it is an inherently sonic object. Several memoirists – Johnny Marr, Elvis Costello, Moby, Patti Smith, Carole King, Bruce Springsteen and others – have released their own unabridged recordings of their texts. Audiobook versions of musicians' memoirs stand at the interface between the printed word and performance. Although in this context the voice is an instrument of speech rather than song, its sonic essence or grain remains unchanged. Morrissey, however, delegated the narration to the actor David Morrissey. Only a few other musicians have hired actors to tell their stories: for example, Sean Penn read Dylan's book, while Rosanna Arquette voiced Chrissie Hynde's memoir. To compartmentalize the subject and the speaker as separate entities is to outsource what is a form of time-consuming, unglamorous performance labour – such a move seems a popstar's prerogative or, alternatively, a projection of his or her imagined alter-ego. In Morrissey's case we could cite an additional rationale. In their reading of 'Speedway' as a text that conflates the singer's martyrdom with that of Wilde, Devereux and Dillane argue that Morrissey uses Wilde 'in a kind of performative ventriloquism' (2011: 195, 201). Via the audiobook, this artist engages in another type of ventriloquism that underlines the constructedness of his public persona. Cracks appear in the veneer of authenticity as his autobiographical account is transformed into an actor's script.

This performance embodies the ambiguity often identified in Morrissey's songs. Even author and actor identities are blurred: born five years apart, they share the same surname, northern origins and soft Mancunian accents. 'I read the book very slowly to get the rhythms right', David Morrissey said (Ayers 2013), thereby conveying his sensitivity to the musicality of the prose. His studied delivery reminds us how everything about this memoir mediates and remediates Morrissey's art and persona. Nothing is unfiltered: the text channels his songs, the visuals (re)present the materiality of the albums and the audiobook's presentation acknowledges the artifice of performance. Speaking to the listener as well as to the reader, the book redraws the boundaries of literature and popular-music performance.

Furthermore, from today's perspective, *Autobiography* exposes Morrissey's propensity for framing his views via the lenses of his lyrics. 'There Is A Light That Must Be Switched On', he preached by way of headline to an incendiary interview published on his blog on 16 April (2018a). That rhetorical construct of rephrasing a track title is familiar from *Autobiography* – but here a Smiths' track is co-opted for inflammatory propaganda purposes. Responding to social-media denunciation of his apparent far-right politics, the singer posted a blog four days later titled 'I've Been Dreaming of a Time When / the English / Are Sick to Death of Labour and Tories' (Morrissey 2018b). Again, he refashioned his lyrics to fit the tenor of the post. Paradoxically taking his cue from 'Irish Blood, English Heart', a paean to the assimilated immigrant, he appealed to fans to join him in supporting For Britain. In curating a political presence online, Morrissey may be indicating that he intends to continue expressing himself in the prose medium, a form he first really explored in the memoir.

References

Ayers, M. (2013), 'Morrissey Asked David Morrissey to Record *Morrissey*', *Rolling Stone*, 14 November. Available online: https://www.rollingstone.com/movies/news/morrissey-asked-david-morrissey-to-record-morrissey-20131114 (accessed 3 March 2018).

Brooks, L. (2011), 'Talent Borrows, Genius Steals: Morrissey and the Art of Appropriation', in E. Devereux, A. Dillane and M. J. Power (eds), *Morrissey: Fandom, Representations and Identities*, 257–70, Bristol: Intellect.

Clark, A. (2015), 'List of the Lost by Morrissey Review', *Guardian*, 24 September. Available online: https://www.theguardian.com/books/2015/sep/24/list-of-the-lost-morrissey-review-novel (accessed 30 April 2018).

Connor, M. (2011), '"My So Friendly Lens": Morrissey as Mediated through His Public Image', in E. Devereux, A. Dillane and M. J. Power (eds), *Morrissey: Fandom, Representations and Identities*, 139–50, Bristol: Intellect.

Crouch, D. (2013), 'Morrissey Launches *Autobiography* with Single Book Signing in Sweden', *Guardian*, 17 October. Available online: https://www.theguardian.com/music/2013/oct/17/morrissey-autobiography-book-signing-sweden (accessed 30 April 2018).

Devereux, E. and A. Dillane (2011), 'Speedway for Beginners: Morrissey, Martyrdom and Ambiguity', in E. Devereux, A. Dillane and M. J. Power (eds), *Morrissey: Fandom, Representations and Identities*, 207–23, Bristol: Intellect.

DiBattista, M. and E. O. Wittman (2014), 'Introduction', in M. DiBattista and E. O. Wittman (eds), *Cambridge Companion to Autobiography*, 1–22, Cambridge: Cambridge University Press.

Dillane, A., M. J. Power and E. Devereux (2014), '"I Can Have Both": A Queer Reading of Morrissey', *Journal of European Popular Culture*, 5 (2): 149–63.

Eagleton, T. (2013), 'Autobiography by Morrissey – Review', *Guardian*, 13 November. Available online: https://www.theguardian.com/books/2013/nov/13/autobiography-by-morrissey-review (accessed 2 March 2018).

Goddard, S. (2016), 'Smith vs. Smith: Reading the Morrissey and Marr Memoirs', *Pitchfork*, 5 December. Available online: https://pitchfork.com/thepitch/1381-smith-vs-smith-reading-the-morrissey-and-marr-memoirs (accessed 2 March 2018).

Hawkins, S. (2011), '"You Have Killed Me": Tropes of Hyperbole and Sentimentality in Morrissey's Musical Expression', in E. Devereux, A. Dillane and M. J. Power (eds), *Morrissey: Fandom, Representations and Identities*, 307–23, Bristol: Intellect.

Keightley, K. (2001) 'Reconsidering Rock', in S. Frith, W. Straw and J. Street (eds), *Cambridge Companion to Pop and Rock*, 109–42, Cambridge: Cambridge University Press.

Madden, P. (2014), 'The "New Memoir"', in M. DiBattista and E. O. Wittman (eds), *The Cambridge Companion to Autobiography*, 222–36, Cambridge: Cambridge University Press.

Marr, J. (2016), *Set the Boy Free*, London: Century.

McCormick, N. (2013), 'Morrissey, Autobiography, First Review', *Telegraph*, 17 October. Available online: https://www.telegraph.co.uk/culture/books/bookreviews/10385321/Morrissey-Autobiography-first-review.html (accessed 2 March 2018).

Michaels, S. (2013), 'Morrissey Inks Memoir Deal with Penguin Classics', *Guardian*, 4 October. Available online: https://www.theguardian.com/music/2013/oct/04/morrissey-smiths-memoir-published-penguin-classics (accessed 5 March 2018).

Morrissey, S. (1981), *New York Dolls*, Manchester: Babylon Books.

Morrissey, S. (1983), *James Dean is Not Dead*, Manchester: Babylon Books.

Morrissey (2013), *Autobiography*, London: Penguin Classics.

Morrissey (2018a), 'There Is A Light That Must Be Switched On', 16 April. Available online: https://www.morrisseycentral.com/messagesfrommorrissey/there-is-a-light-that-must-be-switched-on (accessed 30 April 2018).

Morrissey (2018b), 'I've Been Dreaming of a Time When/the English/Are Sick to Death of Labour and Tories', 20 April. Available online: https://www.morrisseycentral.com/messagesfrommorrissey (accessed 30 April 2018).

Niven, J. (2015), 'Was There No One to Stop Morrissey Publishing *List of the Lost*?', *New Statesman*, 1 October. Available online: https://www.newstatesman.com/culture/books/2015/10/was-there-no-one-stop-morrissey-publishing-list-lost (accessed 30 April 2018).

Power, M. J., A. Dillane and E. Devereux (2016), '"I Sing Out to the Youth of the Slums": Morrissey and Class Disgust', *Popular Music and Society*, 39 (5): 547–62.

Rukes, F. (2017), 'The Disruption of Normativity: Queer Desire and Negativity in Morrissey and The Smiths', *Gender Forum: An Internet Journal for Gender Studies*, 64: 4–22.

Smith, S. and J. Watson (2010), *Reading Autobiography: A Guide for Interpreting Life Narratives*, 2nd edn, Minneapolis: University of Minnesota Press.

Stein, D. and M. Butler (2015), 'Musical Autobiographies: An Introduction', *Popular Music and Society*, 38 (2): 115–21.

Sutton, M. (2015), 'Amplifying the Text: Paratext in Popular Musicians' Autobiographies', *Popular Music and Society*, 38 (2): 208–23.

Tonkin, B. (2013), 'Book Review: *Autobiography* by Morrissey – Droning Narcissism and the Whine of Self-Pity', *Independent*, 17 October. Available online: https://www.independent.co.uk/arts-entertainment/books/reviews/book-review-autobiography-by-morrissey-droning-narcissism-and-the-whine-of-self-pity-8887301.html (accessed 2 March 2018).

9

'Glory Days': Memory-related processes and the performance of memory in the work of Bruce Springsteen

Nicola Spelman

In accordance with Liedeke Plate and Anneke Smelik's observation that 'memory is embodied performance [that] does not function in a vacuum but needs a medium to be trained, shared and transmitted' (Plate and Smelik 2013: 2), this chapter examines Bruce Springsteen's performance of memory in both recorded and live contexts. It discusses his recurrent use of autobiographical memory during on-stage monologues, his performed acts of remembrance and how his past repertoire is continually enlivened through considered constructions of self-history (recently exemplified by the *Springsteen on Broadway* concert residency). Songs with a factual basis illuminated in Springsteen's autobiography *Born To Run* (Springsteen 2016) and the content of his live song introductions are examined with a view to demonstrating their role in promoting audience authentication of Springsteen's working-class performer identity, while those centred on fictional characters are referenced to demonstrate his creative employment of memory-related processes from a compositional perspective.

Throughout Springsteen's career, reflective monologues have been a notable feature of his live concerts and serve a variety of purposes. The vast majority entail autobiographical recollections that comprise what Plate and Smelik refer to as 'performative acts of memory generating an experience of the past in the present' (Plate and Smelik 2013: 2). Two notable examples included on the *Bruce Springsteen and the E Street Band Live* (Springsteen 1986) album occur within 'Growin' Up' and the preamble to 'The River'. The former is humorous in tone and recounts scenes of minor parent/teenager disagreement that hold common currency: Springsteen recollects his father telling him to turn down his guitar in the house, and describes how his parents' hopes of him becoming a lawyer or author were dashed by his unswerving commitment to rock and roll. The latter is concerned with more serious father-son conflict where a sudden threat of permanent separation provides an unforeseen means of reconciliation. Springsteen describes spending time out of the house to avoid fights, recalls telling his father he hated him, and progresses to the eventual disclosure that, when he failed his army physical for the Vietnam draft, his father responded with the words, 'that's good'.

Both monologues demonstrate causal coherence and possess satisfying endings. In the first, Springsteen calls to his parents (in the audience) that they are 'both just gonna have to settle for rock 'n' roll' and follows it with full band re-entry, creating a high-energy rhythmic drive in support of the defiant closing lyric – 'When they said "pull down", I pulled up! Ooh ... growin' up'. The close of the second monologue supports the idea of an unbreakable bond between father and son, and gains further meaning as a consequence of the opening harmonica of 'The River'. The effective segue between the two encourages listeners to reflect on their conjoint relevance, which Michael Neiberg and Robert Citino claim illuminates 'the limited choices available to young working-class men in a rapidly deindustrializing America at the end of the twentieth century' (Citino and Neiberg 2016: 42).

While imbued with a narrative realism that stirs an empathetic response from his audience, the self that is remembered through such monologues is, as Ulric Neisser and Robyn Fivush observe in relation to autobiographical memory, 'not the historical self of yesterday, but only a reconstructed version' (Fivush and Neisser 1994: 8). This is not to imply that the events related in such monologues lack factual validity, simply that it is important to acknowledge the performative aspect of these acts of memory and the fluid relationship between past and present entailed therein. Springsteen's performance requires the selection and organization of remembered materials from the standpoint of the present, a process Jürgen Straub identifies as requiring agency:

> People do not simply memorize objectively existing things (events, etc.), which thereafter can be neutrally perceived, captured in a universal symbolic system, and preserved in a static form. Rather, already in the act of perception and reception, they transform a given thing into a phenomenon which can be and is worth being memorized, a *meaningful* and *therefore* communicable experience. (Straub 2008: 221)

The aforementioned monologue endings provide an insight into the performative aspects that transform past events into worthy phenomena, as do the openings and the physical and verbal gestures employed in their effective delivery.

Dave Marsh's account of Springsteen's monologue preceding 'The River' provides a useful insight into its theatrical properties. He describes: the stage going black; Springsteen striding forward into a single spotlight and gazing into the darkness; Springsteen buttoning up his jacket and crossing his arms to demonstrate the cold winter evenings of his youth, and his enactment of his father's authoritative stance – pointing straight ahead at the audience, arm rigid yet shaking while delivering the line 'Man, I can't wait 'til the army gets you' (Marsh 2004: 595–6). Such gestures attest to Springsteen's skilled performance of memory and are sometimes enhanced via pre-prepared audio backdrops and prompts that are equally well crafted. The scene is set for 'The River' monologue via picked alternating major chords (I and IV) on guitar in simple triple time (3/4) producing a relaxed, consonant feel. After eight bars a synthesizer melody is introduced, employing expressive use of non-chord tones in a developing two-bar motive that progressively descends to the dominant chord. At this moment of harmonic change, Springsteen asks the audience, 'How ya doin' out there tonight?'. Their responding cheers are accompanied by a move to the tonic chord, allowing the resulting perfect cadence to impart a sense of resolve and completeness before the alternating I IV harmony begins anew, its comforting predictability supporting Springsteen's reply, 'That's good, that's good'; the exact same words (of his father) that are used to close the monologue. In contrast, the opening of the 'Growin' Up' monologue is signalled via a dramatic prompt: pausing mid-song, the instruments gradually fade while a repeating piano note creates a contrasting metre, as if mimicking the bell of a passing train. Its presence underlines the sense of departure, indicating that Springsteen has alighted the song to impart his story.

As a global rock artist, Springsteen is remarkable in terms of the attention both he and those who commentate on his work pay to 'memory talk'.[1] Katherine Nelson first employed this term (1993) and, used here, it means to talk about someone or something from the past. Springsteen is renowned for his storytelling abilities both in spoken and written form (his autobiography *Born to Run* was nominated for a Grammy and won Best Autobiography in the 2018 Audie Awards). Specialist fan websites contain meticulously transcribed and referenced sections of his spoken monologues/song introductions, and biographers are compelled to incorporate his autobiographical recollections within their interpretations of his artistic and personal development (see Dolan 2012; Marsh 2004; Masur 2009).

Springsteen's introduction to 'Born to Run' during his 16 May 1988 New York City concert reveals the thought and prominence he gave to the spoken segments of his live shows at that time: 'I was sitting at home thinking about what I wanted to come and sing about, and talk to you about' (Pirttijärvi c.1996–2018). Marsh claimed his song introductions were an 'art in themselves' (2004: 301) and, following the release of *The River*, reported that Springsteen was 'celebrated and loved as that last true believer in the possibility of speaking meaningfully to a mass audience' (2004: 295).

With regard to content, Springsteen's monologues have focused on specific themes, the most fantastical being his humorous account of the E Street Band's mythical formation following the prediction of a Jersey Shore gypsy woman. Occurring in the middle of 'Tenth Avenue Freeze Out' during his 12 June 2000 New York City concert, that particular monologue possessed a quasi-preacher vocabulary and intensity reminiscent of the late James Brown: 'I wanna go to the riverside, I wanna go to that river of life … and I want you to go with me … one evening I stood as a young man before a dark grove of trees, and just like a child, I was frightened to pass through … then a gypsy woman called me onward and she said "what you need, Son, is you need a band to walk beside you"' (Pirttijärvi c.1996–2018). In accordance with his comedic introductions to 'Glory Days' – which typically focus on his advancing years yet undiminished potency: 'Oh where has youth gone? Anyway, 36, I feel handsome tonight, I'm at my sexual peak' (2004).[2] The purposefully immoderate and whimsical nature of these modes of address helps to establish Springsteen's showman persona. Aside from injecting fun into the performance, by way of contrast, they also serve to illuminate the serious tone of those which impart an ostensible sense of truth and realism, those monologues designed to be perceived as offering genuine insight into the man himself where the performance of memory plays a crucial role in defining Springsteen's performer identity.

Many of the serious monologues recollect events from his youth, a common trait according to Dan McAdams's observation that 'people tend to recall a disproportionately large number of autobiographical events from the ages of approximately 15 to 25 years' (McAdams 2003: 196). In the mid-1980s, performances of 'I'm on Fire' were often preceded by an account of his parents' limited financial means despite working hard:

I can remember growing up, and my folks working so hard all the time ... I remember my mom always going down to the finance man, borrowing money for Christmas, getting it paid off just in time to borrow money for Easter ... I remember it bothered my dad, and he'd sit at the table at night like something was dying inside. I got to feeling like there was something dying inside of me, and I didn't know how to keep it alive. (27 September 1985, Los Angeles, CA, introduction to 'I'm on Fire' transcribed by Pirttijärvi c.1996–2018)

Like the aforementioned River monologue from *Live*, some focused on the tensions resulting from his father's depression and his own bid for independence. For example, Springsteen's cover of the Animals' 'It's My Life' in the mid-1970s was preceded by a lengthy spoken introduction of this nature, culminating in a depiction of non-compliant escape: 'I'd end up running out the back door screaming, telling him, telling him how it was my life and I was gonna do what I wanted to do' (22 March 1977, Boston, MA, introduction to 'It's My Life' transcribed by Pirttijärvi c.1996–2018).

His later monologues on the same subject were more reflective in tone and linked to his own composition 'Independence Day'. Examining three such song introductions delivered just days apart demonstrates Springsteen's flexibility to utilize and adapt the same essential subject matter – in this case, an acknowledgement of his father's life having been constrained by external forces. In May 1981 Springsteen spoke to an audience in Brighton of how both his father and grandfather, being small-town factory workers, were victims of something they didn't understand. Four days later in London he spoke again of his enhanced perspective on his parents' lives and how it took him thirty years to tell his father he loved him. Just five days after this, again in London, the ending of the monologue referred to his father losing his sense of self-worth and added that songs from artists like The Drifters played an important part in saving him from a similar fate: 'in the whole world where people are telling you that you weren't worth nothing, it seemed like these songs said that was a lie, they just reminded you that you were worth something, and I guess there's two kinds of people in the world: the kind that remember that and the kind that forget that' (Pirttijärvi c.1996–2018). In all three cases, 'Independence Day' is introduced prior to the commencement of the monologue, meaning the audience foresee the destination, and there is nothing to detract from the sincerity of its placement. The monologue speaks for itself as a self-contained entity, yet its meaning informs the audience's reception of the subsequent song.[3]

With reference to the above flexibility, Springsteen's record producer, Chuck Plotkin, remarks:

> The stuff isn't canned. He tells stories; the stories are a little different each time. I've heard stories for the seventh time that I thought I knew, and you'll see this funny expression on his face and you realize he's remembering some detail of that story that he didn't remember before *that moment*. And you realize that there is a live thing taking place. That it's not simply some guy getting up and repeating a series of songs – that it is a live celebration, in that moment, in real time. (Marsh 2004: 622)

It is precisely this skill that illuminates Astrid Erll and Ann Rigney's observation that memory 'is as much a matter of acting out a relationship to the past from a particular point in the present as it is a matter of preserving and retrieving earlier stories' (Erll and Rigney 2009: 2). The steadfast message of Springsteen's introduction to 'Independence Day' is not dependent on a scripted reproduction of past events but on providing fitting depictions of self-revelation and discovery relevant to both him and his audience. The progression in theme from adolescent rebellion preceding 'It's My Life' to the later adult contemplation for 'Independence Day' demonstrates the importance of the present moment in how the past is recalled and for what purpose.

With respect to the purpose of recalling the past, McAdams explains that, by the emerging adult years, 'autobiographical memory and narrative understanding ... have developed to the level whereby they can be called into service in the making of identity' (McAdams 2003: 193). This naturally leads to his conclusion that identity is, in part, a product of self-selection since 'We choose the events that we consider most important for defining who we are' (2003: 196). It is therefore unsurprising that many of Springsteen's performances of memory centre on his roots and consequently serve to promote audience authentication of his working-class performer identity. As Allan Moore makes clear, 'authenticity is ascribed to, rather than inscribed in, a performance' (Moore 2002: 220). The detailed accounts of his working-class upbringing in both monologues and recent autobiography[4] ensure Springsteen's expressions of working-class issues are perceived to be authentic, and effectively negate the incongruity of his rich superstar status and blue-collar performer identity. Springsteen uses his autobiography to stress the importance and permanence of his roots: 'the piece of me that lived in the working-class neighborhoods of my hometown was an essential and permanent part of who I was ... There on the streets of my hometown was the beginning of my purpose, my reason, my passion ... I would travel far, light years from home ... but I would never completely leave' (Springsteen 2016: 264–7).

Katherine Nelson's explanation that autobiographical memory 'develops not only through social language practices, but in the context of cultures that value the individual personal histories of their members' (Nelson 2003: 20) accounts for Springsteen's audience being somewhat preconditioned to appreciate his autobiographical musings, though the additional functions of his onstage monologues necessitate further explanation. As indicated above, monologues appearing mid-song are intentionally framed by the surrounding materials, while those serving as pre-song introductions purposefully set the emotive context for what will follow; their repetition and causal development attest to this. And yet their content is not focused on literal detail (narratives/characters) of the songs in question, but on aspects of Springsteen's own life history so as to ground a song's subject matter in some imagined reality and illuminate its relevance to those issues shared by all people, such as the life changes/stages passed through, the changing relationship to the ***town/city*** one was born or grew up in, and to families and partners. Consequently, the monologues have the potential to enhance the perceived applicability and appeal of surrounding songs by attempting to guide audience interpretations.

Louis Masur points to their role in enabling Springsteen to tackle emotions he wishes to purge (Masur 2009: 22) while Marsh similarly describes them as personal disclosures and justifications to oneself (Marsh 2004: 301). Whatever the personal motive, the monologues permit audiences to assume a close affinity with Springsteen since their focus on seemingly private thoughts creates the impression of a personal connection and a level of intimacy not afforded in the songs themselves. Moreover, the audience's audible reaction to such monologues with cheering and applauding significant pronouncements demonstrates Michael Rothberg's observation that memory relies on 'the active agency of individuals and publics ... recognizing and revealing the production of memory' (Rothberg 2010: 8). Springsteen's audience acknowledge and bring testimony to his performance of memory and, in so doing, legitimize its placement in the concert proceedings.

It is this assumed level of intimacy that, alongside Springsteen's longevity and standing as a global artist, permits not only the performance of autobiographical memory but also the initiation of large-scale communal acts of remembrance.

During live concerts he has paid tribute to numerous deceased artists, playing cover versions of their signature songs (The River Tour 2016 incorporated tributes to both David Bowie and Glenn Frey).[5] Occasionally, these are preceded by stories indicating a particular artist's historical relevance to Springsteen, as typified by his 1985 introduction to 'Can't Help Falling in Love With You' where, following a humorous account of his efforts to breach the outer security of Graceland, he described Elvis as his idol, somebody whose music had 'given people a reason to live and to look for whatever promise there is' (3 July 1985, London, transcribed by Pirttijärvi c.1996–2018). Occasionally an artist is commemorated in this way because a concert takes place in their home city, as in Springsteen's cover of 'Highway to Hell' in memory of AC/DC's Bon Scott during his 2014 Perth concert. Such acts promote a degree of respect and thoughtfulness that surpasses the mere insertion of a city's name into the welcoming stage banter, and, in so doing, present unexpected yet poignant opportunities for audiences to reminisce.

Live tributes for mass audiences are evidence of popular music's ability to generate communal memory practices since a cover 'invites, if not insists upon, a comparison to the original ... rousing residue of musical memory, engaging the listener in a historical duet with lyric and lineage' (Plasketes 2005: 157). The death of a notable performer ordinarily prompts a flurry of tributes as touring artists of similar standing and/or musical genre suspend business as usual to insert an appropriate cover in honour of the departed.[6] Being such a prolific performer and someone who prides himself on years spent developing his musicianship skills as a bar band musician, where flexibility and scope of repertoire is prized, Springsteen has been perfectly situated to engage in such practices. On 23 April 2016 he opened his Brooklyn concert with a tribute to Prince, performing an understated version of 'Purple Rain'. Eyes cast down, his lack of direct engagement with the audience evoked a sense of solemnity and personal reflection not customary in opening numbers where statement gestures pertaining to one's own artistry are the norm. Its impact prompted one journalist to declare his homage a 'lesson in public mourning' (Rose 2016).

To date, Springsteen's tribute to saxophonist Clarence Clemons provides the most striking and habitual example of his ability to incite practices of remembrance in live concerts. Clemons, described by Springsteen in his autobiography as 'The Emperor of E Street' (Springsteen 2016: 243) died on 18 June 2011. His appearance alongside Springsteen on the *Born to Run* album cover (1975) and celebrated solos within eminent songs such as 'Jungleland'

and 'Bobby Jean' made him E Street's most conspicuous and venerated member. Springsteen routinely culminated his band introductions with a comic-book style narration designed to entertain and enhance Clemons's mythical presence within the band, hailing him as 'the king of the world ... the master of the universe ... emperor of all things ... he's faster than a speeding bullet ... more powerful than a roaring locomotive' (5 June 1981, London, transcribed by Pirttijärvi c.1996–2018).[7]

Post-2012, the Wrecking Ball Tour incorporated archive video footage of Clemons during live renditions of 'Tenth Avenue Freeze Out', enabling a virtual reunion of Springsteen and 'The Big Man'. The start and end points of this act of memory were carefully choreographed: following the song's bridge, Springsteen would announce 'This is the important part'. The band would then cease playing, allowing Springsteen to sing the first line of the subsequent verse alone: 'When the change was made uptown and the big man joined the band'. In place of Clemons's customary sax riff response, Springsteen held his microphone in the air and looked toward a large video screen, directing the audience to view a visual montage of live performance clips of Clemons and him performing together. The crowd's whoops, whistles, claps and cheers were eventually brought to a close by Springsteen raising and pulling down his right arm to signal the band's re-entry. Lasting 1 minute 30 seconds and devoid of sound, the video provided a fitting resource for communal remembering.[8] Its presence linked the present moment to the past, while the recruitment of Clemons's nephew, Jake Clemons, on saxophone connected both to the future continuation of the E Street Band. During the customary band introductions, Springsteen would ask five times 'Are we missing anybody tonight?'. The resulting tension would be routinely dissolved by his reassuring declaration that 'If you're here and if we're here (holding up his microphone) they're here ... I can hear him in your voices', implying the summoning of Clemons's performing spirit through collective commemoration. This supports Astrid Erll's assertion that, in order to exist and have impact, 'a "memory" represented by media and institutions must be actualized by individuals, by members of a community of remembrance' (Erll 2008a: 5).

Aside from commemorating the life and work of Clemons, this performance of memory equally functioned as a means of strengthening his fans' sense of connection and belonging in accordance with Jan Assman's observation that 'Remembering is a realization of belonging, even a social obligation. One has to remember in order to belong' (Assman 2008: 114). Springsteen has long understood the benefit of appealing to and enhancing a sense of community spirit during his live concerts. The aforementioned tribute to Clemons encourages fans to acknowledge a shared past – from those who experienced Clemons's work only in recorded format to those who witnessed his contribution to countless live concerts – all draw on associated memories and feel, if only transiently, a sense of kindred identification and appreciation with the potential to bind them.

Communities hit by misfortune have received targeted tributes from Springsteen that acknowledge their bravery and resilience while provoking memories of the hard times experienced. His selection and re-arrangement of 'When the Saints Go Marching In' for the first post-Katrina New Orleans Jazz and Heritage festival is one such example where he describes purposefully slowing down the tempo and sourcing all lyrics to create 'a meditation on resilience, survival and commitment to a dream that lives on through storm, wreckage and ruin' (Springsteen 2016: 450). The song most often utilized in this way is his composition 'City of Ruins'. Originally written as a statement on the decline of Asbury Park, New Jersey, its theme of devastation and plea for renewed strength – 'Come on, rise up!' – has been appropriated and applied to numerous occasions. As well as the aforementioned New Orleans festival, it was played during the 2017 New Zealand Christchurch concert, dedicated to those who suffered the 2011 earthquake and, most notably, the national TV telethon *America: A Tribute to Heroes* for the victims of 9/11 on 21 September 2001.

Songs such as 'Into the Fire' and 'Empty Sky' from *The Rising* (2002) were specifically inspired by the events of 9/11 and constitute examples of what Erll defines as 'memory-shaping media' (Erll 2008b: 395). They are 'viewed by a community *as* media of cultural memory' (2008b) due to their surrounding contexts, which grant them memorial status. For example, Kurt Loder's *Rolling Stone* review defined *The Rising* as 'a requiem for those who perished in that sudden inferno, and those who died trying to save them' (Loder 2002). Springsteen's commitment to representing those directly affected drew creative impetus from obituaries in the *New York Times* and conversations with the families of those who lost their lives. This gave the album an integral collective dimension and gravitas.

This dedication to evoking and confronting aspects of a shared American past is evident in many of Springsteen's compositions; from the frequently misunderstood single 'Born in the U.S.A.' to the unequivocally provocative 'American Skin (41 Shots)', both of which demonstrate Erll's assertion that 'media of cultural memory … are rarely uncontroversial. Their memory-making effect lies not in the unity, coherence, and ideological unambiguousness of the images they portray, but instead in the fact that they serve as cues for the discussion of those images' (Erll 2008b: 396). Springsteen's performance of 'American Skin (41 Shots)' in Atlanta (4 June 2000) was markedly controversial since its apparent reference to the tragic death of West African immigrant Amadou Diallo was interpreted by many as instituting overt criticism of the New York City Police Department. Forty-one shots were fired at Diallo while he was reaching for what police officers mistakenly believed to be a gun but was later found to be his wallet.[9] Following the results of a grand jury indictment a year later, in which the officers involved were found innocent of any criminal charges, the song served to invigorate public memory. This demonstrates what Plate and Smelik identify as one of the important consequences of the live act of performing cultural memory: that it 'blurs the boundaries between past and present, by bringing the past to and in the here and now' (Plate and Smelik 2013: 11). The negative reaction to Springsteen's performance – two police unions calling for a boycott of his impending concerts in New York – further illustrates the potential for the performance of memory to 'unsettle the present' (Franko and Richards 2000: 2) by highlighting unresolved problems, dangers and injustices.

'American Skin (41 Shots)' is one of the few songs in Springsteen's autobiography for which he provides a detailed account of his artistic aims: 'I wrote as thoughtfully as I could, trying to take in the perspective of not just the Diallo family but the officers as well' (Springsteen 2016: 434). He outlines the content and intended meaning of the song's individual sections before explaining that 'the idea was: here is what systematic racial injustice, fear and paranoia do to our children, our loved ones, ourselves. Here's the price in blood' (2016: 436). Springsteen recounts the audience and media reaction, selecting relevant aspects of his experience to justify his actions, make sense of the event and inform future readings of the song. It is in a similar manner that his past repertoire is continually enlivened through considered constructions of self-history. His live monologues, song introductions, autobiography and recent Broadway concert residency present aspects of his past that find literal representation in songs such as 'My Hometown', 'The Wish' and 'The River'. But all songs possess a rootedness in his autobiographical reflections concerning his family, his childhood and the town he grew up in, since the majority are, in his words, 'emotionally autobiographical' (2016: 267) and this is presented as a considered decision: 'I determined that there on the streets of my hometown was the beginning of my purpose, my reason, my passion ... I wanted my music grounded in my life, in the life of my family and in the blood and lives of the people I'd known' (2016: 266–7).

Memory-related processes are, of course, also located in the songs themselves. Many of Springsteen's fictional characters use memory as a basis for discerning the present and realizing either the possibility for change/redemption or the tragedy of their immobility. The protagonist in 'The River' recalls moments of youthful abandon that have been quashed by the responsibilities of marriage, fatherhood, work and the impact of industrial decline. His denial of memory, 'Now I act like I don't remember', is presented as his only means of coping with the predictable and limited possibilities of the present. The comparative vigour of the subsequent reminiscence, 'But I remember us riding in your brother's car, your body tan and wet down at the reservoir', is conveyed via a strengthening of accompanying rhythm as side snare hits are replaced by full snare drum hits to produce a more driven, dynamic sense of motion in support of this defiant act of memory.

Memory dreams are a further way in which Springsteen illuminates the sometimes-hurtful consequences of an insistent nostalgia for past events, loves and liberties. 'Downbound Train', 'My Father's House' and 'Shut Out the Light' all contain such sequences; in the first of these the drum kit drops out entirely, resulting in an abrupt decrease of momentum suggestive of stopped time, while the lyric sentiment is supported by sustained synthesizer harmonies that create an emotive, wistful atmosphere. The use of short-term phrase repetition in the vocal melody 'I rushed through the yard, I burst through the front door / My head pounding hard, up the stairs I climbed / The room was dark, our bed was empty' builds a sense of tension and expectancy that enhances the ensuing disappointment of the protagonist's realization that what he actually experienced was merely the past coming back to haunt him in his sleep: 'Then I heard that long whistle whine / And I dropped to my knees, hung my head and cried.'

In relation to autobiographical memory, Harald Welzer explains that it 'forms the temporal feedback matrix of our self, with which we can measure where and how we have changed and where and how we have remained the same' (Welzer 2008: 292). Springsteen has created numerous songs in which characters perform acts of autobiographical memory as a means to reflect on their former selves. The first-person confessional narrative of 'With Every Wish' presents a life story in which memories of particular events are used to demonstrate the moral of the refrain, that 'before you choose your wish you'd better think first / 'Cause with every wish there comes a curse.' Following evocative vignettes of childhood and early adulthood during verses one and two, the third verse moves to the present and, while hinting at the possibility of release, avoids definite closure by omitting the words 'there comes a curse' from its final refrain. Secure in their recourse to the past, Springsteen's narrative expositions often employ this device, leaving the listener to imagine possible futures and lessons learnt.

'My Hometown' expresses the threat of the present (economic recession) through an emotive key change to the relative minor before returning to the major (home) key to reveal the protagonist's recognition of his sense of place and belonging. Following the disclosure that he and his wife might be packing up and moving south, the protagonist repeats his own father's actions relayed in the opening of the song, sitting his son up on his lap behind the wheel of their car and delivering only the first line of the refrain 'This is your hometown.' The accompaniment continues to play out the song while listeners are left to contemplate the protagonist's undefined future, albeit safe in the knowledge that his hometown will never leave him. This is the same message Springsteen has imparted in numerous song introductions relating to his hometown of Freehold.

Springsteen's work provides consummate examples of the ways in which popular music artists perform affective memories to generate compelling experiences for their audiences and reciprocal emotive responses. His autobiography ends with the admission that 'Writing about yourself is a funny business. At the end of the day it's just another story you've chosen from the events of your life. I haven't told you "all" about myself' (Springsteen 2016: 501). It further demonstrates his understanding of how the performance of memory is an active, discerning and fluid process, one that remains an integral means of shaping, conveying and perpetuating his unique performer identity.

Notes

1 The term 'memory talk' was first employed by Katherine Nelson in her 1993 article 'The Psychological and Social Origins of Autobiographical Memory'. Used here, it means to talk about someone or something from the past.
2 Introduction to 'Glory Days', 27 September Los Angeles 1985. It ends with the recurrent tag line 'In the end, it ain't nothing but glory days'.
3 In the first two cases, Springsteen has to subdue the predictable cheers following

his verbal introduction of 'Independence Day' in order to commence the monologue: 'I need, I need a little quiet for this song, please, thank you'. His not uncommon requests for quiet further demonstrate the value he has placed upon autobiographical recollections in live performance.

4 Springsteen uses his autobiography to stress the importance and permanence of his roots: 'the piece of me that lived in the working-class neighborhoods of my hometown was an essential and permanent part of who I was' (2016: 264). 'There on the streets of my hometown was the beginning of my purpose, my reason, my passion ... I would travel far, light years from home ... but I would never completely leave' (2016: 266-7).

5 Springsteen performed David Bowie's 'Rebel Rebel' in his opening show in Pittsburgh (16 January) and delivered a solo acoustic version of 'Take it Easy' as a tribute to Glenn Frey just three days later in Chicago.

6 Cover tributes to Prince were incorporated into existing tours by Pearl Jam and Coldplay, the latter featuring a guest vocal performance by comedian and actor James Corden.

7 In the early years, the band introduction would appear as either an intro or mid-song break to 'Rosalita', and later became the staple monologue aligned to 'Tenth Avenue Freeze Out'.

8 Its presence linked the present moment to the past, while the recruitment of Clemons's nephew, Jake Clemons, on saxophone connected both to the future continuation of the E Street Band.

9 For a detailed account of Springsteen's engagement with this and other political issues, see Harde (2013).

References

Assman, J. (2008), 'Communicative and Cultural Memory', in A. Erll and A. Nünning (eds), *A Companion to Cultural Memory Studies: An International and Interdisciplinary Handbook*, 109–18, Berlin, Boston: De Gruyter.

Citino, R. M. and M. S. Neiberg (2016), 'A Long Walk Home: The Role of Class and Military in the Springsteen Catalogue', *Boss: The Biannual Online-Journal of Springsteen Studies*, 2 (1): 41–60.

Dolan, M. (2012), *Bruce Springsteen and the Promise of Rock 'n' Roll*, New York: W. W. Norton.

Erll, A. (2008a), 'Cultural Memory Studies: An Introduction', in A. Erll and A. Nünning (eds), *A Companion to Cultural Memory Studies: An International and Interdisciplinary Handbook*, 1–15, Berlin, Boston: De Gruyter.

Erll, A. (2008b), 'Literature, Film, and the Mediality of Cultural Memory', in A. Erll and A. Nünning (eds), *A Companion to Cultural Memory Studies: An International and Interdisciplinary Handbook*, 389–98, Berlin, Boston: De Gruyter.

Erll, A. and A. Rigney (eds) (2009), *Mediation, Remediation, and the Dynamics of Cultural Memory*, Berlin, Boston: De Gruyter.

Fivush, R. and U. Neisser (eds) (1994), *The Remembering Self: Construction and Accuracy in the Self-Narrative*, Cambridge: Cambridge University Press.

Franko, M. and A. Richards (eds) (2000), *Acting on the Past: Historical Performance Across the Disciplines*, Hanover, London: Wesleyan University Press.

Harde, R. (2013), '"Living in your American skin": Bruce Springsteen and the Possibility of Politics', *Canadian Review of American Studies*, 43 (1): 126–44.

Loder, K. (2002), 'The Rising', *Rolling Stone*, July 30. Available online: https://www.rollingstone.com/music/music-album-reviews/the-rising-248610/ (accessed 10 November 2017).

McAdams, D. P. (2003), 'Identity and the Life Story', in R. Fivush and C. A. Haden (eds), *Autobiographical Memory and the Construction of a Narrative Self: Developmental and Cultural Perspectives*, 187–207, Mahwah, NJ: Lawrence Erlbaum.

Marsh, D. (2004), *Bruce Springsteen: Two Hearts the Definitive Biography, 1972–2003*, London: Routledge.

Masur, L. P. (2009), *Runaway Dream: Born to Run and Bruce Springsteen's American Vision*, New York: Bloomsbury.

Moore, A. (2002), 'Authenticity as Authentication', *Popular Music*, 21 (2): 209–23.

Nelson, K. (1993), 'The Psychological and Social Origins of Autobiographical Memory', *Psychological Science*, 4 (1): 7–14.

Nelson, K. (2003), 'Narrative and Self, Myth and Memory: Emergence of the Cultural Self', in R. Fivush and C. A. Haden (eds), *Autobiographical Memory and the Construction of a Narrative Self: Developmental and Cultural Perspectives*, 3–8, Mahwah, NJ: Lawrence Erlbaum.

Pirttijärvi, J. (*c.*1996–2018), 'Storytellers'. Available online: https://brucebase.wikispaces.com (accessed 20 November 2017).

Plasketes, G. (2005), 'Re-flections on the Cover Age: A Collage of Continuous Coverage in Popular Music', *Popular Music and Society*, 28 (2): 137–61.

Plate, L. and A. Smelik (eds) (2013), *Performing Memory in Art and Popular Culture*, New York: Routledge.

Rose, C. (2016), 'Bruce Springsteen's Tribute to Prince is a Lesson in Public Mourning', *NPR*, 27 April. Available online: https://www.npr.org/sections/allsongs/2016/04/27/475870604/bruce-springsteens-tribute-to-prince-is-a-lesson-in-public-mourning (accessed 12 February 2018).

Rothberg, M. (2010), 'Introduction: Between Memory and Memory: From Lieux De Mémoire to Noeuds De Mémoire', *Yale French Studies*, 118 (119): 3–12.

Springsteen, B. (1980), 'Independence Day', *The River*, Columbia Records.

Springsteen, B. (1984), 'Born in the U.S.A.'/'Glory Days'/'My Hometown', *Born in the USA*, Columbia Records.

Springsteen, B. (1986), 'Growin' Up'/'The River', *Bruce Springsteen and the E Street Band Live*, Columbia Records.

Springsteen, B. (2002), 'Empty Sky'/'Into the Fire'/'My City of Ruins', *The Rising*, Columbia Records.

Springsteen, B. (2016), *Born to Run*, London: Simon & Schuster.

Straub, J. (2008), 'Psychology, Narrative, and Cultural Memory: Past and Present', in A. Erll and A. Nünning (eds), *A Companion to Cultural Memory Studies: An International and Interdisciplinary Handbook*, 215–28, Berlin, Boston: De Gruyter.

Welzer, H. (2008), 'History and Development of the Concept of Communicative Memory', in A. Erll and A. Nünning (eds), *A Companion to Cultural Memory Studies: An International and Interdisciplinary Handbook*, 285–98, Berlin, Boston: De Gruyter.

Part Two

Recollections

10

Time machines

Barbara Frost

Things you need to know:

I don't own a lot of records
Most of what I have has been given to me rather than bought by me.
I have spent periods of my life with no way of playing vinyl.
I very, very rarely play music in the house.
There's a lot of dust on my shelves.

Here's the starting point: I'm sitting in a café with two of my oldest friends. Jill: best friend of nearly fifty years: soul mate and serial rescuer; designer; cake maker; and singer. Edwin: her husband whom I've known for forty years: artist; writer; collector; and musician. We are talking about the idea of me writing a piece for this book. I have just made the statement that I find it strange that I have spent so much of my adult life immersed in the music world whilst having little musical ability or even being that bothered by music.

They politely leave the part about me being not musical alone but agree to challenge my assertion that I've never been that bothered.

Maybe it's relative. Compared to Edwin's collection, my one shelf each of CDs and old vinyl doesn't look like much of an interest. Compared to both of them, I listen to a negligible amount or range. As a considerable proportion of my friends are practising musicians, composers, writers or otherwise engaged in music-based pursuits I really can't compete. But as I said, maybe it's just relative. Or maybe it's not about the hpw (hours per week) I listen. Or the gpa (gigs per annum) I attend. If it's about impact then maybe I was, and am still, bothered.

Then we talk about records. It's well understood that us old people can get quite emotional about 'vinyl'. Admit it, we've all bored or been bored by people waffling on about the golden age of the vinyl album or LP. The anticipation, the lingering over the cover artwork and sleeve notes, the hoping for legible lyrics on the inner sleeve and then the sensuous slide of that black disc out of its paper lingerie. The skilled balancing between the finger on the label and the thumb on the outer rim. The practised sweep of the little velvet pad to banish dust. Then the lowering of the disc onto turntable/deck, the positioning of the needle/stylus, the lowering of the arm (automatically or manually) and the stepping back, waiting for those first seconds of gentle crackle to fade and at last the reward, the rush of … the music! Remembering not to dance too vigorously – don't want to make the arm jump and scratch – or to get too comfortable – you'll be back on your feet in 20 minutes to change to side two. The searching for depth and meaning, the switching from first impression to slow burn favourite tracks, the hoping that maybe you'll find someone out there who'll share your appreciation of this band/singer/opus even to the point of agreeing to have sex with you.

Now you don't get all that with your downloads and streaming, do you? Well maybe the sex thing still works.

So we talked about Records. Discs. Albums. LPs. Edwin, bless him, seemed much more impressed with my collection than you would expect given that his knowledge of music can justifiably be described by browsing the 'e' pages of a dictionary – encyclopaedic, erudite, esoteric, eclectic, extensive, expansive, enthusiastic, expensive – you get the gist. Admittedly, he's probably thinking more of my Bowies than my Monkees but I remain encouraged. However, we soon establish – and this is where Jill comes into her own given the five decades etc. mentioned above – that while certain records have undoubtedly played a significant part in my life, my memories of the details of dates, locations, sources and sequences are maybe … questionable? Jill gets to use the word 'no' quite a lot or at least to imply it through the narrowing of the eyes and the tilting of the head in reaction to various assertions. She's not usually so negative and she's sensitive to our age-related paranoia about failing memory and general loss of marbles. But she does seem pretty damn sure about me being pretty damn wrong about some things.

Edwin is ploughing his own furrow by now in avoidance of a conversation that is descending into a, 'You know that shop in Wimbledon, opposite side to the theatre?', 'Not the one in Putney then, along from Woolworths?'

'A record,' he pronounces, 'is a sort of Time Machine'. He had more to say about that and it was worth hearing. However, I'm not going to explain his thoughts here. I suggest you try to track him down and have the conversation with him yourself. I take no responsibility as to whether you end up agreeing with him but I promise you it'll be interesting.

What Edwin meant and what it triggered in me may not be the same thing.

These are my time machines

Five records covering a five-decade timeline. Five records sitting on the shelf. I'm leaping in with five that I believe, on first pass, to have some significance to me. Although, at the beginning of this process I'm not sure why.

I've decided to start with quick descriptions of the objects from memory and then move onto associated memories – a bit stream-of-consciousness. Not digging too deep.

Then I'll take the records off the shelf to check my facts. I'm expecting errors. Finally, I'll ponder on the results.

There may be some passing references to music but probably nothing of great significance.

The records

Nobody Needs Your Love (Gene Pitney)
The Monkees (The Monkees)
The Man Who Sold the World (David Bowie)
Gag (Fad Gadget)
Black Star (David Bowie)

Record 1: *Nobody Needs Your Love* by Gene Pitney

Description from memory: 12" black vinyl. Black and white paper inner sleeve printed with record company details and adverts for other records. Outer sleeve: front – colour photograph of Gene Pitney, be-suited and clean-cut with a half-smile on his face. Plain, pale green background. When held at a certain angle words can be seen incised into the glossy lamination: 'Happy Xmas from Ken and Aunt Lil'. Back – black and white and less glossy. A photograph of Gene – possibly full length and on stage; informational text including facts such as his studio practice of double-tracking his vocals and his childhood hobby of practising taxidermy using road kill collected on his way home from school; track listings and record company logo and info.

How and when acquired: December 1966 as a Christmas present.

Record 2: *The Monkees* by The Monkees

Description from memory: 12" black vinyl. Black and white paper inner sleeve printed with record company details and adverts for other records. Outer sleeve: front – glossy colour photograph of The Monkees shot at an angle. Four young men with hair a little longer than the Beatles cut wearing identical outfits – 'as seen on TV'. Monkees logo – the name forming a guitar shape. Back – black and white, track listings, text and photographs. May have my nickname written on in biro (Bobbie).

How and where acquired: Probably early 1967, possibly bought by self using Christmas or donated money. Most likely bought at the 'electrical' shop at the top of my road near station. Not a record shop as such. It sold household goods including radios and record players but stocked a few records and would order for you.

Record 3: *The Man Who Sold the World* by David Bowie

Description from memory: 12" black vinyl. Paper inner sleeve, can't remember details. Outer sleeve: front – man-in-a-frock photograph of a long-haired Bowie reclining on a chaise longue, crushed velvet draperies and scattered playing cards. Cover had a soft texture that began to wear from much handling. Back – can't remember.

How and where acquired: 1971. Bought by self. Not long after release. Record shop somewhere in South-West London, probably Putney or Wimbledon. Pocket money/paper round earnings.

Record 4: *Gag* by Fad Gadget

Description from memory: 12" black vinyl. Inner paper sleeve with lyrics and writing/publishing credits. Outer sleeve: front – glossy, white background with black and white photograph of the artist (Frank Tovey) 'tarred and feathered'. Title and artist name in black and red lettering. Back – bottom half of same photograph, track listings and label details.

How and where acquired: 1984. Direct from record company as one of a boxful, just pre-release. No money exchanged hands.

Record 5: *Black Star* by David Bowie

Description from memory: CD in jewel case, inside card slip cover. Black semi-gloss star on black satin card. Probably text somewhere – lyrics, track listings, publishing details etc. But not sure what or where.

How and where acquired: January 2016. Not on release but within weeks of. Gifted.

Memories

Nobody Needs Your Love

My first real record.

Ken: The only record player in the house capable of playing vinyl belonged to my older brother (the Ken of the inscription). This would have made it a fairly useless present only a few months previously as I would have no access to the red and cream, mono portable as it lived in his bedroom – a forbidden zone for a little sister. That summer, however, he had joined the RAF and it had been moved to the living room.

I don't think that I had specifically asked for this record but Ken owned several Gene Pitney LPs and as I sort of hero-worshipped him at that age – he was, after all, a real teenager and I was a mere ten years old – his taste influenced my own.

I'm guessing Ken actually bought the record but Aunt Lil will have provided some or all the money.

Aunt Lil: My dad's aunt. Her strange, slightly posh, possessions and habits – jam in a china jam dish with a silver spoon on sliced brown bread for Sunday tea, her huge overgrown garden with apple trees and gooseberry bushes awaiting harvest. Her descent into what was described by the catch-all 'senility' with her inability to smell off-food and asking me if I was from the 'razor-blade factory'. Her talking about operations with my Nan at Christmas and the way she took out her dentures straight after dinner, wrapped them in a large white hankie and stuffed them in her handbag until the next meal. She probably contributed a ten-shilling note for my Xmas present from the many she kept in separate paper bags in a drawer.

Mum: Neither brother nor aunt would have wrapped the present – that would have been my mother. Nothing fancy. A sheet of thin, cheap Christmas paper. Maybe robins, holly or Victorian coaching scenes. The message written directly onto the paper with a ballpoint.

Creating that lasting impression.

The Monkees

I became a Monkees fan when the show began on TV – Dec 66/Jan 67. From top juniors at primary school on everyone had to have an answer to 'Who's your favourite … ?'. Same group united us. Same group member divided. So in the playground we Monkees fans hung around together, talked through the weekend's episode, sang the songs, swapped essential information: Davy's birthplace, Micky's birthdate, Mike's star sign, Pete's favourite food. We bonded.

In the absence of easy access to merchandise, the knowing of facts and the owning of the records gained you top position in the social hierarchy.

Whatever time was spent in school discussing things Monkee, outside school friends were scattered and there was little socializing. The record stayed at home and listening to the music was a solitary thing.

Other random memories triggered by this record: throwing a tantrum – and a plate – when parents proposed going for a nice walk at the same time as The Monkees were on TV.

Playing at being the Monkees. Walking around the playground with my arm around Lesley because I was – for the duration of playtime at least – Mike Nesmith. A role allocated because I was the tallest and had short (for a girl) dark hair. Lesley being slightly shorter and having long blonde hair was my/Mike's wife. Others played the parts of Davy, Micky and Peter. It was a girls' school – we were doing our eleven-year-old best.

The Man Who Sold the World

For half of 1971 I'm 14 for half I'm 15. I'd long outgrown the Monkees. Being bookish and good at maths and science I had discovered sci-fi and Robert Heinlein. One of his books was called *The Man Who Sold the Moon*. One evening while I was occupying my usual spot at the kitchen table grinding my way through whatever homework needed to be handed in the next morning and listening to the radio, John Peel announced a song called 'The Man Who Sold the World'. I pricked up my ears. Someone called David Bowie. I'd heard of him – a couple of years ago there had been a single called 'Space Oddity' which I'd paid some attention to, me being a sci-fi fan and a prospective astronaut. Don't remember if the song caught my attention first and then I got the title/artist or if it was the other way round but whatever. My attention was got. A note was made and the hunt was on.

I wouldn't have had much money at that time. There was a Saturday job serving cheese and cold meats at David Greigs in Wandsworth High Street. I really wanted a job down Kensington Market selling t-shirts and loons like some of the other girls from school but I wasn't cool enough. Other than that there was birthday and Christmas money and occasional small-change handouts from family. What little cash I had went on buying books the local library didn't have but maybe I was prepared to re-direct that small book budget to finance the buying of TMWSTW.

Can't remember how I got hold of the record – when, where or how much. But somehow I did. Don't need to remember the cover much – it's too famous. But my strongest memory is of its feel. Usually covers were glossy, smooth and hard. This was soft, stroke-able. Texture and emotion. I have restless fingers that can conjure the texture of a bedspread from my childhood or the skin of my newborn baby's head. My hands remember carrying this record up and down Augustus Hill (I'll explain that in a bit), holding it gently while I listened. Trouble is, soft is not so hardwearing. If you're one of those people who buys shrink-wrapped vinyl and never unwraps it or spends hours at record fairs searching for rare, mint copies of obscure or classic albums, look away now.

My response to the first signs of wear was to cover it in clear, sticky-back plastic. Yep, the stuff promoted weekly on *Blue Peter* and recommended for keeping your school hymnbook pristine. I know, it's a bit like mending the Magna Carta with Sellotape, but, hey.

Those trips up and down the hill had a purpose. Jill (her again) lived at the top of the hill and I at the bottom (sounds charmingly rural – it wasn't). I still relied on my brother's old record player but by now technology had moved onto the delights of STEREO and my little machine was MONO. Not only was that limiting my listening pleasure but the warnings were that playing a stereo record with a mono stylus (Google it) would damage the record. That was life at the bottom of the hill. However, at the higher altitude was a man with a more serious approach to recorded music. Jill's dad, jazz fan and tech geek, had put together his own – what did we call it? Not sound system, maybe hi-fi. Record player didn't begin to do it justice. It was all separate bits. There was the 'turntable' complete with an appropriate stereo stylus, which was made by Bang & Olufsen (no idea but he said it was a good brand), an 'amplifier', a pair of black, floor-standing speakers and for that perfect finishing touch – headphones.

What's more, he let us use it. At the bottom of the hill if the TV/radio/anything electrical went wrong us female people were expected to wait until Daddy got home to fix it. At the top of the hill music listening became a sacred ritual. The record itself was treated with respect, prepared for placement on the B&O altar. The ritual: add to the un-sleeving, cleaning and placing of the disc on the turntable, selecting speed and volume; tweaking the sound quality – bass and treble – choosing turns for headphones or best positions in the room to listen through speakers. To dance. Or to lie back in companionable surrender. Physical, social, erotic.

And maybe one day someone would notice me carrying the record around, think I was cool, strike up a conversation ...

Gag

This is not really a first of anything. Not a turning point. But it is in many ways the most personal because it is the record I had the most involvement in from beginning to end.

And it makes me think of Berlin.

Biting cold wind on the walk between the bus and the studio alongside the Wall. Shopping and cooking for up to twelve people with limited equipment in a tiny kitchen. Supermarket potato salad sold by the bucketful. Feeling very spooked about doing vocals alone in the studio after we had convinced ourselves that it was haunted. Sitting by an open window late at night, warm on one side, cold on the other. Music on the warm side, armed guards and watchtowers on the cold side. Sun-rise taxi rides through the city after all-nighters. Daughter being baby-sat by a girl who carried her pet rats in her clothes. Nightclubbing. Berlin Zoo. Winter's first snowfall on the Ku'damm and the craziness of pre-Christmas at the KaDeWe. A temporary, extended family living and working together. Missing Marmite.

Back in London: Developing the idea for the cover with Frank and Anton Corbijn. Inventing 'tar' for the tar and feathers out of Pond's Cold Cream and daughter's powder paint. Shooting the cover on Christmas Eve in a studio with no working showers, and having to scrape off a body's worth of black gunk with paper towels. Black gunk that didn't fully wash off until around Twelfth Night and never from the sheets.

Black Star

Knowing something was to be released from internet news. Aware of release coinciding with Bowie's birthday. Waking on Monday morning, after a weekend of family trauma and hospital waiting rooms, to the internet: David Bowie Dead. Much crying. Calling Jill who had also just heard. Calling in to work to ask for day off due to weekend's events, going back in on Tuesday and wondering who thought I'd had time off because of Bowie. People assuming I must have bought it by now but I couldn't. Didn't want to order it from Amazon and have to wait, didn't want to walk into a shop and buy it. Didn't want to talk about it. A week or so of numbness and pain: work, hospital visits and mourning. All mixed up. Feeling like I was struggling to deal with the present and had lost my past. Began to mourn ex-husband again. Bowie was very much a shared thing between us. Regretting not being pushier on New York visit four years earlier to get someone to arrange a meeting – too late now. Finally, Jill gives me a copy of *Black Star*. Not sure I want it. Of course I want it but it's no longer enough. It sits on the shelf for days/weeks unopened. Then I open it. Listen maybe a few times, probably read notes, look at it. Then upload it to laptop and then sync it to phone – the new ritual. Put disc on shelf in place with other Bowie CDs – many bought in recent years as additional copies to original vinyl – on single shelf of CDs – alphabetic then chronological order. Somewhere between Bingham and Brel. Then left there. Music becomes part of daily commute, sometimes as album sometimes as tracks on shuffle. The disc stays on the shelf.

Off the shelf

Finally I allow myself to take the records of the shelf and test some of my memories.

Nobody Needs Your Love – essentially as remembered. Exact inscription reads 'To Barbara Merry Xmas From Ken and Aunt Lil.' Definitely my mum's handwriting. On the back I've added the nickname I was trying out: 'Bobbie' in awkwardly joined letters in red pen. And on checking the sleeve notes I find that he didn't stuff roadkill as a hobby – he set traps for 'small game' and continued to hunt and stuff animals. I'd remembered him as a nicer human being than he was.

The Monkees – The guitar-shaped logo wasn't there – that must belong to later albums. A lot more detail on back cover than I remembered but this was the first source of those valuable biographical band details: height, eye colour, etc. I'm still trying out those identities: 'Bobbie' in red, 'Babs' in black. So maybe I did take the records round to friends' houses or maybe I was just going through a possession-marking phase, like writing my name in books.

The Man Who Sold the World – I hadn't forgotten the details of the inner sleeve – there weren't any. Back cover had another photo of Bowie and lots of text about the tracks and all the people involved: musicians, producers, engineers, designers, etc. I'm finding the sticky-back plastic more offensive than I thought I would.

Gag – Now here's a problem. Not on shelf, not in cupboard or another shelf or in the box of records under the bed that mostly belonged to my son's DJing phase. This record is not a figment of my imagination. It existed. It exists (available online) but not in my house. Somewhere in the sharing out of that original box of discs, in the house movings, in the room re-arrangements, in the divorce division of possessions, in the post-mortem re-acquisition of things, *Gag* has gone. I am distraught. And not just because I can't check the sleeve notes. I've got the CD released seven years after the original. I can always buy one from eBay. Won't be the same though. I've lost a bit of my self.

Black Star – No point in listing what I didn't remember as I remembered so little and there's quite a lot to describe. Except that it's not in a jewel case and there's more white on the front than I thought. And now that my new phone won't sync with my old laptop and my old laptop has lost its ability to make noise, if I want to listen to this again I'll have to handle the CD. Maybe I'm ready.

Musings – Is there anything to be learned from this?

The choice of records was made without much thought or initial analysis. Inevitably, I can't avoid the 'why these?' question. I've done a rough count and there were about 200 vinyl albums on the shelf when I started and some 150 CDs. Some of which I like/listen to more than some of the chosen few. As part of the process of writing, a few of my suspicions about my choices have been confirmed and other possible reasons have surfaced. Four out of five could represent fairly obvious landmarks in the collection: first record, most significant record, most involved in record, last Bowie. If I'd have let myself I could have dropped *The Monkees* for a number of later acquisitions and, in all honesty, if that had been the one missing from the shelf I wouldn't have felt it's loss as much as that of *Gag*.

And thirty-two years between *Gag* and *Black Star* – what's that all about? I bought/acquired/loved a fair number of albums in between but none that shouted out to be on the list.

So here's my fancy, whether I knew it at the time of choosing (deep in my subconscious blah, blah, blah) or whether the process of writing has created the links, these records now represent significant stages and relationships in my life.

So one last time ...

Nobody Needs Your Love by Gene Pitney

This is family at the tale-end of childhood. When things are about to change. Money was not plentiful so, homemade, second hand and knock-down (not knock-off, never knock-off) were more typical. This was something new and shop-bought; first taste consumerism; the last remnants of big brother hero worship; Great Aunts and Nans, Aunties, Uncles and Cousins visiting for Christmas Dinner; my brother leaving home; me elevated to only child status with access to a record player; no competition over early evening TV; a chance to become Dad's workmate rather than Mummy's little helper; being the tallest girl in school; knowing that only girls with long hair got boyfriends but not caring much.

The Monkees by The Monkees

This is transition from childhood to adolescence. First period and first bra. Changing school and exploring identity – Barbara/Bobbie/Babs; making new friends; still being 'childish'; being a 'fan'; having shared tastes and wearing a uniform; still being part of a family but existing beyond it; learning to want stuff and buying into consumerism. This is being too young and too distant from the Summer of Love to know what 'make love not war' actually meant when I scrawled it on my notebook cover. When certain words were just bad and upset Mum. This was when female friendship was all and boys were annoying and somehow unhygienic; boyfriends were fantasies and the man in the park who wanted to take my photograph was creepy but not dangerous. This is when my body was awkward and lumpy but functional and good at sport and I wasn't that hung up on it. This is when my best friend told me I was singing out of tune 'as usual' and my teacher sarcastically allowed me to join the choir as long as I didn't give up like I had with the recorder. So I stuck with it, mostly in the back row (being tall) and mostly miming so she couldn't practise her sarcasm on me again for being out of tune; singing along but no longer singing out. This is when I gave up on music for the reasons above and became a lyrics kinda girl. This is when my imagination let me try out what it might feel like to have a musician as a boyfriend and everyone would be jealous. This is when I discovered Dickens and Shakespeare and Narnia. This is when I loved my family but suspected that maybe they were not quite keeping up. When school intruded into my home through homework and I was on my own with it.

The Man Who Sold the World by David Bowie

Change. Earlier I said that by the time I heard this I had 'long outgrown' the Monkees. Yet only a couple of years separate them. I had grown the hips and the breasts and was ready to find out what to do with them. I was used to being clever and had to figure out what to do with that. Hormones and brain cells were firing on all engines. A time when everything was possible even when nothing much was happening. This is confusion: knowing you can love/hate your body/self at the same time. When being clever wasn't enough. When family and school friends weren't enough. This is wanting to stand out: to not like what friends liked, not read what friends read, not believe what friends believed. Unless I'd liked, read or believed first. This is still upsetting Mum with words but also with clothes and actions and ideas. This is still not making music but consuming it body and soul. This is painting and photographing and writing, writing, writing. This is making out with people whose names you didn't always remember at parties or gigs. This is strutting in six-inch heels (if you're going to be tall, go all out, girl) or skipping along pavements barefoot. This is still liking school but knowing it wasn't everything. This is Genet and Sartre and Burroughs and Fellini and Warhol. This is sex and joy and despondency and darkness. This is lying on the grass staring at the stars and crying because it's all too fucking big. This is love and lust and books and being inside and outside and changing my mind. This is huge and so much follows.

Gag by Fad Gadget

Family again but this time I'm the grown-up. Or rather one of the grown-ups – that musician boyfriend once imagined, though not aspired to, having happened anyway – reader, I married him. There's a daughter and the wonder of watching a child have a childhood in an adult place because she is loved and safe. This is the family business and having so many hats to wear: photographer, costumier, accountant, tour manager, backing singer, opinion-giver, breadwinner, lyricist and cook. This is being part of something extraordinary from first note to sleeve notes drawing on the creative power of the liminal – physical and psychological. Being in Berlin in 1983 – a haunted place. This is secrets and forgiveness and being grown up about it. When I understood that not being centre stage was not thwarted ambition but a preference for being among the backstage machinery. A time of partnership and parenthood, juggling and negotiation. This is a point with a past and many futures. Love. A bubble. This is not going to last.

Black Star by David Bowie

And finally. A time of exhaustion and numbness and powerlessness and guilt. Nothing to do with Bowie's death. Monday morning waking to the habit of the internet and facing something I'd sort of rehearsed for. Bowie's death. Refusing to be drawn into sharing. 'No, you do not know how I feel because I do not feel the same as you.' Trying to understand and explain the scale of my grief. This is a long delayed mourning for that musician ex-husband; a loss of shared memories, private memories and dreams. Feeling old, pissed off and cheated. I'm wallowing in the past and struggling to deal with the present. Then coming to my senses and getting on with it and making decisions and not giving up. Meditating on what's gone and embracing what and who remains. Taking six months to examine a life, to decide 'enough of this shit' and to prepare for another change. Another edge to teeter on.

After all, Time Machines can take you to the future as well as the past.

Oh, and Jill says that I bought *The Man Who Sold the World* in Wimbledon. She seems sure of that.

11

Meeting your idols 1: Growing up addicted in York

Karen Woodall

October brought the smell of sugar beet, sickly and sweet and heralding darker days and longer nights. An infinity of boredom with which we would have to contend until the summer days returned. Cold dark times with nothing much to do but wait for Thursday when there was *Top of the Pops* to look forward to.

Life was not a chocolate box back then in York. There was nothing fancy in the high street other than FineFare or Leak and Thorpe the department store. If you wanted fancy you went to Leeds, the dirty big city down the road. In York in the seventies, there were chocolate factories and working men and women who stood for no nonsense and took no prisoners. Being a 'young un' in York in the early seventies wasn't much fun. In a rigidly working-class society, we knew our place was at the bottom of the hierarchy. We knew not to get above ourselves.

And then there was David Bowie.

'What kind of a poofter is he then?', said my Granddad as Bowie graced the tiny monochrome screen in the corner (colour TV hadn't yet reached my grandparents' council house in Burton Stone Lane). I ignored him and peered through the eye-watering smog that commonly filled that living room. Chain-smoking was the norm back then and bugger the lungs of the young people. We were the last in line for the best cut of meat or to be fed, but were the repository of the waste of our elders' expended smoke. We were the unwilling recipients of their sneering commentary as well.

I was fixated on Bowie singing *The Jean Genie*. The song was powerful enough to drown out the injustice of my working-class youth as well as my grandfather's running commentary about the world going to hell in a handcart.

Back home in the village just outside of York, my father bawled up the stairs to tell me to turn the music down. 'Open the window as well, that stuff smells like a whore house', he finished off with. I doused the joss sticks in water and opened the window, knowing that if I didn't another lecture would start up about how burning joss sticks would lead to taking drugs. I was pretty certain my father had never been in a whore house given he had spent his life making machine parts at the factory down the road but I wasn't going to argue with him. I knew my place and I valued my safety. He wasn't averse to giving us a clatter if he felt like it. Life in a working-class family wasn't much fun in York, especially when it came to middle-class pretensions like burning incense.

The music of my youth is joyous, exuberant and full of sexual promise. The rest of my youth is a drab palette of hard work and not getting above yourself. When I look back, I see those parts that relate to music in day-glo. They are the rainbow relief from a world where children were supposed to turn into adults without much of a fuss. Teenagers had only been invented in my father's younger years and were largely considered to be dangerous hoodlums carrying chains and knives and taking drugs. My family saw drugs as a constant scourge. They were absolutely to be avoided. Not that anyone had ever taken drugs or even known anyone who had done so but it was legend that one dabble in the drug world and you'd be on skid row. I wonder now whether that terror was the product of such a buttoned-up working-class world.

My mother and father were married at age nineteen and twenty and a year later were parents to me. Whilst my father thought he was Elvis, my mother thought she was the 'blue lady' that Nat King Cole brought red roses for. I was a child of the sixties but my mother and father remained firmly rooted in the early fifties. This was a world which was certain and settled and which bestowed expectations of how to behave and what to expect from others. When I turned into a teenager, glam rock and Bowie mixed dressing up and fluid gender roles. For my parents and grandparents, this was evidence that the end of the world was nigh.

Despite the fact that much of what we were listening to back then had its roots in the black music which inspired so much of rock and roll, my father believed that the 'caterwauling' that was going on was directly linked to becoming a junkie. I don't think he knew what a junkie was but he was sure I was going to be one if I wasn't already. This constant suspicion, that I was going to become a cross-dressing, drug-taking, pregnant teenager, appeared to have no reasoning behind it. It seemed to be a fact that I was at risk of this simply by becoming a teenager.

It must have been terribly disturbing for my parents to have this unknown force full of potential debauchery growing up in their household. It certainly seemed to me that it was my father's view that I required a lot of lecturing to keep me in check as I turned thirteen. But, to me, my father was an old fogey and therefore not worth listening to. I developed a particular habit of disassociating whenever he began one of his sermons. Nowadays I'd be told to take my earphones out but back then I simply disappeared into my imagination where *The Jean Genie* played so loud it drowned out all else.

Later in the seventies, I found my real home with Northern Soul. Tracks from obscure black artists from the US were revered in clubs like The Twisted Wheel or Wigan Casino. My first encounter with Northern Soul was actually in the village where I lived. A local dance hall played host to hundreds of teenagers who came from all around York to dance to it.

Throwing my father into another frenzied round of certainty that I was about to become a drug-addled drop out, my first encounters with Northern Soul led me eventually to Wigan Casino. The first Friday night I made my pilgrimage to that holiest of places in the Northern Soul landscape remains imprinted upon my memory as if stored in my DNA. So much so that I only have to hear the opening bars of tracks like *I Walked Away* by Bobby Paris or *I'm Coming Home in the Morning* by Lou Pride and I'm teleported back there by a huge magnetic force. I can hear it, smell it, feel it. That's not a memory; it's post-ecstatic experience re-emerging from my body. My feet want to move, my heart is jumping, my teenage self, liberated from the eternal boredom of a working-class life, is awake again and living.

Wigan Casino was the mecca for so many young people in seventies York and Leeds and all of the surrounding towns and villages. People also travelled from Scotland and Newcastle, Wales and all of the surrounding towns and villages in Lancashire where the Casino was located. That was my first encounter with a wider world beyond the factory door and the grind of living in an inward-looking northern town. It was an opportunity to experience other accents and to learn about other places through the stories of the journeys people made to get there. All of this sound-tracked by the music of black working-class America. It was music that opened the door to wider possibilities than being tied down and married by twenty.

The first time I returned home from Wigan Casino my father was waiting for me and I knew I was for it. I had used the old trick of saying I was staying out at someone else's house and it had backfired on me when that person had turned up on our doorstep looking for me. I had heard before I got back that I was in trouble when I was standing in line for the bus to take me from the station to the village where I lived. It was mid-morning. The all-nighter at the Casino ended at 8.00 a.m. and we were straight back on the coach to be dropped off at York station to disperse to our various far corners. 'Your dad knows you've been to Wigan', said a voice in the line five or six people down. When I realized the voice was talking to me my blood ran cold. There'd be more than a drug sermon waiting for me, I was certain of that.

I think my dad thought that he had some kind of insight into the drug-addled mind of the teenager because he'd grown up in the era of mods and rockers fighting on Margate Beach. Some four hours after I'd left the heaven of Wigan Casino, I found myself immersed in the particular kind of hell reserved only for teenagers in the seventies who grew up in working-class families. The words 'who do you think you are' echoed and repeated and there were dark mutterings about fallen women and the insanity of drug addiction. Letting it all wash over me I switched off and went back to the night before with all of its adrenaline and oxytocin-fuelled love. There was no need for drugs at Wigan Casino (though plenty took them, I never did) and no alcohol either. The music was as powerful a mind-altering substance as I needed. As I grew older, for one night every month from there on I was transported out of the drudge and grime and into a world I will never forget.

Which leaves not much more to say about York other than it went on to develop quite a vibrant music scene in the eighties while I still lived there and I spent some pretty wild nights in various clubs and pubs. When I return there now, I see that some of these places still exist and some form of music and nightlife is still available. York now, though, is different to the city I lived in. The shops are boutique for a start and cater to the tourists and the middle classes who have made it home. The houses that were grimy and smoky and filled with us working-class kids are refurbished and the poverty which prevailed is largely gone.

When I return as I sometimes do, I walk through the city centre and I see so little of the place where I came of age and came to consciousness. The sugar factory closed years ago and when I look for familiar places and see them changed I find it hard to locate the memories of my younger days.

I can't hear the music from my youth in York these days but, as I was driving through south Yorkshire recently, the smell of sugar beet hit me like a shot of adrenaline. The memory ripples revealed a powerful and rich stash of sights and sounds and feelings from my younger days.

It appears my father was right. I am addicted.

12

Meeting your idols 2: Teenage dreams

Steve Leedale

Somewhere around 1983, music stopped being a simple act of defiance and became something much more powerful. Until then the only music I felt passionately about were the hymns in school assemblies. Far from loving them, they allowed me the opportunity to stand silently whilst the rest of the school sang about all things bright and beautiful. As I entered my teenage years, school did provide me with three other avenues to spark my interest:

- Girls; who all seemed to be into Duran Duran and Spandau Ballet.
- School trips; via an endlessly looped Madness cassette that was played thin at the back of every single excursion: whether it be to the local swimming baths or down to Wembley Stadium to watch a schoolboys' international football match.
- The youth club; this saw a naive but enthusiastic boy exposed for the first time to the most significant subcultures of the day and of that place. Interesting that I only remember the male tribes of dancers. The bigger boys dressed as punks who would strut around the centre of the room thrusting arms in every direction whenever The Sex Pistols or King Kurt were played. The lads who were into Ska and would shuffle in beautiful rhythms whenever *Mirror In the Bathroom* or *Too Much, Too Young* came on.

There was only one real place to go to at that time for a young teen who was deliberately seeking music and trying to forge an identity. I armed myself with blank cassette tapes and kept listening to Radio 1, often way beyond my bedtime. I found John Peel. The music was harsh and challenging but soon enough I was latching onto favourites: Echo and the Bunnymen, The Smiths and Billy Bragg.

C90 after C90 filled up with Peel Sessions, Festive 50s and the occasional 45 rpm disc being played at 33⅓ rpm, or vice versa. Weeks, months and years of listening to Peel did more to form who I am than any other influence in my life. His input guided my musical preferences, which influenced the records I bought and the bands I followed. In turn this affected the clothes I wore, the nights out I went on, the conversations I had, the friends I made and, as a consequence, the life I would lead.

I was clearly not the only person who was experimenting with alternative music and our own micro subculture formed. We weren't the exclusive or intimidating gangs of punks, skinheads or goths who had first impressed upon me the power of music to bring people together but a community of (mostly male) 'indie kids', with our jeans, band t-shirts and gatefold vinyl copies of *Hatful of Hollow*. We had arrived at who we were to be throughout the rest of our schooldays, into university and beyond.

Music television at the time was largely pop based. Mimed hits on kids' programmes, mostly. Cool music needing to be sought out via *The Old Grey Whistle Test* or *The Tube*. As eye opening as these latter programmes were, the most exciting times for me were getting to see bands I loved confounding studio audiences on *Top of the Pops*. 'This Charming Man', 'The Cutter' and 'Blue Monday' were iconic performances that I captured on a now degraded VHS tape. I still have that tape stored somewhere in my loft. Excitingly, John Peel became a semi-regular presenter, too. His deadpan style and dry wit were more of a joy to watch than all too many of the manufactured bands that were dominating the charts. My obsession with watching *Top of the Pops* for Peel, rather than necessarily the bands, led to me sharing the surprise of Michael Aspel stepping through the crowd to present him with the big red book for his *This Is Your Life* appearance. My pleasure at seeing my hero recognized in this way was an unexpected thrill.

Live music next. The fourteen-year-old me could not drive and was not yet streetwise enough to get himself to big cities and into gigs on the university circuit.

The first band I ever saw live was King. Who were also the second band I saw. I would love to be able to say that I'd snuck into Rock City to see The Smiths, or that I'd witnessed Billy Bragg playing at a demo during the Miners' Strike. The reality for me is that the only way I knew to go and see a band was to book onto a coach trip organized by a local travel agent and, as was the nature of any business, the options were steered toward the commercial end of the market. So, as cool as my burgeoning music collection was, it was painted Doc Martens and brightly coloured suits performing *Love and Pride* that was to be my formative live experience. The lights, the crowd and the volume all served to win me over. And they were great.

At eighteen I got a job working in the biggest nightclub in Doncaster. Not a cool nightclub. There weren't any. A smoke-filled, sticky-carpeted nightclub where the floor fillers were Luther Vandross and many an offering from the Stock, Aitken and Waterman sausage factory. Sure, every now and again you'd get to hear MARRS' *Pump Up The Volume* or KLF's *What Time Is Love* but only after you'd endured MC Miker G and DJ Sven's *Holiday Rap* three or four times first.

The main room of the club was cavernous, with industrial walkways framing multi-levelled dance floors. My job was to collect glasses, empty out ashtrays, clear away broken glass and keep the bars stocked with bottles. The music, as well as the punters, left me cold. Night after night the same chart hits and cheesy 'classics' were trotted out in the same mind-numbing order. It became a game to always be one step ahead of the DJ. We would pass each other as we went about our duties and would shout our predictions for the next track with a depressingly high success rate. Glorified wedding discos passed as the acceptable soundtrack to your night out. The people of Doncaster and its surrounding villages didn't seem to care about what it was they were dancing to. Drinking lager, smoking fags and copping off with someone before the 2.00 a.m. curfew seemed to be a reward in itself.

In 1989, a whole year into my nightclub career, I was given an opportunity to play a small role in changing popular culture in our town. I had a mutual friend who knew the Leeds band, CUD. I'd adored them since I'd heard their cover of *You Sexy Thing* as part of a Peel Session. My friend said he'd get them to play a gig in Doncaster if I sorted a venue. I moved from Bar Support to Promoter in one afternoon. The club where I worked offered me the main room for nothing providing I did all of the promotion and sorted everything out myself.

All I needed to do was: book a PA system, get tickets printed, design and display posters and other advertising, sort out a DJ and get a local band in as support to draw in their friends. Simple.

This all seemed relatively easy until it came to booking the support band. There were a few upcoming bands at the time so I, along with my friend and now fellow promoter Kash Farooq, needed to select who would be the biggest draw. 'CUD plus support' turned into 'CUD plus six local bands'. We weren't ruthless enough to axe any of contenders for the support slot. The night itself went off surprisingly well. Each band had adjusted set lists to suit their allocated time slot and were respectful enough to the headline act as to not overrun. CUD themselves delivered a set full of joy and energy. It was our Sex Pistols at Manchester Free Trade Hall.

The main lesson I learned from promoting my first gig was that when it came to DJing, having a cool record collection was more than half of the battle. This was a revelation to me as I was pretty sure that I had the best indie record collection within miles of Doncaster. Given my obsessive reading of the *NME* and *Melody Maker* and a decent disposable income (as my dad was not charging me rent), I was most often the first customer at Track Records (Doncaster's only cool record shop) on a Monday morning when new albums and singles were released. No one would be challenging me anytime soon. So the natural step was for me to take up my rightful position behind the Technics SL1210s. First, this was with self-promoted indie discos, then putting on gigs and eventually being hired by venues around the region to DJ in nightclubs, alongside bands and even hosting events such as Scunthorpe's annual summer-long battle of the bands, *The Rock Open*. I had arrived!

John Peel was still with me at this time, even though I had fewer opportunities to listen to his radio show as it was broadcast due to work commitments. Nowadays I would simply choose to 'listen again', but this option would have seemed like science fiction. Peel was, however, a solid discussion topic. Records he introduced you to. Favourite Peel Sessions. Bands you initially misunderstood but gave a chance to because if Peel liked it then there must be something you were missing. I had innumerable such conversations as I knew that his role in my love of music was being repeated in countless bedrooms.

As the indie music scene grew, mostly through the emergence of Britpop as a mainstream genre, demand for my DJ services similarly grew. Albeit on a much less grand scale. Calls came in from around Yorkshire, Lincolnshire and Humberside with some one-off gigs turning into regular bookings. My favourite regular venue to work around this time was Baths Hall in Scunthorpe. A converted swimming baths, it now had a large main room and a sprung dance floor covering the old pool. Events here were intermittent, but regular enough to keep me coming back. Twice a year I would get a call from the manager to tell me what nights they wanted me for in the upcoming season. A potential highlight of my musical career was getting to host *The Rock Open* for a few years in the early 1990s. This was Scunthorpe's traditional battle of the bands competition whereby twenty or so bands from around the region would be whittled down on a weekly basis having performed their chosen songs to a panel of judges and an audience of their fans, friends and family. Over the course of a summer the winners of each heat would progress to a grand final and my role was to introduce the bands onstage and be a member of the judging panel as well as DJ between bands and for an extended set afterwards. This was my first real experience of hosting an event, my preference usually being to judge the crowd and to play my records with no chatter. As I stepped onto the stage for the first time and strode over to the microphone I remember the nerves kicking in. I started to speak and instantly began to relax as I realized that I couldn't see the crowd anyway, the stage lights were blinding me. It was all going rather well, or so I thought, until thirty seconds into my prepared speech, about the format of the competition and the local paper who were sponsoring the event, I heard a yell from Stig, the sound engineer who was behind the mixing desk, 'Stick it in your gob!'. I'd never been in a position to be heckled before and this was certainly not one for which I had prepared a comeback. 'Stick the microphone in your gob!' The penny dropped. With a step taken towards the microphone and a sarcastic cheer from the crowd, I restarted my spontaneous, off-the-cuff remarks.

With plans to finally go to university, I cut back on gigs (or did they cut back on me?) until my only regular work was at Baths Hall. This was fine as it paid well enough and with *The Rock Open* as a regular event I could expect to largely pay my way through university. With hopes high for a busy set of bookings I took my regular call from the manager. 'Hi Steve, it's Terry, have you got your diary handy?'. I had, of course, as it was now our routine whereby Terry would call my house a day or two in advance and leave a message on the answering machine to let me know when he was going to call with the list of potential bookings so that I could be home and waiting.

'Ok, we're starting with The Hoverchairs (a hometown band with a guaranteed following) and the following week The Dylans (an upcoming Sheffield band who never quite made it). *The Rock Open* will run for seven weeks this year and then in October we have Peel.'

'Sorry, could you repeat those for me; I couldn't get them all down', I stammered.

'Sure', Terry responded. 'Something, something, something, something, something and then in October we've got John Peel. Those all ok?'

[Pause] 'Yes Terry, that's great.'

I'd be lying if I said I didn't cry after putting the telephone down. I'd be lying too if I said I wasn't crying now as I type this account and remember how this boy felt at that moment.

Teenage dreams. So hard to beat.

13

Meeting your idols 3: The soldier in the box

Kate Ramsay

When did my love of music begin? I find it hard to pinpoint an exact time, memory or year. Many moments spring to mind. It began sometime during my time living on the outskirts of York city centre in a village called New Earswick. The village was built in the nineteenth century for the workers of Rowntree's chocolate factory. Neither of my parents worked at the factory. That wasn't a criterion by the 1970s. The only requirement was that you had to keep your garden tended as it was known as 'The Garden Village'. My dad was a printer working two shifts in the local factory and my Mam stayed at home to look after me.

I had an amazing childhood; everything seemed magical and exciting. From a mile down the road, the smell of chocolate from the factory used to drift in the air. I am an only child and lived in that house with my parents from six months old until the summer holidays before I started secondary school when we moved a little further north of York to Haxby.

New Earswick was a wonderful and beautiful place and it seems, now I'm older, to maybe have had something in the water as everyone who grew up there seems to have a love of music and dancing. Maybe because it was home to the weekly 'Bop' at New Earswick Folk Hall. This was a venue that over the years has played host to Pink Floyd and Procal Harum amongst others. I used to attend the kids' Bop in my Toyah make-up or denim jacket with AC/DC and Status Quo patches while I danced to Soft Cell's 'Tainted Love' or paraded the routine to 'Prince Charming' by Adam and the Ants while others followed. At home I listened to everything from The Kinks' 'You Really Got Me' to chart music.

So, what was my earliest memory of music? Was it taping *Top of the Pops* on 10 April 1980 on a cassette with a gold label? This recording was made possible by holding the tape recorder to the television and gave me a soundtrack to play at my seventh birthday party on 15 April. The show I recorded that week had had performances by Siouxsie and the Banshees performing 'Happy House' and 'My Perfect Cousin' by The Undertones.

I have so many musical memories that spring instantly to mind, like the gold flexi disc by The Bay City Rollers (the kind sellotaped to magazines), 'Top of the Tots' singles and my already increasing seven inch collection and watching *The Old Grey Whistle Test* with my Dad.

In the 1980s, I loved getting *Number One* and *Smash Hits* magazines with their posters and lyrics; pretending to be Bananarama (always playing the part of Siobhan). I remember my friend and I talking at the top of the street when The Jam split up. A major part of my musical memory involves Kate Bush. I used to dance to her music dressed up in a floaty dress. I was really affected by the haunting 'Breathing' and 'Man with the Child in his Eyes'. I collected the albums and singles on vinyl and cassette. Sharing the same name was great too. No one seemed to be called Kate back then.

In 1980 I invited Kate Bush to my seventh birthday party by sending her one of those cards where you responded by crossing out that you would or would not be able to come. 'I will be seven! WOW!'

She responded.

Kate Bush indicated that, unfortunately, she would not be able to attend. I also received a letter and a photograph.

On Kate Bush's *Never Forever* album with its beautiful gatefold sleeve there was a song entitled 'Army Dreamers'. The lyric mentions a soldier in a tin box so I sent her a small tin box with a little green plastic toy soldier inside.

The following year I had the opportunity to be in the audience of *Razamatazz* which was a children's music programme hosted at the time by Suzanne Dando (the former Olympic gymnast) and Alistair Perrie. I got the train with my parents to Newcastle to the Tyne Tees studio where *The Tube* was also filmed. Depeche Mode were the first act on so you could say that was my first live band. They performed 'Leave in Silence'. I asked someone who was going to be on next. 'Kate Bush', came the reply.

I sat at the edge of the space where she would be performing with my legs tucked up. And I waited. She came around the edge of the performance space to speak to the children there. Then she came to me.

'My name's Kate, I'm from York,' I said.

And she replied.

'Ah! The Soldier in the tin box?'

She performed 'There Goes a Tenner' with two backing dancers. I sat in my *Fame* t-shirt and purple striped skirt with flat studs and a wobbly tooth. While at secondary school, my friends would come around to my house and watch the VHS footage of me on TV. It was quite a talking point.

The other major player was (and still is) Adam and the Ants. They have been a massive part of my love of music since I was a child. In 1981, my Mam and Dad got me tickets to go and see *The Prince Charming Review* at Leeds Queen's Hall. My first proper gig. I sat on my dad's shoulders and watched the show. I met him years later when I worked for Sony Record Company. He came into the office and gave me a signed *Ant Box* that was due for release.

Towards the end of my time at secondary school, my continued love of soul and Motown was joined by a love of hip-hop. Each week, dressed in my hip-hop clothing from Fever in York with Troop trainers that I picked off a poster and had imported, I went to watch my friends present on a York-based pirate hip-hop and soul music radio station called KLFM. There were times when large metal poles had to be carried to discreet locations to enable broadcasting. I had a Honda Vision moped and could drive around town. A competition would be announced and the number of a local phone box would be given out on air. I would get on my moped to go and take the calls. It made it seem a very professional set-up. My parents used to get weekly dedications while they sat in the garden during the summer of 1989.

After school I got a job at a local radio station. I asked to look around and, while sat waiting in the empty studio, the phone rang and eventually I thought I maybe should pick it up and answer. They gave me a job. I was sixteen years old and started interviewing bands for Chrissie Glazebrook's Saturday show. I interviewed Beats International, Lol Tolhurst, Lonnie Gordon (who asked me if I wanted a job as her child's nanny) and the head of Nike in Oregon about their Air Max trainers (which many people were having stolen from their feet at the time). I also interviewed Soho who'd had a hit with 'Hippy Chick'. I thought the interview might almost end before it began when my first question was why they had copied the opening guitar part from The Smiths' 'How Soon is Now?'.

Chrissie was fantastic and presented a show the likes of which was unusual for local BBC radio. I had my weekly pick of vinyl from the station's record library. In the late 1980s and early 1990s my love moved to indie music and especially The Charlatans. I started going to see them whenever I could. As my friends were all into the same music, it was a fantastic time to go to festivals and gigs. My love of The Charlatans remains and I still go to see them whenever I can. They are up there in my personal top three with Kate Bush and Adam and the Ants.

I decided that I wanted an academic qualification in music and, at twenty-three years old, I went to Durham to study Music Industry Management and Business and Finance. While studying, I spent the holidays in Newcastle working for Kitchenware Records who looked after The Lighthouse Family and Prefab Sprout. At the university, I ran straight to the students' union to put my name down on the events committee and to get a job working behind the union bar.

I completed a placement in London at Polydor Records in my first year and loved it. The capital became my goal. After leaving university, and with the help of a directory called *The White Book*, I printed out seventy-five CVs and took myself down to London. With a weekend tube pass and two nights in a hotel, I hand-delivered CVs all over town. I returned to York and waited. Those who hadn't replied I kept on the list and when I updated my CV from a pager number to my new mobile phone I went down and did the same thing again.

This time I got an interview in the head office at Sony Record Company. This was firstly just to be on their books and in with a chance of interviews for any forthcoming positions. I had an interview in January 1999 on a Wednesday for the role of Sales and Promotions Coordinator in the Alternative Department. I got it and I moved to London that weekend. I moved into a hotel and started work on the Monday. Sony Alternative worked across all the labels looking after the Indie and Alternative artists. I described it as covering everything (except Ricky Martin). I loved it there. I always walked through the front doors on Great Marlborough Street (even when I got off the bus on Oxford Street and it was easier to go in the back door). I was so proud to walk through that door every morning. I lived in Camden Town so, between there and the West End, I could go to several gigs a night if I wanted to. My Sony ID card was all I needed.

While working in London I went on a two-week holiday to San Francisco to see the sights. I would have loved to have seen Haight-Ashbury in the 1960s. I am a fan of Janis Joplin, so seeing San Francisco blew me away. On my return to London I decided I needed to be in America. I returned to York to save. Life can be so strange at times; on New Year's Eve 2002 I had a phone call from a friend of a friend who had heard I had left London. He offered me the chance to live in New Jersey for a few months. He owned a company that did online marketing for some of the biggest American artists of the time. I headed out three weeks later. I returned in time for my thirtieth birthday in 2003.

I stayed in York and had my amazing daughter. It's lovely now that we can go to gigs together. Her first being Leeds Festival. She was a Kaiser Chiefs fan then.

14

Meeting your idols 4: Culture Clash

Peter Cook

It was at the 1970 Isle of Wight festival that I started to take an interest in documentary. I was through taking photographs. It quickly descended into chaos. You had to buy a ticket, but the anarchists moved in and tore down the fences and turned it into a free festival. The tickets were about thirty-six shillings – you can see the price on reproduction posters – but it was a time when there were a lot of free festivals. The Who were there, the Doors, Miles Davis, Hendrix, Joan Baez and Richie Havens, which was a highlight for me. I think Donovan was there, Free, Joni Mitchell, just about everyone other than the Beatles and the Stones.

The trip to the festival for us was organized by Barry, who used to run Hull Truck Theatre. He took a charabanc of people from East Yorkshire. We were a group of lads and sat on the back seat. The bus had to get on the ferry at the Isle of Wight and suddenly we were travelling through these country lanes. We knew we were getting near the site when we saw our first hippy – and this was three years after the Summer of Love. There was this guy standing naked in a field with a headband on and two sets of fingers in the air waving them at us. So someone on the back seat threw his fingers in the air in the opposite direction and said, 'Fuck you an' all mate.'

We got off the bus and I instantly lost my friends; there were half a million people. I found one friend walking down a country lane, which was a good job as he had the tent – I was lucky to find him. We didn't find anyone else from the coach until we met to go home on the Monday at the arranged pick-up spot.

There was another festival that year, the Lincoln Folk Festival, and on the line-up were The Acoustic Byrds. It was the Byrds unplugged but after three songs they said, 'sod this', and plugged their instruments in.

With an interest in documentary, I enrolled at the National Film and Television School. You were at the film school and you essentially did what you wanted to do. I graduated as a documentary director, that was how it was expressed, but you did lots of stuff.

The graduation film I made was about the setting up of a free festival in 1976 and the run-in the hippies had with the establishment – freaks vs straights. There were all sorts of issues about festivals at that time. Lord Melchett, who ended up with Greenpeace, wrote a report for the government about the future of free festivals. There was one at Windsor where there had been some violence and the government were half-promising to provide a site. Melchett wrote his report and the government did nothing. But, there was a band of hippies based in Bristol who said something to Melchett about seeing an empty airfield near Tangmere in Sussex. When the people who lived nearby heard that these hippies might invade the airfield, they panicked and within a few weeks people from Arundel had been moved in to the airfield houses to stop the hippies squatting.

The atmosphere at the National Film and Television School was laissez-faire. Colin Young, who was the director, had come from UCLA. He'd been running the film course there – he taught Coppola. I don't know if there was an emphasis on documentary really, but he got some good names in. *Cinéma vérité* was in vogue and he brought in some of the big figures like Fred Wiseman, to talk or run workshops. There were some excellent cameramen, like Charles Stuart who was one of the big British *vérité* figures working for Roger Graf. You'd also get people like Mike Leigh coming and running workshops. Roger Deakins was there at the same time as me. And Julien Temple.

Roger was a year ahead of me and Julien was a couple of years behind me. He might have been in his first year when the Clash came. It was in the January of 1976 or 1977. Julien got them in and they did some recording at the Anvil sound stage. 'White Riot', the album version, was part of that and the National Film and Television School gets a credit on it.

I'd never heard of them but then we'd never really heard of punk much at all.

I suppose it was me always having a camera on me that got me into the studio. I took some photos of them and then printed them and sent them off to the music press. A couple of them were printed. I thought it was the *NME*, but thinking back I'm sure it was *Melody Maker* who printed one, saying that this was an up and coming group called The Clash. It was all very new.

It must have been 1977 – the big year for punk. Which means I was just hanging around there; after I graduated I stayed around for a few months. That's probably why I had the time to do it. At the time music was very bland – all that disco stuff that was around. Rhythm and blues had changed quite a bit and become mediocre. Motown, I suppose, had gone out of fashion. The people who had influenced us, like the Beatles and the Rolling Stones, were fading. Suddenly along comes this vibrant music so it was all very exciting. It was so different.

The Clash came one week and I printed copies of the photos for each member of the group and handed them out. It was the following week they came back to do some more recording. Mick Jones threatened to smack my head in. He thought I'd made a fortune out of them. I made about fifteen quid and it cost me more than that to make the prints. So I went up to Joe Strummer to apologize if I'd caused any offence. He just said, 'Do what you fucking want with them, mate.'

They recorded more there and you can see it in Julien Temple's film about Joe Strummer. Julien Temple became very close to Joe Strummer; they became very close friends. The stuff you see in the documentary is his very crude, very primitive Sony video camera that Julien used. I was the first person to use video at the film school and so the technology wasn't very advanced and the picture is pretty poor. You can see which ones are filmed at the film school. Joe Strummer had flu, his nose was streaming and he was coughing a lot. He pierced the edge of a mic stand with a sheet containing the words to his songs. He left it just hanging there. I've got that on a photo as well.

15

Meeting your idols 5: Goodbye Tupac

Jerry Ibbotson

For four years, from 1996 to 2000, I was a reporter at Radio One's *Newsbeat*, shouting the news at young people. It was a job I'd wanted to do for years, working for what was then the biggest station in the UK, covering news for an audience I could identify with. Part of the job involved producing and reading news bulletins, particularly overnight. And at that time, *Newsbeat* was on the fourth floor of Broadcasting House in London, while Radio One itself was across the road in Egton House, now long since demolished.

One evening in September 1996, when I'm still fairly new, I arrive at Broadcasting House to start a night shift and learn the news that Tupac Shakur has died. I adopt a grave face and nod solemnly, while wondering to myself just who this Tupac fellow is. I'd not joined *Newsbeat* because I wanted to keep on top of the music world, but because I wanted to be part of a team producing news in a creative way. And there was lots of travel.

Anyway, Mr Tupac has died in a drive-by shooting in Las Vegas and people are in a state of shock. I am told that I might have to go across the road to talk to Tim Westwood on the rap show about what had happened. I think the actual words are, 'Westwood might call you', which sounds mysterious.

At around midnight my boss Ian rings from home to say I would definitely be doing my bit with Westwood and he suggests that whatever they might be doing in the studio, to ignore it. My brain goes in to overdrive and I think to myself that if they're jacking up or something I'll just look away.

So I gather up some print-outs off the Wires – from Reuters and PA and the like – and set off. Now, as you picture me descending in the Broadcasting House lift to the basement, then walking through the tunnel under the road to Egton, you have to realize that I had never seen Tim Westwood. I'd heard him lots but somehow I'd never seen him. I'll be honest, I presumed he was black.

To the door of the on-air studios. I press a buzzer. It opens and Westwood is there.

'I'm Jerry from Newsbeat.'

'I'm Anthony, the producer. We're having tea and Hula Hoops. Do you want some?'

So not Westwood, then? And what's with the tea and Hula Hoops? Where are the Class As?

'You can go straight in', Anthony says.

I slide into the studio and sit down. There's an engineer at the back of the room going through some stuff so I concentrate on reading through my material. I know Westwood will be coming in at any time. He's probably just popped out for a wee.

Then the engineer, a very tall and very, very white man (I mean really white), turns around and gets in the presenter's chair. He slips the headphones on, opens a fader and starts talking.

Oh my God. This is him. He's Westwood. And what is that sound coming out of his mouth? It's like speech but at the same time … isn't.

He goes into the next track, slips his headphones off and shakes my hand over the desk. We need to work out how he's going to introduce me. I suggest …

'We're joined now by Jerry Ibbotson from *Newsbeat* with the latest on the death of Tupac.'

Or something.

That's when Westwood starts trying to write down my surname. I, double-b, O, T, S, O, N.

'What?'

I, double-b, O, T, S, O, N.

He struggles with this, so many times, that I'm not even sure how my name is spelled anymore.

The track finishes and Westwood says something solemn. Then.

'Yo! My man Jerry from *Newsbeat*.'

And I'm on.

Somehow, I manage to make stuff come out of my mouth.

But I can hear how ridiculous I sound – like someone's dad talking to their mates. I'm twenty-seven. I sound like I'm on the Home Service. I can't help myself. He's done this to me.

I'd imagined that Westwood might ask some questions. In this situation – it's called a two-way – that's what people do. They ask the reporter stuff. Westwood doesn't. I can see him looking down at the desk. Inside, I'm pleading for him to ask something. Anything. Just ask me a fucking question so I can pause for breath.

But he doesn't, so I play a parlour game – talking for two minutes about a dead rapper without deviation or hesitation but with lots of repetition.

Eventually I run out of stuff to say. Westwood gives me a polite nod and Anthony thanks me for coming over. He's still eating Hula Hoops.

Back in Broadcasting House, I decide I need a copy of this. In the basement is a huge control room for all the networks. I ring them and ask for a DAT copy of the five minutes I was on air. I go to collect it, passing through two huge security doors into a room that looks like NASA. The engineer – and it really is an engineer this time – hands me the DAT. He smiles.

'Have you heard it?', I ask.

'Oh yes', he says.

16

'What Do I Do Now?': Encountering ourselves in music memoir

Jon Stewart, Louise Wener and
Benjamin Halligan

Jon Stewart and Louise Wener founded what eventually became platinum-selling Britpop band Sleeper while at the University of Manchester. After graduating they moved to London and signed to Indolent Records, part of BMG/RCA, in 1993. Their 'Delicious' EP reached #1 on the UK indie singles chart in 1994. Sleeper's 1995 breakthrough UK Top 20 hit single 'Inbetweener' was followed by the gold-selling album *Smart* and the hit single 'What Do I Do Now?' (see Figure 16.1). 1996 saw platinum-selling album *The It Girl* and three additional hit singles: 'Sale of the Century', 'Nice Guy Eddie' and 'Statuesque'. Sleeper's version of Blondie's 'Atomic' also appeared in Danny Boyle's *Trainspotting* movie that year. 1997's *Pleased to Meet You* entered the UK charts at #7, accompanied by two more UK Top 40 singles, although Sleeper broke up the following year. In 2002 Wener featured prominently in the feature documentary *Live Forever: The Rise and Fall of Britpop* (John Dower). She is also a published novelist, having authored *Goodnight Steve McQueen* (2002), *The Big Blind* (2003), *The Half Life of Stars* (2006) and *Worldwide Adventures in Love* (2008) for Hodder & Stoughton. She has also taught creative writing.

Wener's memoir was published as *Different for Girls: My True-Life Adventures in Pop* in 2010, and *Just for One Day: Adventures in Britpop* in 2011, by Ebury/Random House. The book was one of the first insider accounts of Britpop and is still one the best-received works in this genre. The *New Statesman* described it as a 'riveting memoir of that time', about 'a period full of promise which slowly expired' and a 'clear-eyed examination of the realities of fame' (Rogers 2010). Stewart, as Sleeper's co-founder and guitarist, is also one of the key figures in her story. Now widely published as an academic in his own right, Stewart interviewed Wener and discussed their shared experience of memoir

Figure 16.1 Sleeper receive British Phonographic Industry gold discs awards for certified sales of 100,000 copies of their debut album, *Smart* in 1995 (Jon Stewart far left, next to Louise Wener). Credit: Andy Willsher: http://www.andywillsher.com/.

and memory in January 2018 – shortly after Sleeper's twentieth anniversary sell-out reunion show at London's Shepherd's Bush Empire the previous month (see Figures 16.2 and 16.3). Halligan, who attended that concert, assembled a series of provocations in relation to the memoirs to structure the anticipated conversation, which now form parts of the commentary below.

Different for Girls, with its near-neon cover colours and celebrity endorsement, was presented as aimed at a young adult fiction or even 'chick lit' audience. The title referenced Joe Jackson's 1979 single 'It's Different for Girls'. On the back cover an image of a bespectacled twelve-year-old Wener ('I wasn't the coolest of 12 year olds. If I had been, I wouldn't have grown up to be a pop star' runs the blurb) is contrasted to an attitude-heavy image of Wener in the mid-1990s, as a Britpop 'ladette'. *Just for One Day*, with a black and white cover image of a half-loaded Sleeper tour van, signalled to a different constituency altogether. This audience would have been those whose youth had been coloured by Britpop, and with the book presented as providing an opportunity to revisit that period via the perspective of someone who was at its epicentre. That title recalls the lyrics of David Bowie's '"Heroes"' (1977), suggesting a nascent canonical impulse: the time for a reassessment of cultural artefacts, and critical acclaim.

Figure 16.2 Louise Wener (centre) and Jon Stewart (right) on stage at the London Shepherd's Bush Empire sound check, 2 December 2017. Credit: Thomas Brooker: http://www.tlbrooker.com.

Figure 16.3 Sleeper reunion gig, London Shepherd's Bush Empire, 2 December 2017. Credit: Thomas Brooker: http://www.tlbrooker.com.

The book consists of short chapters. At times, like vignettes, these are structured around individual anecdotes or punchlines and elsewhere assembling a series of snapshots that could be read as indicative of Wener's journey. Part

One covers teenage life in a lower middle-class family in the Essex suburb of Gants Hill – the book opens on a 'typical Sunday teatime in the spring of '79' (Wener 2010: 3). This is followed by an escape to Manchester University, and thereafter an increasingly dispiriting period in London in the early 1990s, with Wener and Stewart trying to gain traction with their band. Part Two begins with the early days of the steep ascent into pop stardom, and the recording of the first album, *Smart* (1995) – opening with '[i]t's not time to move to Hawaii just yet ... ' (2010: 149). The picaresque ups and downs of Sleeper, professional and personal, follow – up to the dissolution of Britpop and, with it, the band itself, in 1997/8. A short epilogue returns the reader to the present, noting repaired relationships, and a phase of domesticity and parenthood – opening with '"Damn, the babysitter's cancelled"' (2010: 309) – and casting the moment of Britpop and Sleeper, and by extension the contents of the memoir, as a story that can now be told. And it is this perspective that then allows for a particular take on the subject matter. For the fame years, the rush and adventure and the sense of a long-held dream coming true is tempered by a consideration of the hubristic and cynical nature of the pop scene of the time with its associates and media hangers-on and the beginnings of damage inflicted on members of the band.

Wener's experience of pop stardom was, in some ways, one of frustration, disappointment and displacement. Our narrator seems to fear that she has spawned an enhanced doppelganger over which she has limited control and against which she feels herself judged and found wanting: '[t]he me in pictures is better looking' (2010: 274). Across the years before this turn of events, a fondness for 1980s pop culture endures and a thankfulness for the presence of key pop icons in her young life, such as Bowie and Kate Bush, and the music associated with the New Romantic movement and after. But, at times, entwined emotions of sadness and anger surface. Perhaps the key passage of Part One, which seems momentarily to allow the fusing of a seventeen-year-old's empathy for her sixth-form contemporaries with her future contempt for the machinations of the music and media industries, is one that anticipates a point of a departure from the 'dull Essex suburb ... whose main attraction is its Wimpy Bar' (2010: 5, 29), and describes a silent, condemnatory 'farewell to all that'. This passage concludes a chapter that, with a title referencing Frankie Goes to Hollywood ('Two Tribes', 1984), charts the absolute division and then breaking points of inter-gang tensions and outbursts. But it is the cool kids (who dance at parties) who seem doomed to turn into their parents and remain in those suburbs. The outsiders (who, isolated, draw up exam revision plans in their bedrooms) will break loose and find that aspirations are available and ambitions are achievable.

> Someone puts on 'Perfect Skin' by Lloyd Cole and the Commotions [1984], and the perfect-skin girls, with cheekbones like geometry, get up to dance. But their sheen is fading too. When the summer's over the Donnas and the Haileys are off to work behind the counter in Gants Hill supermarkets. Or local hairdressing salons. Or forget to take the pill and get pregnant. There are four of us going to university from this sixth form. Despite spending half my time drafting and redrafting revision timetables with a multitude of pens and coloured pencils, my results will all come good. And I'll be one of them. (2010: 104–5)

In this respect, the autobiography also hints at what could have been had it not been different for this girl or no Britpop adventure ensued: another suburban life and pinched or diminished expectations within the orbit of Gants Hill and the Essex/London hinterlands. But at the same time, Wener sees this life as noble and dignified. This is exemplified by her parents' lives and is thrown into painfully sharp focus by the early death of her hard-working father. Here, her sense of displacement and rootlessness seems to parallel the experiences of Richard Hoggart's 'scholarship boy' (1957). This figure, plucked from the crowd by dint of intelligence, suddenly finds himself between social classes. He is neither at home in the mostly privately educated strata in which he now finds himself at university and thereafter in the upper quartiles of white-collar professions. Nor is he at ease in his old haunts, where the habits of his school friends and family grate.

The triumph of *Different for Girls/Just for One Day* lies in its articulations of profound distaste for the media experience and media circus surrounding pop stardom: that 'quixotic equation in which fantasy situations become strangely ordinary' (Wener 2010: 251–2) and that '[f]ame is a fiefdom of wank' (2010: 278), respectively. This pop life contrasts sharply with the ordinary struggles of the life explored in Part One. So the ending of the Britpop era offers the chance for escape, and a new life in which the writer is no longer stalked by her doppelgänger but can, some years later and for these memoirs, grapple with the mythology and rewrite it on her own terms.

Jon Stewart: Who is this memoir addressing? The 1980s and 1990s are history now. What does the book teach us about culture and class from that period?

Louise Wener: As a writer, even when you're writing fiction, you don't particularly think about who you're addressing. It stymies creativity if you think too much about your audience. You can become self-aware or self-conscious in a way that inhibits your writing. You just can't think about it too much.

But, I can say it's *not* really for the kind of people who are obsessed with details about B-sides and that kind of thing. I wanted to write something more inclusive. It's much more of a broad-brush commentary about that time, growing up in the 1980s, for people with a general sense of cultural history rather than a detailed analysis of Britpop.

> When my Mum goes shopping in Ilford the following weekend, 'Inbetweener' is playing on the stereo in Clarks' [shoe shop]. Mum is overcome with pride and tells the shop assistant that it's her daughter singing on the radio. The assistant had seen us on the television. She's so impressed, so offers my Mum a free pack of innersoles.
>
> The innersole moment feels significant and in the light of our debut appearance on *Top of the Pops*, our relationships with our families are subtly changing. My Mum has stopped reminding me that I have useful retail experience from my days working at Mothercare and Jon's Dad is no longer asking him if he's thought about getting a job on a cruise ship. (Wener 2010: 191)

Jon: I could see lots of contrasting themes, what you might call binary opposites: self-doubt and self-confidence, artifice and reality, comedy and sadness, future ambitions and the passage of time, everyday problems and the romance of celebrity, innersoles and glamour. Your cultural reference points are much like that: *popular* and *particular*. Quite precise observations are contrasted with generalized cultural touchpoints that anyone of our age would remember – like *Top of the Pops* on TV or Clarks' shoes and Mothercare in the High Street. Was it constructed that way, or was this just how it came out according to your recollections?

Louise: I think the key to good storytelling is to find commonality. You find things to draw people in, moments that people can identify with. But you can't know what those things are in advance. It's hard to construct them because you don't necessarily know what those things are until after the fact. That section about taping the Top 40 as a child – to me, I felt I was the only person who did that. You imagine it's your own unique experience when every kid in the country was doing it. So, I think, all you can do is write about things you care about. If you're lucky you'll find other people have had those experiences as well, and that will resonate. It's the same if you're writing fiction, or lyrics or whatever. It's finding those moments that resonate.

I didn't overthink it. I didn't go, 'Let's go back and find the things that were culturally relevant at that time.' I suppose I just picked things that mattered to me.

I also grew up with some less general reference points. Marx Brothers' films that my Dad loved. *Paper Moon* [Bogdanovich 1973] was a seminal film in my childhood. It probably wasn't to a lot of people. I said, 'God, this child actor [Tatum O'Neal], she's amazing, and you could be something like that.' I obsessed about that film quite a lot. But it's not the specific film that matters, it's the intention. That's what you try to uncover. It's not the reference points in themselves that count, it's that shared desire or ambition.

Jon: I honestly thought you might have Googled some of the history, to research popular culture in the 1980s.

Louise: I didn't Google anything. It's not contrived in that way. I didn't think about any of that stuff because I think you can't be natural about it if it's not real. You can't make it up. If you did you'd be grafting it on. If you graft those things together, people will read it without really feeling it. If it's not true, I don't think you can expect it to have any forward motion.

I get people saying, 'I'm exactly the same age as you. I recognise everything.' They feel it quite strongly. There's something about allowing other people's input. One of the things I took from teaching writing is that reading is not a passive experience. You don't read fiction, or read a biography even, and do nothing. You have input. You, as a reader, visualize what's going on. You imagine what happens afterwards.

It's a two-way process. It's important to imagine writing as a dialogue, rather than: 'I am just presenting my story to you and you are reading it passively.' It doesn't really work like that. People are inputting their own images at the same time as you're inputting yours. They're creating pictures above and beyond what you're giving them.

> We're on *Top of the Pops* again. We're on *This Morning* with Richard and Judy. We're on kids Saturday morning television and in *Smash Hits*, and we're on *The Big Breakfast* being interviewed by two sarcastic glove puppets called Zig and Zag. We go straight from the Zig and Zag interview to the recording studio. Jon lights a restorative spliff. You can see why he'd want to. Sarcastic glove puppets can have that kind of effect on people. They can give you cause to question everything you thought you knew about yourself.
>
> (2010: 243)

Jon: How's it different when you're actually in that picture?

Louise: I almost had to imagine myself as a character to make that work. It's told as a first-person, but in the first-person present. So, it's told as if it's actually happening. I thought if I put myself back at the beginning of my story, and stepped through it, it would reveal itself to me in a way that maybe even I wasn't expecting. I separated it into the periods that were important to me, and stories that left their mark on me in some way.

Jon: That makes it so immediate, as a reader, because you're also living through it with the writer. You become part of it as the audience. It also allows for moments when you step outside of the narrative and fast-forward, then you step back into it. That creates quite an emotional shift.

Louise: Yes. It's nice that you say that. They were almost like short stories. Vignettes that you don't entirely finish, and you sometimes leave hanging. It just sort of flavours things, so other people can layer their own experience over it. Rather than, like, every 'i' is dotted and every 't' is crossed. It's not like that. It's more like you just give a flavour of things, and that allows people to be pulled into the story.

I think the reason that people warm to those things is because they find truths in them. People are very dismissive of 'chick lit' and young adult fiction – of which some is brilliant, and it's a very hard thing to do well, I think. Those things work because they resonate with an audience who put themselves into the characters.

> Someone else is injured. Diid [Sleeper's bass player] has blood spilling out of his head. He has fallen over into a glass table after too much vodka. I am hoping it wasn't rectally administered. Our number one fan, the girl who lives in her car and comes to every single gig we ever do, is sitting alone by the bar with a giant red cake on her lap. The cake is an exact replica of our album cover. It has disturbing little marzipan effigies of the four of us on top of it. We are too scared to eat it. (2010: 258)

Jon: How did it feel to reveal so many personal things? The fruity touring stories, our inter-relationships within the band. It's quite intimate at times.

Louise: I think I could have been much more personal so it doesn't feel that exposing to me. I didn't want to write that sort of book. I was more interested in the notion of this kid from Gants Hill, who came from an environment that didn't lend itself at all to the things we did, and her journey. I thought that was pretty interesting in itself and also probably something that people could identify with.

Jon: That's another one of those binary opposites. From Gants Hill to the West End [of London]. That chapter where you go to the Wag Club, and it's a disappointment, reminded me of *Saturday Night Fever* [John Badham 1977], where they look over at Manhattan from Brooklyn.

Louise: It *was* a disappointment, it was also like a foreign territory. I didn't have access to it, and when you got there, it was a bit shit. So I was kind of unimpressed. I think I took with me, right through what we did, that sort of refusal to be impressed by the people who thought they were cooler than us. I never bought into that. I think that's part of the narrative of the book as well.

Jon: The other thing I think comes over effectively is that we are trying to break through into that world and come up against all these gatekeeper figures who have to be overcome. We get tiny little glimpses, but then the door slams in our face. Then, finally, we find it, the golden key, and the gate opens ... and what you realize is that everyone on the inside is just as sad and screwed up as everyone on the outside.

Louise: It's weird, because if you are lower middle class and aspirational you sort of get the feeling that you don't belong anywhere or deserve anything. Everyone else is special. 'I can't be the sort of person that could be in a band or write a book. I can't be that sort of person. That's not the people that I know.'

It was so far away, wasn't it? It felt like it was impossible. It would never happen. Then you realize that there isn't any special secret, there is no golden key. There are advantages if you've grown up with arty parents that kind of indulged you. It's helpful, but there's no special secret.

Everyone's on an equal plane, once you get there. That revelation is pleasing ... but also, it's like: 'God, why didn't I do stuff like that earlier? Why didn't I know that, and why don't I necessarily have the confidence that those people have got?'. Theirs seemed, sort of, inbuilt – in a way that mine wasn't.

It's an odd mixture. There was this idea that 'it'll never happen, I'll never get there' ... but another sort of feeling of, 'well, why not?'. There was also that incredible confidence that comes with being young, that means you have the guts, nevertheless, to keep knocking at that door. Someone else has done it – they've done it, why not? I'm as good as that person. You have this powerful mixture of, like, 'it's impossible' and 'well, why not?'

Jon: That's another one of those opposites. The personal drive set against the reality of the clock ticking and time passing. You're able to demonstrate that sense of desperation very well, alongside the humour. Being confident enough to be self-deprecating in your memoir is, I think, one of its great achievements.

Louise: The humour was very important. I couldn't look at it humorously until a certain point, so although I got offers to write a memoir earlier, I waited until I could look back at it fondly. Generally, you don't want to see people air their grievances for three hundred pages, so what's the point of that?

> Spend ten seconds in a room with any of the bands poised on the starting line in the early days of Britpop … They are all of them, every man jack of them, committed to being famous, desperate to get to number one. They would all sell their grannies to get a higher chart position than the other and while they're all skulking around in their leathers and Adidas, archly pretending 'the music's all there is, man', a thousand backroom deals and deceptions are taking place. (2010: 163)

Jon: It would be extremely churlish to read that book and not enjoy the humour. However, as an insider, I can also see certain accounts being settled.

Louise: But what you have to remember is, everyone has that kind of hassle in regular everyday life. There's really nothing special about it. People go to work and they hate their bosses, and life is difficult …

Jon: You've been through an experience that not everybody gets to live through. Did you feel also a responsibility to portray that reality? This book is clearly not a celebrity memoir.

Louise: When you're standing in front of a huge crowd and singing, playing your music and seeing people respond to it, being in a studio seeing a record take shape, they're extraordinary things. You step utterly outside of your regular existence. However, a lot of what was around it was striking in its ordinariness too. That was one of the things that really surprised me. The music industry is very conservative, traditional in lots of ways that I hadn't expected. The desperation to put people in packages and boxes.

Jon: There is one memorable section when you methodically lay things out about the supposedly rebellious anti-establishment popular music world. The race for media attention.

Louise: Yes. I just say in careful order some things that need to be said. It's another of the contradictions: you weren't allowed to admit or say that you wanted to be commercially successful, even though that desperation was everywhere around you. It was literally seeping out of people's pores but you couldn't address it.

Jon: My favourite chapter is the one about being on tour. It's so well constructed; the reality of the pure chaos that occurs when everything is finally happening.

Louise: I wanted to represent that chaos: that feeling like those days are just coming at you. And there's barely time to digest them. And touring, it becomes this strange state, the very ordinary repetitiveness is mixed with these exceptional episodes. Drug taking. Bad behaviour. This sensation that you can behave like children and there's always someone there to clear things up.

> The moments that have stayed with me are, generally, the most colourful. So they might also be interesting for other people to read. The things that are the strongest moments, the craziness – like that guy in Boston, Oedipus, with his pet wolf [Edward Hyson, US radio personality, at that time Vice President of Programming for WBCN]. They all represent something, and they stay in your own filing cabinet as memories.
>
> One afternoon I break my curfew and go to buy a packet of biscuits at my local Spar. A boy is buying the paper with my face on the front. He sees me standing next to him in the queue and he just sort of stares and looks confused.
>   'What are you doing here?' he says finally, when he works up the courage to speak. 'What are you doing, you know … in *the Spar*?' (2010: 194)

Jon: As events outpace your control you have a touching encounter with someone who represents yourself from the past. You run into a girl who idolizes you. She cries when you talk to her and you realize this is you when you were younger.

Louise: I think those are the moments when you become very self-conscious because, suddenly, you realize you've now got something to live up to. You're just going about your day and you cross over into this realm where there are these expectations of you. You represent something to someone else, which isn't at all to do with who you really are.

It has actually to do with them. It's to do with their narrative. It's not to do with yours. You've then got this weird sort of crossover. How do you break down that barrier? You realize, at that point, that other people's reactions to you are about their own stories and not yours.

Jon: It's almost Freudian. You're writing a memoir while being on the couch. You're recognizing other people in yourself.

Louise: I think that's true. Absolutely true. Fiction as well. You look to fiction to illuminate truths for you. Quite often, when you're writing you don't recognize what part of yourself you've put into the characters until after a book is complete. I think of reality television in the same way because people are looking for, 'Oh God, she's doing that, I wouldn't do that in that situation … or maybe I would.' Or, 'I feel her pain.' Or whatever it is. That is all about communication and looking for truth, and illuminating the world in some small way, I think.

Jon: Is there a challenge in writing a memoir in terms of which 'Louise' you're writing about?

Louise: When I'm writing I'm much more interested in whether I've made a nice sentence, or something humorous. … something that's going to communicate with people. I'm not thinking 'who am I writing this as?'. This is my story. All I want is to put it down on paper and make it sing in some way.

After publication people would say to me, 'I was interested you wrote that …' or 'I was surprised that you admitted to that …'. I knew, then, they were viewing it through the prism of 'that girl in the Britpop band' rather than me as a writer now.

The only time that you consciously construct an artifice is when you do it as a form of protection. You're doing certain interviews or in certain situations and you need to protect your real self, your private self, because that's not something you want to reveal. That doesn't belong to the journalist concerned, so you need to build a layer of protection.

Jon: But that's also what anybody would do if they're in, say, a job interview rather than a magazine interview. We all behave differently in private and in public.

Louise: Exactly. We're all picking and choosing how we want to be represented all the time. We all conduct ourselves differently in different situations. So, absolutely, it's just a more acute version of what we all do in everyday life.

Jon: This binary of reality and fantasy, everyday life and fame, it seems to be the crux of the book. Everything turns on the sliding doors moment when we get a major label record contract and the point of view is inverted. For the first half you're postulating what it might be like to be successful. Then we become successful and realize it's essentially just the same old nonsense.

Louise: Yes. I also thought it would solve things. I felt it would resolve insecurities that I had, and help me find confidences that I didn't have. Whereas in fact [laughing], it makes them worse. It amplifies all of that stuff rather than helping with it. I was a really shy kid. I thought, being a pop star would change that … but it doesn't. It makes you more self-conscious and self-aware than you ever wanted to be. I think it's just a more extreme version of most people's journeys. I think if you have this critical interior monologue you look for ways to escape it. Everyone feels that at times. I think mine was a fairly acute version of that.

> How does it feel to be a sex symbol? How does it feel to know boys are masturbating over your photograph? Hmmm. These aren't questions I ask myself all that much. They are questions male music journalists ask me. *All* the time … I don't think they're asking Liam [Gallagher, of Oasis] and Damon [Albarn, of Blur] this kind of question. And I'm pretty sure people are masturbating over their pictures too. (2010: 197)

Jon: You were pretty good at staying level-headed among the chaos and the nonsense and the self-doubt.

Louise: I was quite committed to all of that. That's part of the reason that I didn't lose myself in amongst the drink and the drugs and all that stuff. I felt like I couldn't, like I needed to be at the helm of it and make some rational moves. I felt I was holding on to all these strings at the same time, and if I let go it would all fall apart. Maybe that's because I'm a bit of a control freak [laughs].

Jon: One of the things I've reflected on, in hindsight, is how nasty the music business is. You see people get into serious trouble with drug habits and other issues.

Louise: People die, people have lost their lives.

Jon: Losing money, getting ripped off … I thought you were remarkably good at holding it all together. Very mature. That's why it's not a misery memoir.

Louise: I think I had this sensation of being at war with everyone at that time. Like I had something to prove. I was very conscious of not letting it – whatever 'it' was – get the better of me. That's also why I needed the distance to write about it.

Jon: How does it feel now that you've got some distance from the memoir itself?

Louise: Actually, I really love it. It's like when you've written songs. In time you forget what you've written. Then you get some distance from it, and go back to it, and you can almost read it like someone else's work. That's really nice. It makes you smile, it makes you feel sad. It actually affects you. You are now the observer, one person away from the experience. It's not something that belongs to you. It's something that you've put out there and now you can let it affect you too which is a nice thing.

I think that's what I like about it. It wasn't thought about too much. I wrote those things just as they came out. They came ready-formed. They do represent to me actually how I felt at that moment. It all came together in a very organic way. I had to trust it, and let it be, and not overthink it.

I'm also proud of it because I wasn't sure if I could do it. In a way, I'm prouder of it than I am of the fiction that I've written. I think memoir is harder to write. In fiction, you can inhabit anything you like and go anywhere it takes you. The memoir is truthful; it's not indulgent. It represents who I am and it's got my personality in there.

Jon: Now, of course, we're another generation on. Have you thought about this at all? 'Here, kids, this is your Mom.'

Louise: I'm really glad it's there, because they can read it – rather than going online and reading other people's approximations of us. I think that is part of the joy of writing. I think that's why I turned to writing after the band, because you spend so much time being written about, with people having views on you and sort of creating you. The idea that you could push all that away by saying: 'Here's the reality.' You get control of it, of every part. It belongs to you in a way that is very real, in a way that none of that other stuff does, because – essentially – all that other stuff is other people's narratives, not yours. It's very important to have your own narrative put down in the way that you recognize. To find the important little bits and pieces you want to underline. I read old interviews and I don't see myself in those interviews. I just don't recognize myself. Whereas I read that book, and I recognize myself. That's who I am.

References

Blondie (1980), 'Atomic', 7" single: CHS 2410.
Bowie, D. (1977), 'Heroes', 7" single: PB 1121.
Frankie Goes to Hollywood (1984), 'Two Tribes', 7" single: ZTAS 3.
Hoggart, R. (1957), *The Uses of Literacy: Aspects of Working Class Life*, London: Pelican.
Jackson, J. (1977), 'It's Different for Girls', 7" single: AMS 7493.
Live Forever: The Rise and Fall of Brit Pop (2002), [Film] Dir. J. Dower, UK: BBC.
Lloyd Cole and the Commotions (1984), 'Perfect Skin', 12" single. COLEX1.
Paper Moon (1973), [Film] Dir. P. Bogdanovich, USA: Paramount Pictures.
Rogers, J. (2010), 'Different for Girls: My True-Life Adventures in Pop', *New Statesman*, 9 July. Available online: https://www.newstatesman.com/books/2010/07/wener-pop-different-girls (accessed 1 February 2018).
Saturday Night Fever (1977), [Film] Dir. J. Badham, USA: Paramount Pictures.
Sleeper (1994), 'Inbetweener', CD single: SLEEP 006CD.
Sleeper (1995), *Smart*, CD album: SLEEPCD 007.
Sleeper (1995), 'What Do I Do Now?', CD single: SLEEP 009 CD1.
Sleeper (1996), *The It Girl*, CD album: Indolent Records 74321 36477–2.
Sleeper (1996), 'Nice Guy Eddie', CD single: SLEEP013CD.
Sleeper (1996), 'Sale of the Century', CD single: SLEEP011CD.
Sleeper (1996), 'Statuesque', CD single: SLEEP014CD1.
Sleeper (1997), *Pleased To Meet You*, CD album: SLEEPCV016.
Sleeper (2019) *The Modern Age*, CD album: SLEEP19CD.
Trainspotting (1996), [Film] Dir. D. Boyle, UK: Channel 4 Films / PolyGram Filmed Entertainment / Miramax Films.
Wener, L. (2002), *Goodnight Steve McQueen*, London: Hodder & Stoughton.
Wener, L. (2003), *The Big Blind*, London: Hodder & Stoughton.
Wener, L. (2006), *The Half Life of Stars*, London: Hodder & Stoughton.
Wener, L. (2008), *Worldwide Adventures in Love*, London: Hodder & Stoughton.
Wener, L. (2010), *Different for Girls: My True-Life Adventures in Pop*, London: Ebury.
Wener, L. (2011), *Just for One Day: Adventures in Britpop*, London: Ebury.

17

Exploding the myth

Tom Hingley

The initial drive to compose *Carpet Burns* was to set down a record of the most rewarding, artistically successful and publicly lived year of my life in written form; to recount just how it felt to be part of that iconic nineties ensemble who contributed a great deal to popular culture. To construct an understanding of what happened in those pop days and to arrive at a state of emotional control that was lost in the 'fame years' and the come downs that followed the highs and lows of both the band's initial demise in 1995, and then my expulsion from its reformed iteration in 2011. A motivation to create the memoir was, that by creating a written log of those pop years, I might draw a line under that epoch and allow both me and the band's fans to comprehend what actually happened, seal it in a box and get on with the rest of our lives.

Writing the memoir was also driven by a desire to change the way in which fans viewed Inspiral Carpets and myself within it. True, we had already provided a soundtrack to their lives, but now we owed them so much more in the form of a book of explanation of the phenomenon. You see, no band belongs to its members solely: the fan base is equally entitled to share a sense of ownership over the artist, too. For they were the acolytes, the early adopters of the band ethic, catchphrase and zeitgeist, it was them who got beaten up behind the bike sheds at school for having the psychedelic bowl haircut and derided for their underdog music choice. After all these years I owed them an honest evaluation of what our music and band was about.

Another aim of my book was to show by implication how much the internet has changed pop music and fandom through the creation of a new aesthetic reality. It is a study of the old ways pop music functioned for its exponents before technology gave over to new consciousnesses and methods of consuming the arts. It is a potted history of a small piece of fabric of the past in its dying analogue age. It provides a map and critique of memory for those who 'measured out their lives' in hit singles, *Top of the Pops* and *Chart Show* appearances, *NME* interviews and concerts. It captures a time long before the advent of email, mobile phone video recordings and Facebook came along to complicate and alter the fissure between art and audience or between pop star and fan. It recalls the historical moment before the digital babble consumed our collective attention span and eroded art's ability to be truly oppositional. Back in the analogue days, art could still exist as sub-genre without the post-digital threat of 'going viral' eviscerating and diluting its very uniqueness or the contexts that made new art forms brave new endeavours in the first place. All of that was present in the naivety of the way the band functioned and created its image and fame.

Personal motivations also lay behind the writing process. Completing the work represented an atavistic goal to establish my right to self-expression. It was a chance to develop a fuller sense of my own identity prior to my subsuming it within Inspiral Carpets' creative amalgam. It offered a way to affect a change on the way others observed me. It was an opportunity to cease towing the official line.

I was aware when structuring the memoir that there were several different types of reader whose disparate needs required to be addressed. There were the regular literary readers who might buy the book in order to learn more about the Madchester scene. Their hunger was for a book that was varied, humorous, fast-paced and contained different modes of writing to stop it becoming dull and lumpen prose. I was equally aware of what the non-traditional fan reader's needs were. They required inclusion of modes and structures to make the book readable for them, too. These non-traditional readers might have been bought the book at one of my shows (I'm a really persuasive salesman, I'm afraid) or for a birthday or Christmas present, or might chance upon it simply because they loved the band's aura and past. The needs of the fan-reader audience were taken into account in my construction of the book, indeed the memoir could only be deemed to be a success if I served the needs of all readers. So the structure of the book needed to provide differentiation for traditional and non-traditional readerships. Let's discuss how I managed those separate constituencies.

I served the needs of the fan-reader by including shows, songs and album cycles. Once hooked, I was free to go deeper on the emotional side of being a successful Pop artist by investigating the down side of constantly being locked into writing, recording, touring schedules, bust-ups and business problems; not just the good times and self-aggrandizement. The readership could enjoy the tension of the external superficial attractiveness of being in a successful Indie band in conflict with the internal reality of the over-worked musician caught on a commercial and creative treadmill. I served the needs of the more traditional reader by including details of cities visited (such as the U-Bahn in Berlin), the business of negotiating deals and the politics of being signed to a successful Indie label (how to ensure your promotional video got an airing on the terrestrial television channels, for example).

Self-editing of content led to avoiding the inclusion of content such as personal whingeing or expressing that misfortunes were everybody else's fault. These details would have switched the fan-reader off. The fan-reader who has a lot of latent knowledge of the band would want to know the what-and-why of the songs and records they enjoyed; how they came into existence. The aim was to hold the reader's interest by focusing on well-known aspects of my music career that they already knew but then to take them further down the rabbit hole into the band's hitherto secret musical motivations and influences. In these ways, readers would be encouraged to change the way they viewed the achievements of the band and even re-evaluate their own lived experiences and emotional memories that had been stimulated by the band's music in the first place. And in that process, even change the way they feel about themselves.

I included details that had hitherto been kept secret by Inspiral Carpets, such as who had written particular songs or contributed particular musical accompaniments to compositions. This content was included with the specific intent of holding the interest of the non-traditional fan-reader. As followers, they previously would have based their love of Inspiral Carpets on songs and emotional memory of concerts, videos and t-shirt designs. They would be fascinated by who in the team actually created the initial ideas that went on to form the songs. A less involved reader wouldn't necessarily be as interested in this process of lifting the Inspirals' stone up and seeing what crawled out from underneath.

Utilizing various modes of writing led me to include tour diaries, photos and explorations of song styles and their lyrics in the book. These sat alongside longer descriptive autobiographical passages. It was central to my structuring of the memoir to remember that there was a whole spectrum of readers out there. They were coming to the book with differing entry-level requirements and many separate degrees of skills in consuming written texts; hence the overlaying of different modes. Inclusion of photos, tour diaries and song lyrics kept some of the narrative light and made it easier for the less traditional reader, so they would not feel they were getting bored with long-winded prose. It also made the book more of a 'pop' art form and this reflected the subject matter; a double good, then! This shifting between modes lends *Carpet Burns* a dynamic narrative structure. I managed to switch between modes by working on the book in three distinct sections comprising of several chapters each.

The descriptive passages describing my life were written and these were interspersed with sections about each album's songwriting, recording and release schedule as well as songs' lyrical meanings. Halfway through writing the book I included some tour diary excerpts. I felt that autobiographical sections written from memory contained a more impressionistic nature that were then thrown into rough contrast when presented up against the tour diaries' economic prose. The contrast between these two modes affording the reader a greater circumspection of precisely how I saw my place in the band at the time, and later in retrospect (once it was all over). The sections describing the songs' musical qualities and lyrical meanings contained a more compact style of writing. Explaining the innate messages contained in the lyrics hopefully provided some insight to the casual reader as to the emotional approaches I took as a singer in the band (aggressive attack vocally on songs of frustration, for example; softer tone for songs of regret or love) and what we were attempting to achieve by placing each of them on our four albums.

Balancing the various modes of writing involved composing the autobiographical sections with appropriate (but not too much) detail and, with there being only a relatively small amount of tour diary to go from (three weeks from a thirty-year career), there was no choice but to include all that I had of them. However, unlike the autobiographical sections, I include them exactly as I found them to catch the immediacy of the time. These tour-diary sections are less romantic and less consciously constructed than other sections of the book. Their verisimilitude gives the book an air of immediacy with regards to what it felt like to be in your mid-twenties on an American tour (with news from home such as the outcome of The Stone Roses court case against Silvertone going on in real time). The news from home foregrounds a sense of alienation and distance, it is a reminder of just how far away we were from British shores, but still doing something we loved doing. Rewriting the diaries as retrospective description could have done none of that.

The immediacy of the raw tour diary sections contrasted with those where I investigated the composition, music and lyric of each song or the underlying themes of each of the band's four albums. These more consciously composed modes of writing are where I could allow myself the luxury of being more elegiac and poetic in my approach. Here I could allow my voice as an artistic creator to be more clearly demonstrated. I wrote these passages as carefully as I could because nobody had ever set out any written explanation of what each song was about before. This makes these sections unique texts and in that they hold the power of enhancing the enjoyment of long-time listeners of Inspiral Carpets songs. Once digested, the fan, reader or listener could hear our music in a new context with additional nuances informed by reading these texts.

The movement between these modes of writing was designed to make the book more layered, more diverse and to make the reader feel that the narrative was forever shifting, that their gaze was always being directed at different elements of my life, my art, my muses, my successes and failures. Like the call and response of a blues song, the modes moved away from one subject to another and then back again. It was vital to keep the reader engaged; which is one's primary purpose as an author.

The structure of the book changed quite a lot over the course of the twists and turns of its creation. I began by composing the chapters around distinct periods of my life: early years, first musical experiences, joining the band, initial success rise, four major albums, decline and fall and the disappointment felt in the wake of band's demise in 1995, its reformation in the early noughties and my eventual ejection from it.

The balancing of the various modes and methods of writing, the descriptions of songs, inclusion of tour diaries, was achieved through my own over-production. My wife Kelly carried out the initial edit and then the book's editor Ian Daly created the shorter (much better structured and polished) narrative with supreme artistry and a much fuller word cull. He swapped round the order of chapters and created a far more readable narrative. The relationship with the editor is a complex one because they had to carry out a thorough speed read and research job on my musical and family life before reading any of the prose of my book. They had to calculate what the untold story was that would be interesting to both the avid fan and the previously non-traditional (Inspiral) fan-reader. I left out any content that would have upset or had a detrimental effect on others, although there was one story that was removed between the initial publishing of the hard back and its reissue as paperback because it detailed a death someone distantly connected with the band had caused. One family member was unhappy with my description of my early family life, but that's to be expected as that was their family life, too – they have a right to feel a sense of ownership over it. To answer a theoretical question, 'would I write the book differently now knowing what I know now?'. 'No. I wouldn't.'

As a writer you never really control the ultimate meaning or reading of texts – that is constructed by the reader. You communicate more effectively when dealing with historical events that lead to personal upset, anger or feelings of betrayal through careful use of language. In these kinds of instances, you're better using methods of communication such as implication and hint rather than laying the narrative down with a trowel or hammering the nails down with a claw hammer. You can't write in a way that demands the reader feel one hundred per cent on your side, they have to decide where their feelings lie. Some of that depends on how good a job you've done in convincing them that the narrative is engaging and that you are worthy of supporting. For example, in the case of the recollection of the meeting in which I was sacked from the band, you can't expect the reader to have sympathy for you by trying to tell them how to feel in the narrative; you have to write it dispassionately. This is the quality in speech that the ancient Greeks termed rhetoric. Think of Mark Anthony enraging the Roman crowds to overthrow Brutus by coming to 'bury Caesar rather than praising him'. An attempt to write in an angry or over-emotional way simply produces bad writing and will lose your readership. The art of suggestion, hinting and implication will get you much further than a vain display of anger. Some of this process of leaving out content took place at the time of writing; some of it was achieved by editing some offending pieces out – both by me and by the editor – and by rewrites. All this gave the book a much better and more dynamic narrative drive. If it's a significant part of the book, the reader will work harder to ascertain what you mean in your disengaged, detached unemotional description of the worst moment of your musical career.

I spoke to a student on a creative writing course once and repeated the adage that you should listen to the way that people speak to one another in everyday mundane speech as a spur for writing when you're stuck for ideas or have writer's block. What people say to each other is usually more fantastical in its content or rhythm than anything we could ever dream up. Being alive to all these aspects of language helped me in the process of writing my book. Listening to people has helped me become a writer. Being a journeyman musician affords the nascent writer the ability to hone their storytelling skills. You can simply repeat jokes and anecdotes and refine the punch line until the piece works better. All that can exercise the authorship muscle. Repetition helps in all creative arts, so live performance helps one develop one's linguistic skills. Many interviews I have given on radio, TV and in the press also offer the opportunity of learning how to use brevity, staying on message and relevant. They also help you to get a headline for an interview (useful when trying to come up with chapter headings for a memoir) and how to throw a curve ball at the denouement of a story so it ends on an unexpected twist. My maternal and paternal grandfathers were both men of the cloth and I believe there is a generic way of preparing liturgical sermons in a boomerang structure where the opening premise of a lesson or story or humorous anecdote is returned to unexpectedly or ironically right at the end of the story. I am unconsciously aware of this narrative structure and employ it instinctively in my authorship and lyric-writing alike.

A central approach of my memoir composition is to demystify both the glorifying impulses of rock-and-roll myths and the tendency of musician-cum-authors to self-aggrandize. I set a personal mission in my book to stake a claim for any unique contribution that I made artistically to Inspiral Carpets and to describe the contributions other band members made. I attempted to be brutally honest about the ups and downs of a rock-and-roll band. Dennis Healey once said that all politicians' political lives end in failure; I believe that it's equally true of rock-and-roll careers. I felt that the steady decline of the fortunes of Inspiral Carpets ought to be reported in terms as honest and as un-starry as possible.

This process of demystification served three purposes. Firstly, to strip rock and roll of its glamour and excesses in a punk style; the Inspirals were always down to earth, always shrugged off all concepts of stardom in its most clichéd baggage (our business cards, for example, stated free underlay and fitting!). Secondly, the honest approach could lance the boil. It could challenge the view held by the band that there was any need to suppress the idea that we had fallen from fame's pedestal. It might allow the band's significant achievements to be viewed in a new and historical light. Thirdly, the reduction of the band myth might make it easier for me to get on with the rest of my life. If one aim was to demystify the band, then the other one was to explode and rewire my own image as part of it.

The band originally hailed from Oldham, the mill town seven miles outside Manchester city centre. The Inspiral Carpets original singer Stephen Holt was in the band from its formation in 1983 until he left in 1988. When I passed the audition in 1988, the band had already cemented their core image as a Northern working-class band immured in Garage Rock, Punk and Psychedelia. They had supported indie cohorts such as Spacemen 3 and The Wedding Present and had appeared in John Peel's listener vote-based annual Christmas

Chart, The Festive Fifty. The continuation of Inspiral Carpets under what was to become the 'Classic' or 'Hits' line-up required me to act the part of a working-class northerner from Oldham when, in fact, I was a middle-class southerner from Oxford. So the purpose of the honesty in my memoir was to explain this mismatch between the image I had as being the lead singer in one of the big three Madchester bands (Happy Mondays, The Stone Roses and Inspiral Carpets) and the actuality that I was a journeyman musician squatting some 180 miles north of my home town Oxford. The construction of any successful band's image is produced by a combination of the artists themselves, their record company and their promotional staff, so in many ways the absolute honesty I undertook when writing *Carpet Burns* saw me undo the confection of the band's image that had been constructed in those late eighties days. The constructed authenticity of my 'northern' and 'working-class' roots were disambiguated by the demystifying approach of my memoir. This established a newer authenticity based around my own individual experience within that myth-making machine.

The physical process of writing the book involved a variety of approaches. I began by writing prose on a laptop. My employment at the time of writing afforded me some down time in a busy life that was split between academic positions at a couple of northern Universities and Higher Education Colleges, and live performance – both solo and in a group – with many of the shows requiring stays in hotels, guest houses and waiting around between sound check and performance. On a couple of long journeys up to far-away locations such as Inverness or London on a National Express Coach or train, I committed some anecdotes to self-addressed emails composed on a Blackberry mobile phone. Content-wise I began with a potted family history of both sides of my family going back to grandparents and then focusing on the past and then present generations. I focused chapters around significant experiences that could be roughly divided into: descriptions such as early musical experiences, first band, college band, semi-successful indie band (John Peel play, New Order support) meeting the Inspirals, joining the band, pre-major label tours, negotiating record and publishing deals, recording the band's four major label released albums, US tour diary, then decline and fall of the band, post-band life, reformation and then sacking from the band.

I have an irrational fear of losing electronically produced work, so was always cautious in archiving my writing using multiple processes such as immediately storing it to a memory stick, saving it to the computer's hard disk, cutting and pasting each chapter and sending it as an online message to two of my own email addresses. I had heard of authors who had lost whole books through being careless about archiving their work and teaching had taught me the perils of too many students who had lost their work due to the appliance it had been stored on becoming corrupted by a virus, the hard disk failing or the operating system going into melt down. I had no idea whether anyone would enjoy my book beyond my hubristic desire to create it, but I didn't want to fall at the first post by the digital dog eating my homework.

Once I had completed a chapter I would forward it to my wife Kelly who, in a previous life, had been a script editor for ITV's drama department. Kelly has a surgeon's eye for grammar, sentence construction and clarity. She would print out the draft chapters and annotate them and I would then carry out detailed rewrites. Kelly also removed any content she believed might cause undue upset to family members, other band members or partners. She was unaware of the history of Inspiral Carpets to any greater degree, which meant that she was in a good place to question if a story was relevant or interesting enough to merit inclusion, or whether my prose made any sense at all.

When the first draft was complete I emailed it to Ian Daley at Route Publishing. Ian carried out the extensive and professional editing job. The process of book editing and the relationship that evolves and develops between the author and the editor is very complex. I was so pleased to have found a home for my little book that I was more than happy to entrust an editor with the task of chiselling the first rough draft into a more readable shape. I trusted the editor implicitly in his suggestions; it would be hard to work with any editor where ideas and trust don't flow so freely.

The editor suggested moving some chapters around to make the flow of the narrative better. He removed some 130,000 words that concerned the post-Inspiral Carpets years of 1994–2001 and this made the book more focused, more commercial, and replaced woolliness with a vibrant visceral narrative drive in which the book shifts up a gear every chapter and keeps the reader engaged.

The editor also shifted stories around to maintain a constant sense of tension in the book and so that the narrative isn't constantly shifting backwards and forwards in the history. This sounds like a simple process; I can assure you that it isn't.

I have honed my writing by telling stories both on and off stage, by making strangers into friends at the hundred or so shows I perform each year, using a combination of anecdotage and humour to make them feel at home. I repeat stories endlessly, which aids their improvement and economy and brevity. This in itself is a similar process to song writing or rehearsing a set with a band. I have an innate sense of rhythm of end rhymes and poetry. All these processes helped me along the path of writing. People assume that singing is like talking, but it isn't talking – it's much more like writing than music-making.

18

Remembrance Sunday

Bill Drummond

When I heard the news that David Bowie had died I felt little. Even less when it was Prince. When the news was announced, in June 2009, that Michael Jackson was dead, I think I thought – 'Well of course.'

As for George Harrison, there was a time he was my favourite Beatle and I had worshipped The Beatles. They are still the artists – in any sphere of the arts – who have had more influence on my life and work than any other. But when the news was announced that George Harrison had died of cancer, back in 2001, I just thought, 'that is what happens to people'.

People die of cancer or heart attacks or strokes or any number of other things. Plenty of people in my extended family have died of such things. Many of those members of my extended family had died before their three score years and ten were up. Why should pop stars be any different? And anyway they have had rich and fulfilled lives, so what's the problem?

When I was young, rock stars died at the age of twenty-seven from drugs and fast living. It was part of the career path. When that did happen to someone close to me, and for whom I felt responsible, it was different. It was a motorcycle accident and he had just become a father for the first time and was getting over his breakdown and life was mending and sorting. And then he had a motorbike accident. And he was dead. And the band played on, but never the same.

Not a month goes by without him being in a dream of mine. We talk about this and that. But motorbike accidents happen to young men who drive motorbikes fast through the night. They know that is the risk and part of the attraction. Even young men with new baby daughters.

When I first learned that Pete Burns had died it wasn't, in any big way, different. What Pete Burns had supposedly put his body through over the years, with all the nips and tucks, no wonder it responded with a heart attack. What was he thinking it would do?

But in the next four days something grew in me. Some major sense of loss. No, that is not quite it, I have lost nothing personally. But his death has created some landmark in my own life. Like when Tony Blair first became Prime Minister and Tony Blair was seven days younger than me. From that point on, those running the world would be younger than me. This was a difficult thing to comprehend. Barack Obama was not just seven days younger than me, he was more than seven years younger than me. From now on this was going to be the way things were. But Pete Burns is dead.

The day after the news broke, my very close friend and colleague since 1978, Dave Balfe, sent me an email and I quote: 'Hi Bill – bearing in mind the recent sad news, I thought you might like this old photo that just popped up on Facebook.' I don't do Facebook so had not seen it. Had never seen it.

It was a photograph of Julian Cope, Ian Broudie, Budgie, Pete Burns and myself playing music together. When he first sent me the photo, I had no memory of what or when or why we might have all been playing together on the same stage at the same time. We were never a band. And although one cannot see much more than Budgie's elbow, one knows it is him, as I am sure the others in the photo would concur. Who else would it be?

But over those next few days, memory upon memory came back to me. And as those memories revealed themselves to me, the effect of Pete Burns's death grew in significance.

The trouble is I do not do nostalgia. I have no truck with it. But the further the late 1970s recedes, the more I know I was part of something in Liverpool. That something is a thing that does not happen that often and only in a few cities. And whatever that thing was that happened in Liverpool in the last few years of the 1970s and the very early 1980s, I was very lucky to be part of.

The roots of whatever that thing was can be traced back to whoever is doing the tracing. If the tracing was left to me I would trace it all back to a certain manhole cover, in Mathew Street, at the centre of where it was all happening. Nothing of significance occurred more than 100 yards from that manhole cover. And it can all be traced back to some point, in early 1976, when I first stood on the said manhole cover. But that is my version.

It was a scene, a classic scene, with its rifts and fall-outs and opposing sides and factions within factions. The thing is, at most, there were probably no more than forty of us in this scene. And, of course, none of us knew it was a scene at the time. Scenes are only observed by those outside, who maybe want to be part of it. Those that were part of it could only know of its existence when it was all over.

In 1980, the founding father of the greatest UK rock magazine ever, *ZigZag*, came to Liverpool to make and create one of his *Rock Family Trees*. This was Pete Frame. Pete Frame had been a sort of hero of mine in the late 1960s when I was a schoolboy into rock music. Pete Frame knew his stuff. He knew his shit. Or at least he knew what was shit and what was cool in a late 1960s sort of way. And here he was, in the spring of 1980, coming up to Liverpool and proclaiming we were a scene worth his while documenting in one of his, by then legendary, *Rock Family Trees*.

When it was done and published that August, I could not believe it. And I quote, and the reason why I can quote has nothing to do with my memory or even Google, but because I have the original of what Pete Frame did framed on the wall in front of me: *Liverpool is about to explode again – in the first unforced geographical rock boom since San Francisco mushroomed in 1967*. It never really did explode like San Francisco but …

I want to rewind a couple of years, before Pete Frame arrived and proclaimed. I want to go back to the photo mentioned above. On seeing this photo, a photo I had never seen before, I did know the unseen drummer was Budgie and that we were playing on stage in Eric's and it was sometime in the spring or early summer of 1978. It was the person playing bass that was the giveaway. Budgie, Ian Broudie and myself were then in a band called Big In Japan. If it had been earlier than the spring it would have been our then bassist, Holly Johnson, playing. It was in early spring that we had sacked Holly for turning up late to rehearsals and not seeming to take the whole thing seriously enough. The trouble was we all liked Holly and him and me lived near each other so we would get the bus into town together. But you can't have someone in the band if they are going to turn up late.

So it wasn't Holly and it wasn't either of Holly's replacements – Steve Lindsey or Dave Balfe, it was someone else. It took me a bit of time to realize it was a very young Julian Cope on bass. A Julian Cope before I knew Julian Cope proper. I then realized that it was probably this Julian Cope that had instigated this performance. Julian Cope had already formed a band with Pete Burns called The Mystery Girls, with Pete Wylie on guitar and Phil Hurst on drums.

The greatest achievement of The Mystery Girls was to start a petition for Big In Japan to split up. Or was that The Nova Mob? Anyway, it was a band with Julian in. They proclaimed that if they got 1,000 signatures we would have to split. Of course, they tried to stop us members of Big In Japan also signing the petition.

I look at the photo some more and I think. I vaguely remember how there had been a rift between Julian Cope and the guitarist in The Nova Mob, the guitarist being Pete Wylie.

I remembered having a conversation with Julian Cope, sometime around then, about the chord structure of The Kingsmen's version of 'Louie Louie'. How although it was one of the simplest traditional chord structures used in rock music – A to D to E to D and start again and no shifting until you decided the song has ended. But what made 'Louie Louie' different to all other rock songs that may have used this chord structure was the E in question was not a major chord, not even one with a flattened seventh, it was a minor, maybe even a minor seventh. This is what Julian told me, and I remembered correcting the way I was playing it, from then on, even though the E Minor always sounded strange. Exotic strange. Was that the song we were all playing in the photograph?

Then I remembered something else. I had always wanted to play 'Paint It Black' by the Stones in a live band situation. There is no way we could have played it with Jayne Casey singing it. Jayne being the singer and front person of Big In Japan. Jayne would not have had the voice or temperament, and anyway we only played our own songs.

And then I remembered us playing 'Paint It Black'. And how brilliantly Ian Broudie could play the riff. And the commanding presence Pete Burns had over the vocals. And Budgie's pounding on the drums.

Had Julian Cope's rift with Pete Wylie – and the failure of the petition for Big In Japan to split – caused Julian to have other plans? Julian had become friendly, he had a totally different musical perspective to what we collectively had in Big In Japan. His musical perspective was very refreshing. Our perspective had been filtered through The Beatles, The Monkees, filtered again through our idea of Andy Warhol's Factory. Julian's perspective was all these American bands from the 1960s that I had never heard of like The Seeds, Red Crayola and The 13th Floor Elevators.

However, back to the photograph and what was going on and why. I am now remembering Julian orchestrating this performance. But not in some cynical, string-pulling way, but in a let's-have-some-fun sort of way. But was he trying to move in?

We all knew that Pete Burns would be, could be, should be a brilliant frontman. He had it all – the looks, the attitude, the presence. We had sacked our bass player, Holly. Julian would have known how great Budgie was as we had stolen him from The Nova Mob. Budgie, Ian Broudie and myself were a solid band that could play tight and fast and on time. Whatever you may have read about us, we were the tightest band in all of the North West. Was this Julian making his move? If he was on bass and Pete Burns was out in front, it was bound to happen.

But that is just conjecture. We all loved Jayne, our frontwoman. Pete Burns loved Jayne. Julian Cope loved Jayne. All of Liverpool loved Jayne. And we all still do. She is our collective mother or at least the caring big sister we never had. Or the wayward auntie. She was the one we could all go to. And she still is. She is the leader of the gang.

So in the photograph we are playing 'Paint It Black', in Eric's, sometime in the spring of 1978. Things are happening and things are changing.

A couple of months later we knocked Big In Japan on the head, but before we had played our farewell gig at Eric's. And before the idea of The Zoo, as in Zoo Records, started to evolve and become a reality.

I have just remembered something else …

Pete Burns and I shared a bus ride back towards L8, or maybe Sefton Park way, but out of town, back to our respective living quarters. And we discussed future plans. We discussed the idea of forming a band together, as I am sure others must have discussed with him. This was a serious discussion. Pete was not the Pete of legend. There were no quips and one-liner putdowns. This was the real Pete. Or maybe one of the many real Petes, because we are all many.

But nothing happened, or Zoo happened and a backwater of rock 'n' roll history followed its course.

Pete Frame came to Liverpool and made his *Rock Family Tree* about all of us. Tucked away is the following paragraph that I have just read and maybe have not read for thirty-six years:

> Pete Burns is a strange character – probably the most bizarre fucker on Merseyside: a psychedelic Sitting Bull with rings in his nose, a cosmetic blitzkrieg of eye shadow and rouge, cascades of elaborate ear-rings, several pounds of beads and bones hanging around his neck, and a tonsorial superstructure like a rasta Tony Curtis modified by 5,000 vaults of live wire up his anus.

And just for the sake of historical clarity a 'Tony Curtis' is a haircut.

The years move on and times shift and the centre does not hold. It was March, 1985, I had a very small office in the middle of Soho, just off Wardour Street. I was an A&R consultant for a major record company. Thus I was working for the man.

This was not how it was supposed to be. This is not what I had hoped or even planned – not that I had ever planned anything.

It was just gone ten in the morning and I walked into my office and sitting on the chair, waiting for me, was Pete. But no, not Pete Wylie, or Pete De Freitas, or Pete Frame, or even Pete Burns. Or even Pete from the Libertines, as he had not been invented yet.

This was Pete Townshend.

By the time I had turned seventeen, I had seen every living rock act that history deemed were … anyway, I had seen The Stones, Hendrix, The Doors, Zeppelin, Floyd, Dylan and all the other ones and they had all been disappointing, I had walked away from them all thinking: Is that it? Is that all there is?

If that's all there is, my friends Then let's keep dancing

And that is what I thought the first time I saw The Who, in 1969. But the second time I saw The Who, in the summer of 1970, they were everything that The Who should have been. Not that I was ever bothered about buying records by The Who. But Pete Townshend was, and still is, the only live rock guitarist that had ever delivered for me as a teenage boy. I might have wanted to play like Peter Green, but it was Pete Townshend who made me want to smash the world up. Or at least my bedroom.

And here he was sitting in my office, unannounced and waiting for me. Did he want to smash my upright piano – it would have been a pleasure. The, 'I am not worthy line', in *Wayne's World Two*, must have been based on this very moment. What do you offer a rock god? A cup of tea? A mug of Camp coffee?

But Pete was not bothered by any of that. He didn't want to talk about the best way to smash up a guitar, or how old is the old before which you should die.

He wanted to talk about books.

Pete Townshend kept talking … he told me whatever it was that I was involved with in Liverpool was over.

Pete Townshend was now Faber & Faber's celebrated editor at large. Pete Townshend thought I should write a book about the whole thing I had been part of in Liverpool, in the late 1970s. Pete Townshend knew who I was. He knew about Eric's and he knew about Zoo. Pete Townshend was talking to me. This was the same Pete Townshend who … And … What can you say … ? What has he not seen … ? What offering should I give him? I am definitely not worthy! Over and over again in my head.

But Pete Townshend kept talking, he was not listening to what was going on in my head. He told me whatever it was I was involved with in Liverpool was over. Scenes do not last for that long; that whatever bands came out of that scene had now run their course, had delivered whatever they were going to deliver. And the best thing I could do was take stock: look back, write about it all. Write about it now before I forgot about it all.

And I was the person to do the writing. I should start writing that very day. Walk out of this record company and start writing now. And next week send him everything I had written. And do that every week until I had nothing left to write. And then we would get together and pull apart what I had written and he would help me then try and pull it back together again in a way people would want to read. And he told me it had to be me. No one else could do it.

This was Pete Townshend talking to me. Pete Townshend from The Who. Not the one that nearly married Princess Margaret. Or any other Peter Townshend. The real one. The one from The Who.

I tried to challenge him. I tried to ask why he continued to do music, if not The Who stuff, then his own stuff. If he believed all of what he was telling me, he should have quit making music back in the early 1970s. I held back from saying that nobody listened to his own albums anyway.

He tried to explain. He felt he had a duty to carry on making records for a small group of people in the USA who seem to need what he did. If it was just down to him, he would stop today and just get on with writing books.

Then he shook my hand and told me to send what I had written by this time next week.

And that was that – Pete Townshend was gone. I have never heard from him since, or for that matter seen The Who play live since or bought any of his records. But those forty minutes he spent in my office have had a long and lasting impact on me. Even if I never sent him anything I wrote.

So, after composing myself, I walked out of the building and went to the café on Berwick Street which I used regularly when I wanted to disappear. I got my notebook and pen out my bag and I thought.

Pete Townsend was right. Everyone from my class of 76/77 in Liverpool had done whatever they were going to do. The Teardrops had imploded, *Ocean Rain* by The Bunnymen was obviously going to be their high point. Pete Wylie had done his 'Story Of The Blues'. Holly Johnson and Paul Rutherford had trounced us all with the Frankie hits, but even they were over. Jayne had left the building for a better building, Budgie had joined Banshees and Broudie was a record producer down in London. As for Orchestral Manoeuvres in the Dark …

There was only Pete Burns left and it seemed that I had been wrong when I thought back in '78 he was going to be the one. Pete Burns had tried, but to no avail. Every record he had made had sounded shite and did nothing. I had been wrong.

It was time I stopped wasting mine and everybody else's time trying to be interested in bands that were never going to do anything or go anywhere. I had even signed some of these bands to this major label, knowing full well they were not going to amount to anything.

One of these bands was called Brilliant. They were managed by Dave Balfe. He was the only reason I signed them. In reality they were another turgid London band. Their only point of interest was they were a band with two bass players – I mean, who needs two bass players?

Then, just as I was about to start my book about those Liverpool years – the opening page was going to be my resignation letter to the music business – a record comes on the café radio.

I recognize the voice. And the record is a record, if not of genius then one of marked distinction. It is the voice of Pete Burns and the record is 'You Spin Me Round (Like a Record)'. This is the first time I had heard it.

This is the record that Pete should have always made. It had ditched all pretensions of rock or goth or any sort of guitar shit. And it did not need any of the glorious pomp of the Frankie records. This was just a pure pop dance record, with no shit or poetry or pretensions or … Anyway, this is what pop music should be, could be, can be. And it is the voice of Pete Burns telling us all that.

You spin me right round, baby Right round like a record, baby Right round round round. You spin me right round, baby Right round like a record, baby Right round round round

Over and over and over and over again. And in this café in the middle of Soho, it sounded like the best record in the world at that very point in time.

I never started the book, didn't even get the resignation letter done. And nor did I finish off the cheese omelette, chips and beans I had ordered. I headed straight back to my office so that I could find out more about this record and how Pete Burns had made it.

When I got back to the office, there was a man sitting in the chair Pete Townshend had been sitting in only thirty minutes earlier. He was neither a rock god or anybody that I had ever met before. If he actually introduced himself in any sort of polite way, I am not sure, before launching into a whole tirade of reasons why I should hire him as a producer for any of my second-rate acts that needed to have a hit.

He could do me a deal on using his studio at the same time and it didn't matter if my second-rate bands could hardly play because his lads would play all the music on the records and it would be a hit and the kids would love it and he knew what the kids were dancing to. And if it wasn't a hit here in the UK it would be a hit in France or Norway or somewhere else and they could start tomorrow. And had I got anything to play him?

'What did you say your name was?' I asked when I could get a word in.

'Pete Waterman.'

'And what hit records have you produced already?'

'"You Spin Me Round" by Dead or Alive.'

'What? That record that Pete Burns sings on, that I have just heard in the café?'

'Yes and every other café and every club and on every radio station in the country. That record is an all-time classic and it will be number one next week, or the week after or maybe the week after that. And if it is not number one here it will be number one in France or Norway or … '

The conversation took twists and turns and provocations were leapt over and we were talking about Betty Wright playing the Locarno in Coventry, circa early 1975, where I was in the audience and this Pete Waterman was the DJ. But wherever the conversation went it always came back to this Pete Waterman telling me he knew what the kids wanted to dance to and what records they would ask for and what records they would buy on a Saturday morning. And you could keep your art and your shit and your reviews in rock papers and your supposed … because all of that was crap and had nothing to do with … And had I got any bands that needed a hit? And …

As it happened I had a band that needed a hit and they were shit.

I played this Pete Waterman the first single we had released by Brilliant. He told me to sack the band but keep the singer and he had just the song for her. It would be a cover version of 'It's a Man's Man's Man's World' by James Brown, but done totally different, so it would be like a feminist anthem. How this might work I had no idea, but it surely was a sign of vision if he thought this song could be sung by a woman, a modern woman, an intelligent woman. But anyway …

I told him I could not sack the band. And after talking with Dave Balfe on the phone a compromise was arrived at. We keep the singer but also the bass player, as he had formed the band and had vision, and the guitarist because 'he was good at artwork and could play like Jimmy Page'.

Two weeks later 'You Spin Me Round' was at number one, not only in the UK but in loads of other countries if not France and Norway.

And two weeks after that Brilliant were down in this Pete Waterman's studio in South London. And I didn't resign from the music business or whatever, and I didn't start that book that Pete Townshend told me to.

The way Pete Waterman and his boys, Mike and Matt, worked was a total revelation to us – nothing to them was sacred. Everything could be scrapped or changed. Nothing could stop them.

That said, 'It's a Man's Man's Man's World', which this Pete Waterman and his boys made with Brilliant, never made the Top Forty in France or Norway, let alone the UK. Nor did the subsequent album that they recorded with him. It was all shit.

But something else did, very much, happen. The bass player out of Brilliant was called Youth, he started to learn how to really produce records and has been producing records ever since, from The Verve to Kate Bush.

Dave Balfe learned what a hit smelled like, and that sense of smell which he developed was a major part in his success with Blur. As for the guitarist in Brilliant, who could draw and wanted to play like Jimmy Page, that was Jimmy Cauty. It was where he and I got to know each other.

What Jimmy and I both learned in those few months, in Pete Waterman's studio, we were then able to use and abuse in our subsequent quest as The KLF and all the other names we chose to use.

You might hate the subsequent records Pete Waterman made with the likes of Kylie and Jason and the rest. But if Pete Burns had not made 'You Spin Me Round' with Pete Waterman, my journey would have gone in a totally different direction.

And I did resign from it all and left music behind, so as to get on with writing just as Pete Townshend told me to. And the world turned and the winter solstice passed and the sun rose and it was January 1987 and the question had to be asked:

'What The Fuck Is Going On?'

On Thursday – as in the Thursday after Pete Burns died and not some Thursday back in the mid-1980s – I was contacted via text by a friend of mine. An old friend. A very good friend. A friend who I had known from that time in London. A friend who had been very much part of the early 1980s London scene of Boy George and all that Blitz crowd thing. She wanted to know if I knew, and how I felt, about the passing of Pete Burns. And I told her how it affected me more, far more than I was expecting.

She was surprised: surely he was just a one-hit wonder, with barbed tongue and too much attitude? There is no doubt Pete Burns was basically a one-hit wonder and his wit was acerbic. But my mind was focused. That trashy one hit can leave more legacy of standing and lasting artistic merit than a whole lifelong career of well-received long-playing albums.

I had, and still have, no interest in what Pete Burns became for viewers of reality TV or the readers of tabloid papers.

Pete Burns may have been the last out of our class of Aunt Twackies and O'Halligan's Parlour and the Liverpool School and Probe and Eric's and that manhole cover I keep going on about; the last of that class to make a record that clawed its way into the Top Ten and then the number one spot and into …

Nevertheless, if it was not for hearing that record in that café, in Berwick Street, between being confronted by Pete Townshend and Pete Waterman on a March morning in 1985, I may have never thought it worth trying again to use pop music as a medium to make art, great or otherwise. And 'You Spin Me Round (Like A Record)', by Dead or Alive, is great art. As great a work of art as anything else produced in the twentieth century. And if you can't see, hear or understand that, then there is something sorely missing in your imagination.

Now roll over Chuck Berry and tell E. H. Gombrich the news.

Before reading through everything that I have written above and trying to make sense of it, I will look at the photo again and see what else I might be able to remember. Nothing much. I don't even know who took the photo. Most probably Hilary Steele, she was always taking photos. And I liked the photos she took. I like this photo. But I do know while that photo was being taken, while we were all on that stage in Eric's blasting out our version of 'Paint It Black', or whatever it was, some other things were going on in Liverpool.

Somewhere there would have been a brooding Pete Wylie, planning his next Wah! move to outmanoeuvre Copey.

There would have been Mac backcombing his hair in the mirror, knowing he had the greatest voice in all of Merseyside if not the universe.

There would have been Holly, with his voice and his songs that none of us had ever heard, knowing that he knew what was needed and how it should sound and where it should go.

And Jayne will have been standing a few feet away goading us all on.

The world moves fast and within a very short time we would all be over and done with. Part of a fading history, not even of an interest to the likes of Mojo. Not even up there with the Blitz crowd of new romantics, or the synth pop wave, or the shoe gazers, or those that signed to Creation, or the Madchester gang, or the ravers, or Britpop bands or the end-of-pier indie boys and girls hoping for one last hurrah, when guitars and their jangle no longer meant anything to anybody.

I had not spoken to Pete Burns since sometime in those very early 1980s. We had little in common. But we were in the same trench when our officer blew the whistle and it was time to go over the top and meet whatever the enemy had for us.

Pete Burns may have been the last over the top, but he was the first to fall.

Rest in peace, Pete, and on this Remembrance Sunday we that are left to grow even older will remember you.

This chapter was initially published in Liverpool Confidential. https://confidentials.com/liverpool/remembrance-sunday-by-bill-drummond.
It is reprinted here with the permission of the author.

19

Confessions of metal and folk: Remembering and contextualizing the creative process

Kimi Kärki

I know that I've been here before
And I swear, sometimes you were with me
In different times we witnessed places
Returning there I'll always find you

(Lord Vicar 2015)

I am an academic with a serious professional relationship to music, both as a researcher and a musician. I wrote my Cultural History PhD (Kärki 2014) on stage designing in arena and stadium environments, trying to capture a cultural history of technological and theatrical change in high-end music performance from 1965 to 2013. In this research, I was partially relying on first-hand performance experience on both small and big stages, and the related music technology. But the links between my academic and artistic careers are deeper than that. I have knowingly mixed my studies and creative process in order to find new angles to both. I started this chapter with a lyric fragment from a song I wrote back in 2015. 'Accidents' is a heavy metal song, but the song narrative is removed from the most usual clichés – but also a great narrative tradition – of the genre, such as battles, graveyards, evil, death and destruction. Instead, it is introspection on how people meet and fall in love and how that feels both accidental and yet sometimes premeditated. I wanted to touch the old mythical idea of rebirth found from many religions and cultures. As part of my MA I also studied Comparative Religion, and found a wealth of potential song topics. The song, among other issues such as cruelty in relationships, touched the idea that the places that feel intuitively meaningful for us would be manifestations of love from 'past lives'. In the microcosmos of a song anything is possible and this is how I imagined that kind of 'meaningful' place be part of a chain of love and memories that transcend generations and individual memory. Even if there was no such thing as reincarnation – very likely there is no such thing, I remain agnostic – places can still be containers of 'Cultural Memory' as defined by Jan Assmann (2008: 109). Perhaps also recorded music can be such a container.

As a form of experimental autoethnography, I will analyse my own creative process through two case studies of two different music styles. I have played guitar since the early 1990s, been in bands since the mid-1990s and released my first full-length album in 2002. Since then there have been more than thirty releases within a variety of genres, including doom metal, progressive rock, folk, psychedelic pop and electronic ambient. My bands include heavy metal band Reverend Bizarre (1995–2007, Spinefarm Records/Universal Music), progressive rock band Orne (1997–, Black Widow Records), heavy metal band Lord Vicar (2007–, The Church Within Records), electronic ambient band E-Musikgruppe Lux Ohr (2008–, Svart Records) and psychedelic pop band Uhrijuhla (established 2010, I have been their guitar player since 2013, Svart Records). I have also released two acoustic folk albums under my own name (2010–, Svart Records). Having toured in most European countries and the USA for fifteen years, I also have a lot of experience on international live playing. You can find the full discography of my bands at the end of this chapter.

Intimacy, storytelling, tradition

Not only has my music career influenced my research, but my music writing has also been influenced by my research career and the methods of critical inquiry I have learned. This hermeneutic and heuristic circle is a starting point to look at and listen to my own songwriting history; the memories, influences and their impact on creativity. It is actually a really demanding task – as I found while writing this chapter – to go beyond the 'grand narratives' that join my own memories together and try to grasp the individual moments of creativity and realizations about the emergence of something potentially good or interesting in individual instances. My main interest is in the fluctuation between the private/intimate, and the public/shared.

My music has always been filled with intertextual tributes to my influences and my lyrical themes come from a multitude of sources including products of popular culture, books on history and religions, but also the events that shaped my life. I also use my dreams as creative fuel. It is the logic of dreams that mixes the different contexts in surprising and surreal ways. This web of meanings is always elusive as there is unpredictable associative bridging between different contexts and how I relate and remember them during the songwriting process. The relation of performance and memory can be a fruitful meeting point of cultural historical inquiry, as Peter Burge (2010: 105) claims. Artistic re-enactment and interpretation of the past is certainly something that I am interested in. This works as a link between tradition and creativity. My musical narratives move from the personal and intimate to widely shared cultural events, symbols and monuments.

To elaborate this idea further, the two things that are usually intertwined in my songwriting are storytelling and confessional intimacy. Songwriters can wear many masks in the act of distancing themselves from the songs' narratives. But at the same time many songwriters also use songs for introspection. There is a long history for the idea of 'confessionality' in autobiography, from the religious and philosophical thinking of Saint Augustine in his *The Confessions* (written between years 395 and 400, see Saint Augustine 1997) to Jean-Jacques Rousseau's autobiographical work of the same name (1782, see Rousseau 2001). But when it comes to music and confessional expression, an especially important category of musicians is the singer-songwriter. Sung storytelling, of course, goes back to oral transmission of history, and for example the bardic tradition, but, in its current form, it is a North-American tradition:

> Singer-songwriters have been seen critically and commercially as a 'movement' within popular music, and the term has been privileged as a distinct category contained within an Anglo-American rock perspective. The music of singer-songwriters has tended to adhere to folk, rock and North-American pop styles, and to include personal or observational concerns in its lyrics. The term can be viewed as aesthetically loaded, as it connotes particular attributes of a performer – such as emotional honesty, intelligence, authenticity and artistic autonomy. The singer-songwriter has also come to be associated with lyrical introspection, confessional songwriting, gentle musical arrangements and an understated performance style. (Strachan and Leonard 2003: 198)

The big question, then, is how much honesty is there in confessional songwriting? I pour a lot of my insecurities, fears, expectations, sometimes also matters of intimacy, into my lyrics, but to speak directly about that process is very difficult. It is an attempt to get at the felt essence behind the masks of social identities. Analysing it directly could also potentially hurt those around you if you have based some of your narratives on possibly traumatic real life events and personae. But that does not mean there would not be an actual felt honesty in the music. Or, as Joni Mitchell answered to Cameron Crowe in her 1979 interview for *Rolling Stone*, honesty can also be affective in the vocal delivery.

> The *Blue* album, there's hardly a dishonest note in the vocals. At that period in my life, I had no personal defenses. I felt like a cellophane wrapper on a pack of cigarettes. I felt like I had absolutely no secrets from the world and I couldn't pretend in my life to be strong. Or to be happy. But the advantage of it in the music was that there were no defenses there either. (Crowe 1979: n.p.)

The amount of vulnerability and openness varies, but seems particularly to be a question and measure of artistic integrity and this depends on the psychological situation in each phase of an artist's life. Some performers seek turmoil in their private life, and then use that as a fuel for creativity. Others try to escape their inner demons and use music as a form of exorcism, release or therapy. Music journalists and artists themselves have also heavily mythologized this side of creativity. Artistic suffering can also be a mask, a role that is ritually reserved for the 'exceptional', charismatic or half-crazy people sometimes in the music industry.

As a researcher/practitioner I am in a dialogical position between musical traditions and the unknown future; there are circulating themes, narratives and intertextual repetitions that anchor me to a tradition but with the touch of my very own 'persona', something new emerges. However, the research side of my work brings more awareness of the cultural history and socio-political conditions of music making. Every new artist nowadays stands on the shoulders of giants and acknowledges this as a necessity. Tradition helps us to stay orientated; the twist of newness keeps us safe from 'yawning boredom' (Koselleck 2010: 51–2; see also Koselleck 1985: passim). How can this process be honestly analysed as part of the musical traditions that creative work is part of? Is this simply, as some academic autobiographical work is accused of, a case of navel gazing?

Methodological tools

Before I go on to explore my own creative processes through the two case studies it is necessary to outline some key methodological tools. The 'research-as-creation' model that Sophie Stévance and Serge Lacasse (2018) have developed in the context of music research/practice is useful for theorizing the relationship between my academic work and creative practice. Usually it involves a practitioner or a group undertaking a commercial or artistic enterprise in collaboration with researchers, in a 'practicetheoretical' setting (Chapman and Sawchuck 2012: 5; Loveless 2015: 41). This expands from an autoethnographic model so that the two sets of motivations and methods (artistic and theoretical) are embodied in at least two people and the emerging group motivations and methodologies are a negotiated compromise. Most of the band activity works like that anyway, but the conscious element of involving the research makes this really interesting. In my own creative practice this connection has only become fully realized since 2015, when I started lecturing and giving conference presentations – sometimes also involving live music – on my own compositions, instruments and playing style. But the connection between what I have studied and how I have written music has been strong ever since I started playing guitar back in early 1990s, especially after I entered the University of Turku in 1997 to study Cultural History.

The idea of 'playing' with history has become an integral part of what I do creatively. But I think the creative mind should also be critical in order to engage with exactly how the past is being played with. In this sense I follow historian Raphael Samuel (1994: 429–30; see also Kärki 2014: 35) in his claims that past has become the plaything of the present, a postmodern metafiction that is used as a resource for popular culture, 'Disneyfied' theme parks and all kinds of phantasmagoric entertainment. Creative practice rooted in critical self-awareness can mine the past in an extremely anachronistic and humorously playful way to create new meanings.

I also have to be aware of the social implications, though; as well as the difference between intentions and interpretations. Once artistic work becomes social, it escapes from the 'author' and becomes a process of endless interpretations and cultural play. This can be compared to the process of looking into a mirror. Each reflection is different, depending on who is looking and from what position. (On the notion of play, in the context of interpretation, see Gadamer 1999: 101–2, 139–40; Kärki 2014: 51–3.)

If we take this social expansion further, we should think about 'memory' as a social container. This is the other side of the coin, the social matrix that can be seen as a deep structure of each culture. Jan Assmann (2008: 109–10, 116–18) differentiates between 'communicative memory' and 'cultural memory'. The first one of these is autobiographical and social in its nature, attached to the living, embodied memory and the recent past. Cultural memory, in contrast, is monumental, structural, hierarchical, formulated, mythical and ceremonial. What are popular music records in this sense? Aleida Assmann (2011: 137) has noted that human memory co-evolves with the technical progress of media history. Thus, the physical records, with their packaging and liner notes included, are indeed carriers of shared cultural heritage, containers of ideas, memories and creativity. As an example, think of Pink Floyd's *The Wall* (1979). It contains a conceptual narrative inspired by the personal childhood trauma of Roger Waters losing his father in WWII mixed with powerful ideas regarding the problems of communication in rock entertainment, totalitarian aesthetics and cultural critique. The narrative was then re-enacted and re-packaged in live performances (1980–1981), a film by Alan Parker (1982) and so on (Kärki 2015: 60–1).

Communicative memory can be related to both live performances of music and recordings, but some records and notable performances just might transcend to the realm of cultural memory. Mainly this is due to the reception, reputation and successful narrativization of popular culture products. Elvis, The Beatles, Led Zeppelin and the like are quite possibly canonized to such an extent that they have become general symbols of the 1960s and 1970s. Festivals like Woodstock (1969), and museums like The Beatles Story (Liverpool), Graceland (Memphis) and The Rock and Roll Hall of Fame (Cleveland) solidify this kind of Classic Rock 'totem' building. Bob Dylan won the Nobel Prize for Literature in 2016, bringing popular music lyric writing to the realm of institutionalized 'high art'. Most popular music records are, however, bound to have their biggest impact within a year of the release and some are released to small underground scenes only, sometimes reaching long-term appreciation within them. I mostly operate in this field and happily see my own artistic work within the framework of communicative memory.

Aleida Assmann (2010: 35, 37, 41–4; see also Burge 2010: 106) expands this framework with the notion of collective memory that differentiates from individual memory because of the variety of 'social frames'. It offers more variations of Jan Assmann's communicative memory, including the monumental cultural memory. The social frames include ideological, political and cultural elements, and, even if they offer long-term memory systems, are not permanently fixed. According to Aleida Assmann (2010: 44), it is this challenged, contested nature of our collective memory that keeps it alive.

Through the two case studies that follow, I aim to show how the critical and creative influences interact in my musical practice.

Doom metal and three explorations of totalitarian willpower

Just to illustrate the actual processes of creative work, I will now try to remember what I had in mind when writing some of my more accessible works. As I mentioned, I have had trouble writing on my more intimate work as a complete revelation of the personal content hidden in metaphors feels like taking away the magic of those songs.

As I am a cultural historian, it should be no surprise that I often use the past as a creative fuel. And epic historical storytelling resonates well with the ideas conveyed by the conceptual varieties of cultural memory. A song can become a 'monument' in itself, something that brings the idea of the past close and awakens an interest in the listener. In addition to past as a fuel, I also tend to focus on cultural extremes, mostly the cruel, evil and violent aspects of our culture. This creates tension to the way I write, makes it possible to play with darker aspects of our culture and also my own personality.

When I was writing some of the songs for the second Reverend Bizarre album *Crush the Insects* in early 2004, I came up with an idea of writing about English Puritanism and especially the figure of Oliver Cromwell (1599–1658). He managed to turn England into a republic for a while and lead it as a 'Lord Protector' after getting Charles I beheaded in 1649. I immediately named the song 'Cromwell'. The chain of ideas started from the English doom metal/new wave of British heavy metal band Witchfinder General, who took their name from the film of same name, starring Vincent Price (*Witchfinder General*, Michael Reeves 1968). I wanted to touch the era and the aesthetic of the film, but also make a sonic portrait of this man who had the will to change a whole regime, one of the leaders of the 'Ironsides' of the New Model Army in the English Civil War. Indeed, the past became my anachronistic plaything.

I often have a few songs in various states of completion and, when I come up with a good riff or a chord sequence, I intuitively know which song it should go in; even the place within the song structure (intro, main riff, something under vocals, a bridge, b-part, solo, outro and so on). With 'Cromwell', the main riff was a fast one with a 'galloping' feel, and it fell into place with a middle part that followed very naturally. I felt it worked well with the idea of the Ironsides and Oliver Cromwell arriving in London. I also had a b-part that had a long evolving sequence. US doom metal band Pentagram and their song 'Burning Saviour' heavily influenced this idea. With Reverend Bizarre it was never a secret that we were, in our way, doing a tribute to the 'old school' doom metal bands. For this part I had a simple riff and then milked it by changing the key upwards, thus building the intensity until it climaxed back to the main riff. The lyric was directly about Cromwell, but I added a graveyard on a hill and the idea that everyone who does not kneel will be buried there, and a consciously anachronistic reference to British occultist Aleister Crowley (1875–1947): 'Love will be my law, love under will. But first there is the law of Crowell'. This simple song is still perhaps the best known of my compositions. It has been covered by several bands around the world such as Conviction (France), Psygothic (Finland) and Witching Altar (Brazil). There is even an 8-bit version done by Miles_Metal, and a few solo players have posted videos of them playing 'Cromwell' with bass or guitar to YouTube.

This song was also a start of a 'Tyrant Trilogy', as I call it, where I wanted to study powerful leaders. The second song, called 'Caesar Forever', would appear on the third Reverend Bizarre album *So Long Suckers!* and the third one, 'The Spartan', on the first Lord Vicar album *Fear No Pain*, even if it had indeed originally been written for Reverend Bizarre.

These three songs indeed form an oppressive triangle in my mind and each song travelled further away in time. If 'Cromwell' touched the Civil War period, 'Caesar Forever' studied Imperial Rome around the time of emperor Nero (Nero Claudius Caesar Augustus Germanicus, AD 37–68), and 'The Spartan' dealt with the battle of Thermopylae and Spartan king Leonidas I (*c.*540–480 BC). Obviously the idea of the trilogy came to me around the time I was composing 'Caesar Forever' in late 2005. I then had 'The Spartan' composed before the last Reverend Bizarre album *So Long Suckers!* came out. When the band unfolded, the song came out on the first Lord Vicar album, thus destroying the idea of having a trilogy of songs featured in successive albums of Reverend Bizarre.

'Caesar Forever' was primarily about the clash of Christianity and Roman belief systems. The idea was to look at Christian martyrdom from the Roman perspective: 'They believe in a virgin mother, that's why they must be crucified'. I obviously had to throw in another anachronism, which comes in the last chorus: 'Christs may come and Christs may go, but Caesar is Forever'. This comes from the Social Darwinist pamphlet *Might is Right* or *The Survival of the Fittest* (1890) by 'Ragnar Redbeard'. I wanted to emphasize the continuity of anti-Christian thinking and proto-fascism that links the racists and even the current populists and neo-nazis to a manufactured 'ideal' of Roman empire: 'Come my son, and I will show: Tonight we hunt together', followed by cheesy 'anthemic' fanfare, played by our drummer 'Earl of Void', with a Casio I had bought with two pounds from a flea market at Liverpool in 2006. Anyone who knows me might understand the subtle layers of satire here, but obviously there could not be a disclaimer about that and that's a risk I felt I needed to take. The song can just as well be interpreted as something that longs for the glory of hunting and killing Christians.

Going back even further, 'The Spartan' refers to the battle of Thermopylae (480 BC) during the Greco-Persian wars where King Leonidas and his famous 300 Spartans – also 700 Thespians, and 400 Thebans, perhaps some others as well in the end – were defending Greek city states at this narrow pass from the attack by the Persians led by king Xerxes I (519–465 BC). This time I wanted to examine the idea of martyrdom as experienced by a tyrant, thus turning the table from 'Caesar Forever'. Of the three songs, this might be the one that was less a study of evil or power as corruption and more a study of admirable guts and willpower in a truly hopeless situation. Needless to say, going past the area of Thermopylae on a train from Athens to Thessaloniki in 2005 and later seeing the excavated arrowheads from the battle itself at the Athens Archaeological Museum made a lasting impression on me.

Confessional acoustic folk

Perhaps the biggest challenge as a songwriter and performer I could give to myself was about two great 'fears': trying to write honestly about my innermost thoughts and confronting the audience alone with only my acoustic guitar as instrumentation. With no wall of distortion or a band to hide behind, every sound you make becomes both meaningful and potentially terrifying. Confessionality in storytelling has been an interest of mine for a long time, actually since I started reading books at the age of seven. I felt the magic of the stories, and 'lived' the roles. Obviously, this is hindsight.

Around 2010 was also the beginning of the period when my lyrics started moving from epic grand narratives towards something more personal. But the intimate and personal can actually lead back to the universal and culturally shared. And universal themes hide direct personal references. A lot of the current lyrics reflect my own inner world. They are a sort of purification or banishment of the negative aspects of my personality: frustration, hate, sadness and fear. That ritualistic quality extends also to reflecting my dreams. Other than that, religion, war, nature, history and the seemingly bleak future of this planet – and life on it – offer endless inspiration. The nocturnal side of our culture has always been interesting to me.

My first solo album *The Bone of My Bones* (Svart Records, 2013) begins with the song 'I Am Aries'. I wanted to start with a song that would reflect both myself – Aries being my astrological sign – and something more universal. I had been having dreams about the boats that crossed the Mediterranean from Africa to Europe, some of which never made it through to either Lampedusa or any other relatively safe harbour. I was thinking about the National Socialist idea of *Festung Europa*, the fortress Europe, population overgrowth and the reduction of clean water and other means of survival in a lot of the developing world. I wanted to write a song about the incredibly lucky position of having been born within the safe haven of Finland, still able to travel freely to almost anywhere and looking at the global situation with both ecological and moral considerations. We live behind walls, mostly ignorant, protected by coastguards, detention centres, migration bureaucracy, radars, weapon systems and privileged citizenship legislation. Those born in poor areas of the Earth are sometimes in a situation where moving is the only means to survival. But they don't have the same liberties as me. The song also got additional layers from my trip to the island of Lesvos in Greece just two weeks before the Syrian refugees started crossing from Turkey. My family and I were swimming at the lovely beaches of Eftalou that soon become filled with the life jackets of those who made it across. The same life jackets later became an installation at the columns of Konzerthaus Berlin by Chinese artist Ai Weiwei. This fitted with my original idea of ignorance and Fortress Europe perfectly. I now remember the beaches where I was swimming and the installation every time I play the song. For the video of the song, I shot images of travelling in the aeroplane above Europe and flowing water at the Acheron river in Epirus, Greece. According to Greek mythology, this is the earthly manifestation of the river of death.

This river is connected to another song as well, 'The River of Shadows', on my second solo album *Eye for an Eye* (Svart Records, 2017). I wanted to write a tribute to Jason McCash, the late bass player of Indianapolis doom metal band The Gates of Slumber. We had done several tours with them, with Reverend Bizarre and Lord Vicar, and Jason was like a brother to me. He overdosed in April 2014 at the age of 37. He was three days younger than me and his passing was really hard to take. He was the first one of my really close friends to die. And also to die in that miserable and clichéd rock and roll way was something that could have been avoided. This made it especially sad as he left behind a wife and three children. I knew him as a gentle and intelligent man and as someone who went through several religions in search of the meaning of life and peace of mind. Unfortunately, he also sought peace through opiates. And so I remembered him; how we played on a former church altar in Lansing, Michigan, back in 2005, or how we wandered through nocturnal Paris in 2007, just us and some distant street gangs around, musing about the statue of Charlemagne outside Notre Dame. Or how we stood on the tribunal of Zeppelinfield in Nuremberg, thinking about the 'Blue temple', a 'dome' constructed with anti-aircraft lights, designed by Albert Speer and Eberhard von der Trappen, which was one of the more impressive moments at the Nazi propaganda rallies. And I remembered him as I pissed at the area where Hitler's remains had been burned in Berlin, now a parking lot near the massive holocaust memorial full of oppressive monoliths. I was thinking about all that when composing the song and making the lyric about him descending the Acheron river in a boat with coins covering his eyes. I was thinking about the oracle that was supposed to have resided there – it was a place for communication with the dead, *nekyia* (ἡ νέκυια). This is the place that, according to Homer, wise Odysseus visited on his travels when searching his way back to Ithaca. At the Acheron, freezing, crystal-clear water bursts from the underground fountains, making it a place of contemplation, cleansing and spiritual healing. In my mind, it was the most suitable reference for a proper and heartfelt farewell to a friend and a fellow searcher. At the end of the song I described the land of the dead as a beautiful but joyless field of ashes full of silence and solemn sorrow. For this I remembered not only *Odyssey*, but also Ursula K. Leguin's description of afterlife in *Farthest Shore* (1972), the third part of her Earthsea cycle. It is the most impressive account on the subject I have ever read. Homer's epic description feels connected with Leguin's fantasy.

My second solo album starts with 'Entangled in Pleasure'. It is both a tribute to Leonard Cohen's genius and a description of an old man feeling regret over the choices he has made in life. I started the songwriting process with the term nostalgia. The word that comes from two Greek words, *Nostos* (νόστος), homecoming, and *Algos* (ἄλγος), pain, suffering. The 'old man' is a powerful mythological motif and the idea of looking back resonates with me as a historian. But at the same time, I was thinking about the personal side of this taking place, me as an old man, looking at all the wrong choices I had made that forced me to be alone, fully nostalgic – in pain and longing for the past that by now was beyond my reach – at the end of my days. It was meant to be a possible future that I would not want to experience. The idea of being entangled in pleasure is to be an uncompromising searcher for personal joy through lust, satisfaction, sleeping with everyone, eating and drinking too much and basically fulfilling all the carnal urges most people feel every now and then. Such a life can hardly be lived without destruction of personal relations and physical and mental health. Thus the central words, 'And you try to feel something beyond sorrow / But there's no way back home / There's only pain'. By fulfilment of all desires the capability to feel anything else but pain through nostalgia has disappeared. And this, to me, would be the ultimate personal tragedy. I hope the protagonist of the song won't be me and that I live my life with that awareness trying to live a healthy and ethical life. The celestial female voices of Pirita Känkänen and Anna-Elena Pääkkölä add the needed polar opposite to my rather crude baritone delivery. I played the guitar parts of the album mostly with a nylon string guitar to add as much intimacy as possible. In the chorus I introduced both bass and 12-string guitar to drive home the central message of the song – *trying* to feel something beyond the pain and longing for the past glories.

During the writing of this chapter I found out there are songs I can't talk about. They cut too deep and were indeed conceived to offer a form of inner reflection, banishment and therapy from real pain. Their very power to me is in the silence that surrounds them. Hopefully they offer comfort, release and peace of mind to others as well.

Conclusion

Everything I do is somehow connected in my mind. It's all about loving different musical styles and genres and about the challenges variety of framing offer me both as player and writer. The heavy metal of Lord Vicar, progressive rock of Orne, cosmic ambient of E-Musikgruppe Lux Ohr, psychedelic Finnish pop of Uhrijuhla and the acoustic folk I play and record under my own name all contribute to my understanding of music. But similarly, my academic work, especially on popular music history, further reveals new combinations of creative approaches.

I think it's a wonderful source of inspiration in both directions and, during the last few years, I have been able to combine the two roles (or, rather, realities) more and more, sometimes combining playing a gig with giving a talk. I think my academic work has been profoundly changed by my experiences as a musician and in relation to what I have seen of the cultural industries. And I think of music making and live performance as hermeneutic layers as well as research and a means of asking questions and feeling the vibrations of life and death. I am really interested in intuition and creative impulses. I am fascinated by the combination of tradition and the always-surprising appearance of the new.

How to summarize a personal bundle of memories from three decades? How can all this be developed into some kind of new creative step in the future, for the future? I am working on new music for all of my bands. There are several albums in the various stages of production, including *Black Powder* for Lord Vicar, and *Eye in the Pyramid* for Orne. As the biggest step into new territory, my plan is to compose and record my third solo album, *The Spiral Mirror*, based on the idea of combining my work as a cultural historian, the history and bodily learning of Aikido (a Japanese martial art created by O-Sensei Morihei Ueshiba between 1930s and 1940s) and musical practice that is affected by this training. This is movement from visually based thinking to holistic, multimodal awareness. In a way this is an extension of the phenomenological ideas of Maurice Merleau-Ponty, the new awareness of the methods discussed under the umbrella of 'research-as-creation' and playful audio-visual hermeneutics. I am aiming for the combination of the visual aesthetics of Aikido with singer-songwriter storytelling (see Merleau-Ponty 1993 and 2002; Richardson and Gorbman 2013: 23). This ambitious combination of Asian and European Cultural Memory – as transmitted by the bodily training in martial arts, folk guitar playing and singing from the heart – will hopefully resonate with people who seek something other than the usual 'Western' hedonistic way of life.

Coda: Discography

Reverend Bizarre:
In the Rectory of the Bizarre Reverend CD, Sinister Figure, Finland 2002.
Reverend Bizarre/Orodruin 12" split, Hellride Music Records, USA 2003.
Harbinger of Metal CD-EP, Spikefarm Records, Finland 2003. Vinyl version, DLP, Svart Records, Finland 2009.
Reverend Bizarre/Ritual Steel 7" split, Metal Coven Records, Germany 2003.
Reverend Bizarre/Minotauri 7" split, Metal Coven Records, Germany 2003.
Slice of Doom 1999–2002 CD-compilation, PsycheDOOMelic Records, Austria 2003.

In the Rectory of the Bizarre Reverend + Return To Rectory 2-CD remastered reissue + CD-EP, Spikefarm Records, Finland 2004. DLP of In the Rectory, Svart Records, Finland 2010. DLP of *Return to Rectory*, Svart Records, Finland 2011.

Slave of Satan CDS, Spikefarm Records, Finland 2005.

Crush the Insects CD, Spikefarm Records, Finland 2005.

Crush the Insects Double-LP, Metal Supremacy Records, Germany 2006. Vinyl reissue, remastered, DLP Svart Records, Finland 2012.

Thulsa Doom 7" EP, Aftermath Records, Norway 2006.

Under the Sign of the Wolf. Reverend Bizarre/Mannhai 7" split, The Church Within Records, Germany 2006.

So Long Suckers 2-CD, Spikefarm Records, Finland 2007. 4 LP Box, Svart Records, Finland 2014.

Electric Wizard/Reverend Bizarre 12" split, Rise Above Records, England 2008.

Kuolema/Reverend Bizarre CD-split MCR, Japani 2008, 7" split, The Church Within Records, Saksa 2008.

Rättö ja Lehtisalo/Reverend Bizarre 12" split, Ektro Records, Finland 2008.

Reverend Bizarre/Mr. Velcro Fastener 12" split, Solina Records, Finland 2008.

Dark World/Deceiver 7" EP, Primitive Reaction, Finland 2008.

Death is Glory ... Now 2-CD compilation, Spikefarm Records, Finland 2009.

Magick With Tears DLP pre-production demo from In the Rectory era, Emissary Records, Chile. Existing but badly distributed.

Additionally several appearances on compilation albums in England, Finland, Germany and Greece.

First two Reverend Bizarre full-length albums and Harbinger of Metal EP were licensed to Season of Mist Records, USA. Some of the albums were also re-released in England by Spinefarm UK.

Orne:

As Mesmer (pre-Orne, 1997–2000):

Tuonen tytär. A Tribute To Finnish Progressive Rock (Mesmer appeared with Mandala song 'Don't Wake Me Now') Mellow Records, Italy 2000.

As Orne:

The Conjuration by the Fire CD and LP, Black Widow Records, Italy 2006. Prog awards 2007: 'Best Artwork', third in 'Best Foreign Album'. New remastered DLP version, with *A Beginning* demo (orig. self-released in 2000), Svart Records, Finland 2013.

Orne/Blizaro 12" split, Svart Records, Finland 2010.

Tree of Life CD and LP, Black Widow Records, Italy, 2011. New remastered DLP version, Svart Records, Finland 2017.

Lord Vicar:

The Demon of Freedom 7" EP, I Hate Records, Sweden 2008.

Fear No Pain CD, The Church Within Records, Germany, 2008. Hardcover DLP book version 2009.

Lord Vicar/Griftegård 7",Ván Records, Germany 2011.

Lord Vicar/Funeral Circle 12", Eyes Like Snow, Germany 2011.

Signs of Osiris CD, The Church Within Records, Germany, 2011. DLP version, April 2012.

Lord Vicar/Revelation 10", The Church Within Records, Germany, 2012.

Gates of Flesh, The Church Within Records, Germany. CD 2016. LP 2017.

E-Musikgruppe Lux Ohr:

Live at Sibelius Museum. Lux Vitae I CD, Finland, 2010.

Kometenbahn 12" vinyl full-length album, Svart Records, Finland 2013.

Spiralo 12" vinyl full-length album, Svart Records, Finland 2013.

Der Planet der Melancholie Limited edition music cassette mini album, Sea State, Germany 2014.

E-Musikgruppe Lux Ohr/Hisko Detria 12" split, Svart Records 2015.

Tonwald Limited edition music cassette mini album, Sea State, Germany 2015.

E-Musikgruppe Lux Ohr Live at Roadburn 2014 12" DLP, Adansonia Records, Germany 2016. Also as a digital download at http://e-musikgruppeluxohr.bandcamp.com/

Uhrijuhla (with Kimi Kärki):

Jokainen on vapaa lintu CD and LP, Svart Records, Finland, March 2015.

As a solo artist:

Kimi Kärki: *The Bone of My Bones* CD and LP, Svart Records 2013. Tape version, Pléroma, Chile, 2017.

Kimi Kärki: *Eye for an Eye* CD and LP, Svart Records 2017.

References

Assmann, J. (2008), 'Communicative and Cultural Memory', in A. Erll and A. Nünning (eds), *Cultural Memory Studies. An International and Interdisciplinary Handbook*, 109–18, Berlin: Walter de Gruyter.

Assmann, A. (2010), 'Re-framing Memory. Between Individual and Collective Forms of Constructing the Past', in K. Tilmans, F. van Vree and J. Winter (eds), *Memory, History, and Identity in Modern Europe*, 35–50, Amsterdam: Amsterdam University Press.

Assmann, A. (2011), *Cultural Memory and Western Civilization: Functions, Media, Archives*, Cambridge: Cambridge University Press.

Barz, G. and T. J. Cooley (2008), *Shadows in the Field: New Perspectives for Fieldwork in Ethnomusicology*, Oxford: Oxford University Press.

Berger, H. M. (2008), 'Phenomenology and the Ethnography of Popular Music. Ethnomusicology at the Juncture of Cultural Studies and Folklore', in G. Barz and T. J. Cooley (eds), *Shadows in the Field: New Perspectives for Fieldwork in Ethnomusicology*, 69–81, Oxford: Oxford University Press.

Burke, P. (2010), 'Co-memorations. Performing the Past', in K. Tilmans, F. van Vree and J. Winter (eds), *Memory, History, and Identity in Modern Europe*, 105–18, Amsterdam: Amsterdam University Press.

Chapman, O. and K. Sawchuck (2012), 'Research-Creation: Intervention, Analysis and "Family Resemblances"', *Canadian Journal of Communication*, 37: 5–26.

Chapman, O. and K. Sawchuck (2015), 'Creation-as-Research: Critical Making in Complex Environments', *RACAR XL*, 1: 49–52.

Crowe, C. (1979), 'Joni Mitchell Defends Herself', *Rolling Stone*, July 1979. Available online: https://www.rollingstone.com/music/news/joni-mitchell-defends-herself-19790726.

Fisher, C. (2015), 'Mentoring Research-Creation: Secrets, Strategies, and Beautiful Failures', *RACAR XL*, 1: 46–49.

Gadamer, H.-G. (1999), *Truth and Method*, 2nd rev. edn, trans. J. Weinsheimer and D. G. Marshall, orig. *Warheit und Methode. Grundzüge einer philosophischer hermeneutik* (1960), New York: Continuum.

Koselleck, R. (1985), *Futures Past. On the Semantics of Historical Time*. Orig: *Vergangene Zukunft. Zur Semantik geschichtlicher Zeiten* (1979), trans. Keith Tribe, Cambridge, Massachusetts: The MIT Press.

Koselleck, R. (2010), 'Repetitive Structures in Language and History', in K. Tilmans, F. van Vree and J. Winter (eds), *Memory, History, and Identity in Modern Europe*, 51–66, Amsterdam: Amsterdam University Press.

Kärki, K. (2014), *Rakennettu areenatähteys. Rock- konsertti globalisoituvana mediaspektaakkelina 1965–2013*, Turku: Turun yliopiston julkaisuja, Sarja C, osa 397.

Kärki, K. (2015), 'Evolutions of The Wall, 1979–2013', in B. Halligan, K. Fariclough-Isaacs, N. Spelman and R. Edgar (eds), *The Arena Concert. Music, Media and Mass Entertainment*, 57–70, New York and London: Bloomsbury.

Loveless, N. S. (2015), 'Introduction', *Polemics. Short Statements on Research-Creation*, *RACAR XL*, 1: 41–6.

Merleau-Ponty, M. (1993), *Silmä ja mieli*, orig. *L'Eil et l'Esprit* (1964), trans. Kimmo Pasanen, Helsinki: Kustannusosakeyhtiö Taide.

Merleau-Ponty, M. (2002), *Phenomenology of Perception*, London: Routledge.

Richardson, J. and C. Gorbman (2013), 'Introduction', in J. Richardson, C. Corbman and C. Vernallis (eds), *Oxford Handbook of New Audiovisual Aesthetics*, 3–35, Oxford: Oxford University Press.

Rousseau, J. (2001), *The Confessions of Jean-Jacques Rousseau*, orig. *Les Confessions* (1782), Blacksburg, VA: Infomotions Inc./Virginia Tech. ebook. Available online: https://ebookcentral.proquest.com/lib/kutu/detail.action?docID=3314860#.

Saint Augustine of Hippo (1997), *The Confessions. With an Introduction and Modern Criticisms*, orig. *Confessiones (397–400)*, ed. D. V. Meconi, San Francisco: Ignatius Press.

Samuel, R. (1994), *Theatres of Memory. Volume 1: Past and Present in Contemporary History*, London and New York: Verso.

Stévance, S. and S. Lacasse (2018), *Research-Creation in the Music and the Arts*, Abingdon: Routledge.

Strachan, R. and M. Leonard (2003), 'Singer-Songwriter', in J. Shepherd, D. Horn, D. Laing, P. Oliver and P. Wicke (eds), *Continuum Encyclopedia of the Popular Music of the World. Volume II: Performance and Production*, 198–202, London and New York: Continuum.

Strand, K. (2018), '"Let me tell you my life in a song" On Autobiography and Begging in Roadside Ballads of the Blind', *The European Journal of Life Writing, Volume VII*, 34–52.

Index

4AD 40, 49

Adam and the Ants 175, 177
Afrofuturism 67, 74
Albarn, Damon 198
Albertine, Viv 15
Albion 105, 108, 111
Angelou, Maya 66
Animals, The 137
Arlen, Harold 81
Assman, Jan 141
authenticity 48, 49
autoethnography 7
automatic writing 112
Avebury 62

Babyshambles 107, 108
Barât, Carl 101, 103, 108
Barthes, Roland 71
Beatles, The 14, 93
Belly 47
Berlin 83, 91, 92, 158
Bibb, Henry 69, 70
Big In Japan 213, 214, 215
Birch, Gina 101
Black Atlantic diaspora 75
Black Sheep 53
Blondie 187
Bohls, Elizabeth A. 70
Bolan, Marc 92
Bossa nova 66
Boston 47
Bowie, David 6, 81–96, 140, 154–7, 159, 160, 162, 165, 188, 190, 211
Box Brown, Henry 69, 70
Boyle, Danny 187
Bragg, Billy 169–70
Brain Donor 53
Braxton, Joanne. M. 66, 67
Breeders 47
bricolage 5, 40, 127–8

Brighton 25, 26
Brilleaux, Lee 22
Britpop 172, 187, 190–2, 196
Bromley 85
Broudie, Ian 212–15
Brown, James 136
Budgie 212, 213, 215
Burgess, Tim 15
Burns, Pete 211–16, 218–22
Bush, Kate 176–7, 190
Buzzcocks 16
Byrds, The 179

Camden 178
Caponi, Gena Dagel 66
Carlish, Max 103
Carretta, Vincent 70
Cauty, Jimmy 220
Chamberlain, Matt 90
Charlatans, The 177
Chicago blues 91
Child, Lydia Maria 70
Christchurch 142
Clash, The 103
Clemons, Clarence 140, 141
Clemons, Jake 141
Cochrane, Eddie 81
communicative memory 228
composition 42
confession 225–6, 231–3
Conway, Martin and Loveday, Catherine 18–20
Cope, Julian 6, 53–62, 212–15
Corbijn, Anton 18, 33, 159
Cordon, James 35–6
Costello, Elvis 121, 129
Coverley, Merlin 61
Creed, Barbara 77
Crescent Community Venue, York 39
Cromwell, Oliver 229–30
Crosthwaite, Paul 28, 32

CUD 20, 171–2
cultural memory 228
Cummins, Kevin 33
Curtis, Deborah 18, 36
Curtis, Ian 17–18, 22, 26, 31–2, 34, 36
cyborg, the 65–78

Dead Kennedys 14
Dean, James 122
de Man, Paul 55, 56
Derrida, Jacques 21
Dery, Mark 74
desire 120
Diallo, Amadou 143
diary 42, 43
Dick, Philip K. 74
Diddley, Bo 82, 91
Disco 66
Doc Martens 171
Doherty, Pete 101–16
Doncaster 171–2
Doors, The 61
Doo-wop 91
Douglass, Frederick 69, 71–3
Dower, John 187
Dr. Feelgood 22
Drifters, The 91, 137
dub 66
Dublin 124
Dutton, Denis 16–17, 20
Dyer, Richard 66, 76
Dylan, Bob 14, 82, 120–1, 126–7, 129

Echo and the Bunnymen 169
Eddy, Duane 81
editing 205, 209
Eno, Brian 65
Erll, Astrid 141–2
Erll, Astrid and Rigney, Ann 138
E Street Band 136, 140–1
Everything But the Girl 28

Factory Records 30
Fad Gadget 154, 158, 160, 163
Fall, The 26, 30
Family Cat, The 20
fandom 2
Farthingale, Hermione 92

Fiennes, Sophie 66
Fisher, Mark 21, 36–7
Fleetwood Mac 14
Fleischer, Max 93
Fonarow, Wendy 17
Foucault, Michel 33
Frame, Pete 213, 215
Frankie Goes To Hollywood 190
free festival 179
Freehold 145
Frey, Glenn 140
Frith, Simon 94

Gallagher, Liam 198
Gants Hill 190, 191, 194
garage rock 56
Garson, Mike 82, 83, 89, 90, 91
Gates Junior, Henry Louis 66, 68
Gershwin, George 91
Gilmore, Leigh 67
Giovanni, Nikki 74
Glam rock 166
Goude, Jean-Paul 65, 66, 68, 76, 77
Graceland 140
graffiti 99, 104–5, 111, 115–16
Greenpeace 179
Gretton, Rob 17
Gross, Terry 96
Grossberg, Lawrence 82, 86
Gunning, Sandra 70

Halligan, Benjamin 188
Hanchard, Michael 73
Hannett, Martin 26, 33
Haraway, Donna 65–7, 69, 70, 71–3, 75, 77
Haring, Keith 65
Harrison, George 211
Hassell, John 101
Hatten, Robert 81
hauntology 21, 34–6
Hebdidge, Dick 15
hiatus 5
hip-hop 177
historiographic approach 7
Hoggart, Richard 191
Hook, Peter 18, 30
hooks, bell 68

Hoverchairs, The 17
Hughes, Langston 74
Hull Truck Theatre 179
Hunt, Miles 15, 16
Hynde, Chrissie 129
Hyson, Edward 197

imaginative historicism 29, 31
indie 1, 3, 13, 45, 100, 104, 120, 172, 178, 202–3, 207
Indie Daze 14
Inspiral Carpets 201–10
intertextual 129
intertextuality 81, 82, 84–6, 88, 91, 93, 95
Iron Butterfly 61
Isle of Wight Festival 179

Jackson, Joe 188
Jackson, Mattie 70
Jacobs, Harriet 66, 70, 75
Jagger, Mick 82
Jameson, Frederic 21
Jarvis, Brian 88
Jay, Karla 77
Jefferson Airplane 61
Jensen, David (Kid) 60, 61
Johnson, Holly 213
Johnson, Wilko 22
Jones, Grace 65–78
Jones, Mick 103, 108, 181
Joplin, Janis 178
Jourgensen, Al 58
Joyce, James 40
Joy Division 17, 18, 22, 26–37
Judeo-Christian narratives 73

Kaplan, Ann 22
King, Carol 129
King Cole, Nat 166
Kitchenware Records 178
KLF, The 220
Knebworth 20
Kosofsky Sedgewick, Eve 67
Kraftwork 66
Krautrock 82
künstlerroman 40
Kureishi, Hanif 84

laddism 37
Lee, Stewart 58
Leeds 165, 167, 177
Leguin, Ursula 233
Lemonheads, The 47
Lennon, John 60, 84, 88
Lesser Free Trade Hall 16, 20, 29, 172
Libertines, The 100–16
liminal 4
Little Richard 60, 61, 87
Liverpool 55, 212, 213
Loder, Kurt 142
London 178, 187, 190
Lorde, Audre 66, 77

MacInnes, Colin 13–15, 22
Madchester 30, 202, 208
Manchester 26–37, 124, 126–7
Manchester, University of 187, 190
Marine Girls, The 28
Marr, Johnny 119, 123, 129
Marsh, Dave 135, 136, 139
masculinity 32
Masur, Louis 139
Mathers, Ian 34–6
McAdams, Dan 136, 138
McCarron, Kevin 92
McCartney, Paul 93
McQueen, Alexander 103
Melchett, Lord 179
Melody Maker 13, 33, 172
MEN Arena 35
Mercury, Freddie 92
Miller, Nancy K. 27
Ministry 58
Mitchell, Joni 96
Moby 129
modernity 4
Monkees, The 154, 156, 160–2
Moody, Joycelyn 70
Moore, Allan 138
Morley, Paul 28–36, 70–1
Morrissey 6, 30, 119–32
Moss, Kate 102
Motown 177
Moulton, Tom 65
multidisciplinary 3
myth 5

Naiman, Tiffany 83, 92
narrative 5, 128
National Film and Television School 179–80
Neiberg, Michael and Citino, Robert 134
Neisser, Ulric and Fivush, Robyn 134
Nelson, Katherine 135, 139
Neolithic European culture 53, 58, 59
Nevarez, Leonard 33, 35
Newley, Anthony 81
New Musical Express 26, 28, 29, 32
New Order 17, 18
New Orleans 142
New Romantics 190
Newsbeat 183
New Statesman 187
Newton, Helmut 65
Newton, John 66
New York 88, 91, 142–3
New York Dolls 123
Nico 59, 60
NME 172
Norse mythology 57
Northern Soul 167
nostalgia 6, 13, 14, 94, 114, 212, 233–4

Oasis 20
O'Brien, Lucy 28, 36
Old Grey Whistle Test, The 170
O'Leary, Chris 87–9, 91
Olney, James 68, 69, 70
Oursler, Tony 92

Paleari, Fabio 102
paratext 119
pastiche 3
Peel, John 157, 163, 170–4, 207–8
Penguin Classics 122
Perrins, Daryl 92
Pitney, Gene 153–4, 155, 159–60, 161
Pixies 47
Plate, Liedeke and Smelik, Anneke 133, 143
Plati, Mark 88
Plotkin, Chuck 138
postmodernity 82
post-punk 13, 26–30, 36
post-war Germany 62
Powell, Gary 101
Presley, Elvis 140, 166

Prince 140
Prince, Mary 69, 70
psychogeography 32, 61–2, 105
punk 3, 15, 17, 30, 33, 103, 107, 180

Queen Elizabeth (band) 53
queer 119–20

Radio One 183
Radstone, Susannah 36
readership 202–5
Reed, Lou 82
reggae 66
Renck, Johan 93
research-as-creation 226–7
Reynolds, Simon 14, 15, 28, 32
Rhode Island 39–40, 47
Robb, John 15
rock 120
Roeg, Nicolas 94
Rolling Stones, The 14, 56
Rothberg, Michael 139

Said, Edward 82, 86, 91, 95
San Francisco 178
Sardinia 57, 58, 62
Sargent, Roger 100, 102
Savage, Jon 33–6
Saville, Peter 17, 33
sci-fi 156, 157
Scott, Bon 140
Scunthorpe 172–3
self-mythologization 54, 62
Senseless Things 14–15
Sex Pistols, The 16, 20, 29, 169, 172
Shakkur, Tupac 183–5
shamanistic ritual 54, 57, 62
Shaviro, Steven 66
Shiiine On 14
Ska 169
Slapper, Clifford 83
slave narratives 66, 68
Sleeper 187–200
Slimane, Hedi 102
Sly and Robbie 65, 66
Smith, Mark E. 30
Smith, Patti 21, 121, 129
Smiths, The 30, 119, 123, 125–8, 169–70

Sonic Youth 22
Sony Records 178
Springsteen, Bruce 133–45
Stewart, Jon 187–200
storytelling 2
Straub, Jürgen 134
Strickland, Susannah 70
Strummer, Joe 180–1
subculture 8, 170
subjectivity 42, 44
Summer of Love 179
Sumner, Bernard 18, 30
Supremes, The 81

Tagg, Philip 85
Take That 14
Tamworth 61, 62
Taylor, James 96
Teardrop Explodes, The 53, 58
technology 201–2
Teddy Boys 13
teleology 41
Temple, Julien 23, 180–1
Tevis, Walter 94
Thompson, Graham 74
Thompson, L. S. 70
Thorn, Tracey 15, 28
Thornton, Anthony 102
Throwing Muses 39, 46, 47, 49
Tim Westwood 183–4
Tin Machine 84
Top of the Pops 165, 170

Tovey, Frank 154, 159
Townshend, Pete 82, 216–17
Tricky 65
True Faith 17
Tube, The 170
Tyner, Rob 60

Velvet Underground 81
vinyl 151–2, 157–8
Virgin Prunes, The 61
Vivino, Floyd 88

Wallace-Saunders 76
Warsaw 30
Waterman, Pete 219–20
Watts-Russell, Ivo 40, 49–50
Wedding Present, The 15, 16
Weekes, Karen 77
Wells Brown, William 69, 70
Welzer, Harald 144
Wener, Louise 187–200
Westwood, Vivienne 103
Who, The 216–17
Wigan Casino 167–8
Wilde, Oscar 129
Wilkinson, David 36
Wilson, Tony 30
working class 166, 168

Yardbirds, The 82
York 39, 50, 165–8, 175–8
Young, Neil 82, 87, 96

www.ingramcontent.com/pod-product-compliance
Lightning Source LLC
Chambersburg PA
CBHW072139290426
44111CB00012B/1923